Third Edition

Handbook for Public Relations Writing

Thomas Bivins
University of Oregon

NTC Business Books
a division of *NTC Publishing Group* • Lincolnwood, Illinois USA

HM
263
.B538
1995

Printed on recyclable paper

Library of Congress Cataloging-in-Publication Data
Bivins, Thomas.
    Handbook for public relations writing / Thomas Bivins. –3rd ed.
        p. cm.
    Includes bibliographical references and index.
    ISBN 0-8442-3435-4 (hard). – ISBN 0-8442-3436-2 (soft)
    1. Public relations–United States. 2. Public relations–United
States–Authorship. I. Title.
HM263.B538 1995   94-37637
659.2–dc20   CIP

Published by NTC Business Books, a division of NTC Publishing Group
4255 West Touhy Avenue
Lincolnwood (Chicago), Illinois 60646-1975, U.S.A.

5 6 7 8 9 0 VP 9 8 7 6 5 4 3 2 1

Contents

User's Preface

This is a handbook for those who, by intention or by accident, find themselves in the position of having to write for public relations. It is designed to be of aid to both the beginner and the advanced public relations writer. In it, you will find most of the forms of PR writing including news releases, backgrounders, broadcast scripts, magazine and newsletter articles, brochures, and print advertising copy.

This latest edition has been extensively revised to include, among other topics, a new section on how to produce public service announcements specifically for television and how to place them most effectively. The chapter on press releases has been expanded to include information on fact sheets and press kits. You'll also find a new section on how to produce flyers, one of the most-used information formats today.

Examples have been redesigned for readability and additional artwork has been included in most chapters. As in the previous edition, you will find a complete section on grammar and one on style geared toward the PR practitioner working within a business environment. Included in them are examples of work common to such an environment, including sections from orientation materials and most of the everyday types of writing that any public relations practitioner is called on to produce.

Many of the recommendations contained in this handbook are based on years of experience as a writer, both in public relations and in general business practice. It is my belief that any PR writer worthy of the name should become familiar with all forms of writing. After all, good writing is good writing, no matter what the form. The truly good writer is able to work in any medium, like the good artist.

A handbook should be something that you can put on your library shelf, desk, or briefcase and refer to when you have questions concerning public relations writing. This book is an attempt to put most of the reference material that you, as a public relations writer, would need to successfully complete the work which is so vital a part of your chosen profession—writing.

About the Author

Thomas H. Bivins is Associate Dean and Associate Professor in the School of Journalism at the University of Oregon where he teaches public relations and mass media ethics. He received his Ph.D. in 1982 in telecommunication from the University of Oregon, and taught for three years at the University of Delaware before returning to the University of Oregon. Bivins received a B.A. in English and an M.F.A. in creative writing from the University of Alaska, Anchorage, and has nearly twenty years of professional media experience, including work in radio, television, advertising, public relations and editorial cartooning.

CHAPTER 1

Writing for Public Relations

Fine writing is next to fine doing...

John Keats

A ll public relations practitioners write at some time. Public relations is, after all, communication, and the basic form of communication is still the written word.

Regardless of the prevalence of television and radio, the written word is still powerful. Even the events we witness on television and hear on the radio were written down originally in the form of scripts. News anchors on television are not recounting the day's events from memory; they are reading from a teleprompter.

It is no wonder today's employer values an employee who can communicate through the written word. Employers want people who can write and communicate ideas—who can pull complex or fragmented ideas together into coherent messages. This requires not only technical skill, but also intelligence. It also requires a love of writing. Be forewarned: The subjects of public relations writing can seem to many to be crashingly dull; however, for writers who love their craft, the duller the subject, the greater the challenge. Even the most mundane subject can shine with the right amount of polish.

So, the place of writers in public relations is assured. From the president or vice president of public relations to the lowliest office worker, writing will be a daily part of life. From enormously complex projects involving dozens of people and whole teams of writers to the one-person office cranking out daily press releases and weekly newsletters, writing will continue to be the number one concern of public relations. Through it, your publics will come to know you and, for better or worse, develop a permanent image of who you are. It is in your best interest and that of the people you work for to ensure that this image is the one you want to portray.

What is needed before you begin to write, however, is knowledge. Being able to spell and string words together effectively does not make a good writer. A good writer must be able to think. A good writer must be aware of the world around us and understand how his or her writing is going to affect that world.

It is absolutely essential that you think before you write, otherwise your writing will be only empty words, disconnected from reality, or, worse, unintentionally misleading or false.

What Is Public Relations Writing?

All public relations writing attempts to establish positive relations between an organization and its various publics—usually through image-building techniques. Most writing in the realm of public relations falls into two rather broad categories:

- Uncontrolled information;
- Controlled information.

Uncontrolled Information

Information which, once it leaves your hands, is at the mercy of the media, is *uncontrolled*. In other words, the outlet in which you want it placed has total editorial control over the content, style, placement, and timing. Such items as press releases are totally uncontrolled. Others, such as magazine articles, may receive limited editing but are still controlled as to placement and timing.

Controlled Information

Information over which you have total control as to editorial content, style, placement, and timing is *controlled*. Examples of controlled information are institutional and advocacy advertising, house publications, brochures, and broadcast material (if it is paid placement). Public service announcements (PSAs) are controlled as far as message content is concerned, but uncontrolled as to placement and timing.

Naturally, the categories overlap. The trick is to utilize each in a cohesive mix with a single, unified message in mind.

WRITING FOR PUBLIC RELATIONS   3

The Tools of the Public Relations Writer

As with any trade, public relations writing makes use of certain tools through which messages are communicated. The most common are listed here.

- **News releases**—both print and broadcast. This is the most widely used of all public relations formats. News releases are used most often to disseminate information for publicity purposes and are sent to every possible medium, from newspapers to radio stations.

- **Backgrounders**—basic information pieces providing background as an aid to reporters, editors, executives, employees, and spokespersons. This is the information used by other writers and reporters to "flesh out" their stories.

- **Public service announcements (PSAs)**—the broadcast outlet most available to public relations. Although its parameters are limited, additional leeway can be gained by paying for placement, which places it in the category of advertising.

- **Advertising**—the controlled use of media ensuring that your message reaches your public in exactly the form you intended and at the time you want. Advertising can be print or broadcast.

- **Articles and editorials**—usually for newsletters, house publications, trade publications, or consumer publications. In the case of non-house publications, PR articles are submitted in the same way as any other journalistic material. Editorials can be either paid for, as are Mobil's editorials and *Fables*, or submitted uncontrolled and vie for placement with other comments from other parties.

- **Collateral publications**—such as brochures, pamphlets, flyers, and other direct marketing pieces. These are usually autonomous publications, which should be able to stand on their own merits but which can be used as supporting information for other components in a package. They might, for instance, be part of a press packet.

- **Annual reports**—one of the most-produced organizational publications. Annual reports not only provide information on the organization's financial situation, they also act as a vehicle for enhancing corporate image among its various internal publics.

- **Speeches and presentations**—the interpersonal method of imparting a position or an image. Good speeches can inform or persuade and good presentations can win support where other, written, methods may fail.

Although these are not the only means for message dissemination at the disposal of the public relations writer, they are the most used. Knowing which to use requires a combination of experience, research, and intuition. The following chapters do not purport to teach you these qualities. What they do attempt to do is to provide you with a framework, or template, from which you will be able to perform basic tasks as a public relations writer. The rest is a matter of experience, and no book can give you that.

Writing for Public Relations

All forms of writing for public relations have one thing in common— they should be written well. Beyond that, they are different in many ways. These differences are related primarily to intent, style, format, and medium. Corporate magazines and newsletters, for example, employ standard magazine writing style (which is to say, a standard magazine style of journalism). Newsletter writing, on the other hand, is leaner, shorter, and frequently uses a straight news reporting style. Folders (commonly referred to as brochures) are, by nature, short and to the point. Copy for posters and flyers is shorter still, while pamphlets and booklets vary in style and length according to purpose.

There are basically only two reasons for a public relations piece to be produced: information or persuasion. The approach to writing these pieces depends to a great extent on the purpose to which the piece is to be put. But, before you even put pen to paper (or text to screen), you have to begin the whole process from an organizational perspective. This means planning.

Almost all writing goes through, or should go through, several stages before it reaches completion. Before you start writing, a plan by which your message will ultimately reach its intended audience and accomplish its intended purpose has to be developed. One of the most useful techniques for planning written communication is *management by objectives* (MBO). MBO allows you to set objectives in advance for your written communication and provides you with the criteria you need to measure the message's effectiveness all along the way. By adapting an MBO approach to writing, you can derive at least three processes—planning, writing, evaluation—you must go through to achieve success in your written communications.

The **planning process** includes:
- Developing a problem/issue statement,
- Researching the topic,
- Analyzing the target audience,
- Setting objectives and criteria for evaluation,
- Choosing the appropriate medium or media.

The **writing process** includes:
- Setting message strategy,
- Setting a style and organizing the message,
- Writing the message.

The **evaluation process** includes:
- Testing the message in advance of distribution,
- Evaluating the message during and following the program.

The Planning Process

Developing a Problem/Issue Statement

The first step in any MBO-based plan is to define the issue or problem. Working without a precise definition of the issue is analogous to writing a college term paper without a thesis statement—you have no clear direction to show where you are going and, thus, no way to determine whether you have gotten anywhere when you're finished.

The terms *issue* and *problem* are relatively interchangeable depending on how you view the situation. *Issue* is a more generic term and covers both problems and opportunities; however, many in public relations persist in viewing most responses in terms of problems. For our purposes, we will use the term *issue* as being more inclusive.

The first step in defining the issue is to develop an **issue statement**. An issue statement is a precise definition of the situation including answers to the following.

- What is the problem or opportunity you are going to address?
- Who are the affected parties? At this point, it is only necessary to list the concerned parties. A precise definition of publics is the next step in the planning process.

- Is this issue of immediate concern (one needing to be addressed right now), impending concern (one that will have to be addressed very soon), or potential concern (one that you are tracking as needing to be addressed in the near future)?
- What are your strengths and weaknesses as regards this issue?

In answering these questions, you should take care to be as precise as you can. Succinctness is important to clarity, and clarity is of primary importance in the planning process. It is often wise to answer these questions in outline form, then, working from the outline, develop an issue statement. Consider the following example. It is necessarily simplistic for demonstration purposes. Most issue analysis at this stage is far more complex; however, the approach is the same and the need for precision and succinctness is nonetheless important.

1. Issue: Your company has recently developed a new line of educational software targeted to school-aged children from first grade through high school. Development was time-consuming and expensive, and was based on previous research showing a marked trend in education toward computers in the classroom. Marketing and advertising of the new software will be taken care of by your company's marketing department and its outside advertising agency. From a public relations perspective, however, you see an opportunity to capitalize on the growth in educational computers by raising the awareness of key publics as to the importance of this trend and by tying your company's name to that growth.

2. Affected publics: your publics have already been determined in part by the markets who will be using your new line of software. They are: educators, administrators, parents, and students.

3. Because this is an opportunity and not a problem, timing is essential. Most opportunities require that you act quickly in order to capitalize on them. Your software is already developed and a marketing program developed. You need to move in advance of, or, at the very least, simultaneously with, the marketing effort.

4. Your strengths include the availability of existing marketing research that has already determined your target publics, advance knowledge of how the new software will enhance the educational process so that you can focus on those

elements, and a wide-open opportunity to set the scene for your product through some public relations advance work.

Weaknesses might include competition, potential perception of vested interest in any philanthropic effort you might suggest, and the necessity to move almost immediately because of the availability of the product.

An issue statement based on this information might look like the following.

> The recent development of our new line of educational software and the coincidence of current trends in educational computing present an opportunity for our company to align itself as a leader in modern education. To do so, we will need to raise the level of attention of key publics concerning the importance of computers in the classroom in such a way that we become closely associated with the trend. We are in a unique position to alert educators, administrators, and parents to the multiple uses of classroom computers and the availability of educational software as an answer to many current classroom problems. A well-placed publicity effort outside of and separate from our marketing plan could help pave the way for eventual increased sales of our software. This publicity effort should not seem to be connected to our product; however, we should not appear to hide our interests in increased sales either. A joint effort with an educational non-profit organization might be the best approach to take.

This issue statement covers all of the questions posed earlier. The only qualitative difference between the original answers provided to the questions and this statement is the narrative format of the statement. Stating the issue in this form helps others to conceptualize what you already understand, and sets the groundwork for further analysis of the issue. **Exhibit 1.1** describes how to use a direction sheet to plan your written piece.

Researching the Topic

Obviously, as is the case in all forms of writing, you must know your topic. Research techniques can run the gamut from formal research, such as surveys and questionnaires, to simply checking the library.

Most public relations writers have access to organizational research material, and so much of the research can be accomplished in house. You can check with various departments for information on your

Exhibit 1.1—Preparing a Direction Sheet

The first step any public relations practitioner takes before beginning to write is research. Every practitioner needs to understand thoroughly the audience, message, and medium for each communication. Intuition will not suffice. It is important, therefore, to lay the groundwork for any written piece by beginning with a *direction sheet.* A direction sheet is a series of questions you should answer when you begin an assignment. No public relations writer should begin an assignment without one.

A basic direction sheet might include the following information:

• Subject of the piece. Is it going to be a new product publicity piece, an announcement of employee promotions, or news about a special event such as a fund raiser or a grand opening?

• Format. What form will the information take? Is it to be a press release, a magazine article, a television PSA, or a brochure?

• Objective. What do we hope to accomplish by producing this piece? Do we want to educate the general public concerning our hiring policies? Do we want to make engineers aware that we have developed a new product for their use? Do we want to promote the Olympics by associating ourselves with the event?

• Intended audience. Exactly who is our target public? Is it home-makers, businesspeople, children, staff members? Who we decide to communicate with will determine the form of the message and probably the medium.

• Angle. The angle "hooks" the audience and establishes the context of the message. It is all-important and one of the toughest components to establish. The angle must be new and interesting. In a print ad, it could be a bold headline. In a television PSA, it might be a peaceful, scenic shot juxtaposed with abrasive audio. In a radio PSA, it might be a humorous context.

• Key ideas. These are the salient points you wish to make through your communication. Establishing key ideas is important because they serve as an outline for writing a successful message.

• Length. This depends to a great extent on format. The length should be agreed upon in advance by the party requesting the piece and the writer. Press releases, for instance, can be from one to five pages long. Article length is usually determined by the publication for which it is intended. Brochure length varies according to layout.

• Deadline. This element is usually the most inflexible. Unfortunately, in public relations writing as in most writing, the finished product is usually needed "yesterday."

When you receive an assignment, try to get as much information as you can in one "client" meeting. This means, be prepared ahead of time with a complete list of questions. Once you have left your "client," it is usually difficult to get back in touch.

topic and obtain previously published material from in-house and other sources. After you have been at this type of work for a while, you will undoubtedly have a well-stocked "swipe file" in which you have collected everything you (or anyone else) has ever written about your subject area. In essence, you become a standard journalist gathering background information for a story. You should never start writing until you have sufficient background on your subject.

For many articles, human interest is important. This is where interviews come in. First-hand information is always best when you can get it. Interview those intimately involved with your topic and use their information when you write. Interviewing is a special skill and it takes a lot of practice. Whom you interview will determine how informative or interesting your interview will be. Although you can't always control who you interview, you can prepare so that you can make the most out your meeting. **Exhibit 1.2** gives some tips for a successful interview.

Exhibit 1.2—Tips for a Successful Interview

- Do your homework. Collect background information on the people you're going to interview, as well as the topics. Don't be embarrassed by your own ignorance of the topics; however, the better you know the topics, the more time you can save by asking for specific details rather than for in-depth explanations.

- Prepare your interviewees in advance of the interviews. Contact them well in advance, set a convenient time for the interview that is convenient for them, and make sure they know exactly what you are going to cover and why. That way, they can also prepare for the interview by gathering pertinent information as well as their thoughts. Ask if you can "talk with them" rather than "interview them." A talk puts people at ease—an interview can make them tense and formal.

- Write down a list of questions that you want answered, working from the general to the specific. But be prepared to let the interview range according to the interviewees' responses. Often, an answer will open new areas of inquiry or suggest an angle you hadn't thought of before. Be ready to explore these new avenues as they come up.
Ken Metzler, journalist, educator, and author of *Creative Interviewing*, claims that the best interviewers should not only expect surprises, but should ask for surprises in their willingness to explore rather than follow a strict set of questions.

- If you are going to use a tape recorder, check to make sure that your interviewee is comfortable with being taped, and that you have fresh batteries or that an electrical outlet is available. And, even though you are taping, always take notes. This physical activity usually puts the interviewee at ease by showing that you are listening, and it serves as a good backup if your recorder stops functioning or your tape runs out.

Your recorder should not occupy the space between you and your subject. Move it a little to the side, but make sure the microphone isn't obstructed. The space between you and your subject should be free of any object that may be a source of distraction. (You should also keep your note pad in your lap, if possible, or simply hold it.)

• Break the ice. Open your interview with small talk. Try a comfortable topic, such as the weather, or, if you know something about your interviewee, a familiar, nonthreatening topic. For example, if you know your interviewee is an avid golfer, ask if he or she has had a chance to play much lately. Almost any topic will do—in fact, most of the time, something will suggest itself naturally.

• As your interview progresses, don't be afraid to range freely, but return occasionally to your pre-set questions. Although the information you gather exploring other avenues may add greatly to your collection of relevant facts, remember to cover all the ground necessary for your article.

• If you are ever unsure of a quote or think you might have misunderstood it, ask your subject to repeat it. Even if you are taping the interview, accuracy on paper and in your own mind is worth the slight pause.

• Finally, be prepared to have to remember some key conversation after your interview is officially over. Most of us are aware of the phenomenon that Ken Metzler calls the "afterglow effect," when dinner guests, for example, stand at the door with their coats on ready to go and talk for another 30 minutes. The same thing usually happens in an interview. You've turned your recorder off and put your pad away, and on your way out the door, you have another 10 minutes of conversation. In this relaxed atmosphere, important comments are often made. Remember them. As soon as you leave, take out your pad and write the comments down or turn on your recorder and repeat the information into it. However, always make sure that your interviewee is aware that you are going to use this information as well. Don't violate any assumed "off the record" confidences.

Remember, get as much as you can the first time out. Most interviews range from 30 minutes to two hours. A follow-up interview, providing you can get one, will never be as fruitful or relaxed as the first one.

Analyzing the Target Audience

Imagine holding a complex conversation with someone you don't know at all. If you are trying to persuade that person of your point of view, you will have a better chance if you know his or her predispositions in advance. The same holds true for written communication. In order to write for an audience, you have to know that audience intimately.

What you need to know about your target audience depends to a great extent on what your objectives are. As discussed previously, public relations writing is typically used for either information or persuasion. A lot depends on which of these two uses your particular piece will be put to. Persuasive publications, for example, usually rely on the "look" as the element that first hooks the prospective reader. "Slick" brochures or print ads are obviously designed with this in mind. On the other hand, think of all those publications you've seen at government agencies or received through the mail as a result of having requested information. They frequently are less glitzy, more straightforward, and simpler in style. They don't have to be designed to attract your attention or persuade you to pick them up. They are designed to inform you, and they assume that you have already chosen to read them.

Developing a reader profile. Knowing for whom you're writing is probably the most important factor in setting message strategy. The success of your writing will be determined, to a great extent, on how well you've "aimed" your message. The best way to write is to write for an imagined reader, an individual to whom you are speaking directly. In order to understand this individual, you need to know him or her personally. To do this, you will have to develop a profile of this "typical" reader.

Methods for collecting information on your target audiences range from fairly expensive formal research through secondary research gathered from such sources as the library or your own organization, to simply asking the person who gave you the assignment who the audience is. Many writers are put off by the notion of having to gather hard-core information about their readers. Unfortunately, many a message has totally missed its audience because it was not built around this information.

If you can't afford the luxury of a formal survey, try gathering demographic information from other departments within your own organization. For example, if your organization has a marketing department and your publication is external, you might be able to extract some solid audience demographics from existing marketing research. And, don't discount the value of a visit to the library.

Government documents such as the *American Statistics Index* (*ASI*) can be invaluable sources. *ASI* is a compendium of statistical material including the U.S. census and hundreds of periodicals that can be obtained directly from the sponsoring agencies or, often, from the library itself. *ASI* also publishes an alphabetical index arranged by subject, name, category, and title.

Other sources of market information include the Simmons Market Research Bureau's annual *Study of Media and Markets*. This publication includes information on audiences for over a hundred magazines, with readership delineated by demographic, psychographic, and behavioral characteristics. When using secondary research such as this, be aware that you will find much information that is not directly applicable to your target audience. You not only have to know where to look, but you also have to know how to decipher what you read and apply it to your needs.

There is one other important factor to consider at this point: How your target audience feels about your subject. In most persuasive endeavors, there are three types of audiences: those already on your side, those opposed to your point of view, and those who are undecided. Most persuasive appeals are, or should be, aimed at the last group.

As most experienced persuaders know, convincing the hard-core opposition is not a reasonable objective. Persuading those already on your side is like preaching to the converted—unless you want to stir them to some action, it is a waste of time. Thus, most persuasion is aimed at the undecided. Remember, however, that even the undecided have opinions. Those opinions may not be fully crystallized, and this leaves this group particularly open to persuasion.

Anticipating readers' expectations. Once you know who your audience is and how they feel about your subject, one final question must be answered if you expect to be successful: Why are they going to be reading your publication? If you don't know why your audience is reading your publication in the first place, you certainly can't know what they expect to get from it. Ask yourself these questions:

1. What does your audience know about your topic already? Never assume they know anything about your subject; however, don't talk down to them. How do you reach a compromise? Find out what they *do* know. Remember, people like to learn something from communication. It is best, however, to limit the amount of new information so as not to overwhelm your readers.

2. What is your audience's attitude toward you? Remember the three basic audiences for any persuasive piece? You'll need to determine whether your audience is on your side, against you, or unconvinced. To the extent possible, it is also a good idea to

try to determine what your audience's image of you or your organization is. Determining audience attitude is often an expensive proposition because it usually requires formal research. However, if the best you can do is make an educated guess based on a small focus group or even on intuition—that's better than nothing at all. It is much easier to convince others when you know that you already have credibility with them.

3. Is your publication to be used in a larger context? In other words, is your publication part of a press kit, for instance, or a direct-mail package, or one of many handouts at a trade show? This knowledge will determine your readers' level of attention and their receptiveness. Always consider the surroundings in which your piece will be used if you want it to have the maximum impact.

Setting Objectives and Criteria for Evaluation

Objectives relate to the purpose of your message and should be realistic and measurable. For public relations writing, there are three types of objectives: informational, attitudinal and behavioral.

Informational objectives are used most often to present balanced information on a topic of interest to your target audience. For instance, if you are simply attempting to let your employees know that your organization has developed a new health care package, your objective might read something like this:

> To inform all employees of the newest options available in their health care benefits package by the beginning of the October open enrollment period.

Notice that the objective begins with an infinitive phrase. Objectives should always be written this way. Notice, too, that the number of employees is addressed ("all"), and a specific time period for the completion of the objective is also included. In a complete communications plan, this objective would be followed by the proposed tactic for its realization and a method by which its success could be measured. For example:

> To inform all employees of the newest options available in their health care benefits package by the beginning of the October open enrollment period by placing informational folders in each employee's paycheck over the next two months. Personnel will keep a record of all employees requesting information on the new health care plan during the open enrollment period.

If your objective is attitudinal or behavioral rather than informational, your message is probably going to be persuasive. There are three
ways you can attempt to influence attitude and behavior.

- You can create an attitude or behavior where none exists. This is
the easiest of these three because there is usually no predisposition
on the part of your target audience.

- You can reinforce an existing attitude or behavior. This is also
relatively easy to do because your target audience already believes
or behaves in the way you desire.

- You can attempt to change an attitude. This is the most difficult
to accomplish and, realistically, shouldn't be attempted unless
you are willing to expend a lot of time and energy on an, at best,
dubious outcome.

An example of an attitudinal objective might be:

> To create a favorable attitude among employees concerning
> the changeover from a monthly pay disbursement to a
> twice-monthly pay disbursement.

Methods for measuring this type of objective range from informal
employee feedback to formal surveys of attitudes some time after the
changeover has gone into effect.

An example of a behavioral objective might be:

> To increase the number of employees in attendance at the
> annual company picnic by 25 percent by mailing out weekly
> reminders to the homes of employees four weeks prior to
> the picnic.

Obviously, measuring the effectiveness of this objective is easier;
however, if you don't see an increase in attendance, you will have to do
some serious research into the reasons why. Be aware, however, that
these reasons might not involve your message or its presentation at all.
You might simply have picked the Sunday of the big state fair to hold
your picnic. Don't automatically conclude that your message is the
problem without exploring all variables affecting its desired results.

Choosing the Appropriate Medium or Media

Any *assumptions* you make concerning the most appropriate medium
for your message could be disastrous. Selecting the right medium or
media is a decision that should be based on sound knowledge of a

WRITING FOR PUBLIC RELATIONS   15

number of factors. Public relations educators Doug Newsom, Alan Scot and Judy VanSlyke Turk, in their book, *This Is PR: The Realities of Public Relations,* have suggested a series of important considerations to be used in choosing the right medium for your message:

- **What audience are you trying to reach and what do you know about its media usage patterns and the credibility ratings for each medium?** Many target audiences simply do not watch television or listen to the radio. Others don't read newspapers regularly or subscribe to magazines. You need to know, first, whether your intended audience will even see your message if it is presented in a medium they don't regularly use. Research tells us, for example, that businesspeople read the newspaper more than do some other groups, and rely on it for basic news and information. Other groups may rely on television almost exclusively for their news and information. For each of these groups, the credibility of the medium in question is vital. For example, businesspeople cite newspapers as a more credible source for news and information than television; however, for many people, television is far more credible.

- **When do you need to reach this audience in order for your message to be effective?** If time is of the essence, you'd best not leave your message for the next issue of the corporate magazine.

- **How much do you need to spend to reach your intended audience, and how much can you actually afford?** It may be that the only way to achieve the result you're looking for is to go to some extra expense such as a folder with more glitz or a full-color newsletter. Although every job has budget constraints, it's best to know from the start exactly what it will take to accomplish your objectives.

After these tough questions have been answered, you will still need to ask four others:

- **Which medium (of those you've listed in response to your first three questions) reaches the broadest segment of your target audience at the lowest cost?** The answer to this question will give you a "bottom-line" choice of sorts because cost is the controlling factor in answering it. It might be that you can reach all of an employee audience with an expensive corporate magazine, but two-thirds of it with a less expensive newsletter.

- **Which medium has the highest credibility and what does it cost?** Here, the correct answer will give you the additional factor of credibility that is key if your audience is discriminating at all. There are always those for whom the least credible of sources is still credible (otherwise, gossip tabloids would go out of business). But, for the honest communicator, credibility is important to the success of any future messages.

- **Which medium will deliver your message within the time constraints necessary for it to be effective?** Again, a critical letter distributed company-wide may be a lot more timely than a well-written article in next month's corporate magazine.

- **Should a single medium be used or a combination of complementary media (media mix)?** Remember, each element in an overall communications program may require a specialized medium in order for that portion of the message to be most effective.

Obviously, the more you know about your audience, the better you will be at selecting just the right medium for your message. However, you must also understand that media criteria often dictate message and message format. For instance, brochures "demand" brevity, as do flyers and posters; corporate magazines allow for fuller development of messages; newsletters offer more space than folders but less than magazines; pamphlets offer space for message expansion and place fewer demands on style; and annual reports require strict adherence to SEC (Security and Exchange Commission) guidelines. You must also consider cost, lead time for writing, editing, layout, typesetting, pasteup, printing, and distribution.

In short, selecting the most appropriate medium for your message is a complex endeavor. Be forewarned, therefore. No assumptions should be made about the acceptability of any particular medium. Until you have considered, at the least, the questions posed earlier, you will probably only be guessing on your choice of an ideal medium.

The Writing Process

Setting Message Strategy

Message strategy has to do with developing a message, or messages, that will reach and have the desired effect on your targeted audiences. Following the MBO method of organization, your message strategies should logically follow your objectives and contribute either directly or indirectly to them. You will need to develop individual message strategies for each of your target publics, based on what you have learned about them through your research. Remember, the strategy or strategies you employ will be determined, to a great extent, by your audience's makeup, predispositions, and perceived needs.

Sandra E. Moriarty, in her book *Creative Advertising*, has described five basic message strategies (which she calls *stratagems*) that summarize the general orientation of an overall creative strategy.

- **Information**. An information strategy is usually a straightforward statement of fact, best used on audiences interested enough to seek out the information you can provide. This strategy is frequently employed for such messages as new product announcements, consumer awareness campaigns, and public information programs. It is also used for supplemental messages to persuasive campaigns, such as position statements.

- **Argument**. Argument strategy assumes that there are at least two sides to the issue you are addressing. Messages are usually persuasive in nature and require an audience that is already interested in the issue and able to process information fairly well. Argument strategy makes frequent appeals to reasoning and logic and is best structured to reach either those who are already convinced or those who are neutral and open to reasoning.

- **Image**. Image strategy is used to develop or maintain a strong, memorable identity for a person, idea, product, or organization. It attempts to "bundle" perceptions into a single concept or symbol representing the subject of the message. The best image strategies result in a perception that the image itself *is* the subject, not just a symbolic representation of the subject. This technique is frequently used to publicize political candidates and to promote parity products that depend on a connotative association to differentiate them from competitors.

- **Emotional strategies**. Emotional strategies are generally intended to persuade. They are best used for messages aimed at those who are either neutral or already on your side, and will rarely convince the hard-core opposition. Emotional strategies depend on the use of emotionally laden words, images, or style elements, such as the use of "hot buttons" in a message—words or ideas that you know will "turn people on" emotionally. Most of us think of emotional strategies as useful only in the context of emotionally charged issues; however, everything from political candidates to soft drinks can be sold through emotional appeal, or through association of the "product" with emotions, such as patriotism or romance. Even humor can be seen as an emotional strategy because typically it makes us *feel* good about the message.

- **Entertainment**. Entertainment strategy is commonly used in advertising because it is particularly effective when communicating in highly competitive and cluttered environments. Remember, however, that, like humor, entertainment can be an excellent strategy for "selling" your ideas, philosophies, or whatever, regardless of the medium or format. The entertainment value of a message helps it gain and maintain attention.

Persuasive pieces are usually heavy on the positive attributes of your service, product, or point of view. They need to be written in terms the audience can relate to and frequently benefit from a use of words with emotional impact. Information pieces can get away with far fewer emotionally packed words and are frequently longer. After all, their aim is to inform; the assumption is that the audience is already convinced of, or at least interested in, the subject.

An informative piece should be balanced and complete. Its purpose is to let readers in on something they may not know or may have an incomplete picture of. The intent may be to publicize a new product or service, to set the record straight on a vital issue affecting your organization, or simply to let your readers know what's happening in your organization. Whatever the intent, the informational publication has to stick to just that—information. If your point of view is so strong as to evoke opposition, you probably should be writing a piece to persuade.

Setting a Style and Organizing the Message

To a large extent, style refers to format. Style is usually, but not always, predetermined by what medium you will use. If, for example, you are writing for a newsletter or house magazine, your choices will usually be limited to either straight news or feature. If you are writing a press release, your style will always be straight news. If you are writing for broadcast, the style will be that of a script.

Style also refers to grammatical and semantic usage, and to organizing your message.. These topics are extensively covered in **Chapters 13** and **14**. Rather than refering to these two chapters only when you have a question, it is a good idea to familiarize yourself with their contents before beginning to write.

Writing the informative message. Writing informative messages is one of the most straightforward tasks in pubic relations writing. Informative messages should be balanced and unbiased in presentation. Naturally, you can put your own "spin" on anything you write, but in the information piece, you should keep to the facts. Most audiences will see through a persuasive piece thinly disguised as information. This is one of the major objections journalists voice concerning press releases. They often say that much of what they receive is really advertising (persuasion) in disguise.

When writing an informative piece, ask yourself some questions.

- Why would my target audience want to know about this topic?
- What would they want to know about it?
- Is the topic tied to a particular strategy? If so, what strategy? If it is part of an overall persuasive campaign, why am I using an informative approach?
- How much material should I leave for "further information?"
- Am I expecting any results from this approach? Make your objectives clear enough to be measurable so that you can later evaluate the results of information dissemination effectively.

The most valid objective of information is to raise the level of knowledge or understanding of your target audience. The reason behind PR writing may be ultimately to persuade, but in informative pieces, bias should be kept to a minimum.

Writing the persuasive message. Writing a message that persuades is not easy. First, you have to have a crystal-clear understanding of what it is you want your readers to do in response to your persuasive effort. This means that you have to be able not only to convey your message in the clearest possible terms, but also be responsive to opposing points of view.

It is important to note here that the persuasive message is normally audience centered. Persuasive strategy is based on who your audience is and how they feel about your topic. The piece should inform, and while informing, persuade. The approach you use probably will be based on audience analysis—how receptive your audience is to either an emotional or a rational appeal. Historically, audiences react best to a combination of both. There are times, however, when a purely emotional or purely rational appeal will be most effective.

Remember, a hostile audience usually won't be convinced; a sympathetic audience doesn't need to be convinced; and an undecided audience is as likely to be convinced by your opposition as by you. Different strategies will be employed for each of these audiences. For instance, if you are writing for a friendly audience, an emotional appeal may work very well. For an undecided audience, a rational appeal supported by solid evidence may work best. If your audience is neutral or disinterested, you'll have to stress attention-getting devices. If they are uninformed, you'll have to inform them. And if they are simply undecided, you'll have to convince them.

For persuasive messages it is important to understand the psychological state of your audience and build your message around this. This audience-centered approach includes three basic techniques: the motivated sequence, the imagined Q & A, and messages aimed at attitude change. We will discuss each of these briefly.

The motivated sequence. A common tactic used by persuaders is the motivated sequence, which involves the following five steps.

1. **Attention**. You must first get the attention of your audience. This means that you have to open with a bang.

2. **Need**. Next, you have to establish why the topic is of importance to the audience. Set up the problem statement—a brief description of the issue you are dealing with.

3. **Satisfaction**. Present the solution. It has to be a legitimate solution to the problem.

4. **Support**. You have to support fully your solution and point out the pitfalls of any alternatives. Otherwise, your audience may not be able to comprehend completely the advantages of your solution over others.

5. **Action**. Finally, call for action. Ask your audience to respond to your message, and make it as easy as possible to take action.

The imagined Q & A. In the imagined Q & A, the message is structured into a series of questions that the audience might have, followed by your answer to each. Ask yourself the questions your audience might be asking you.

- **Why even talk about this subject**? Tell them the importance of your topic to them. Tie your topic to their concerns.

- **For example**? Don't just leave them with your point of view. Give them examples. Support your proposal.

- **So what**? Let them know what all of this means to them, and tell them what you want them to do.

Messages aimed at attitude change. Many novice writers assume that all they are obligated to do in a persuasive piece is present their side. This is a dangerous assumption, especially if the opposing side has sound arguments of its own. Any persuasion piece should cover all sides. If your arguments really are sound, they will stand up to comparison.

You may assume that your audience is at least familiar with opposing viewpoints. In most cases, it is advisable to address counter arguments only after you have presented your own side. When writing any piece that aims to change audience attitudes, try using the following guidelines.

1. State the opposing view fairly. Make your audience believe that you are fair-minded enough to recognize that there is another side and that you're intelligent enough to understand it.

2. State your position on the opposing view. Now that you've shown that you understand the other side, state why you don't think it's right—or, better yet, not totally right. This indicates that you find at least some merit in what others have to say—even the opposition.

3. Support your position. Give the details of your side of the argument. Use logic, not emotion. Show that you are above such tricks; however, don't avoid emotion altogether. Try to strike a balance while leaning toward logic and emotional control.

4. Compare the two positions and show why yours is the most viable. If you've done your work well up until this point, then your audience will already see the clear differences between the

two sides. Strengthen their understanding by reiterating the differences and finishing with a strong statement in support of your arguments.

The Evaluation Process

Now is the time to test your message. You'll need to test it on several levels in order for your assessment to be accurate.

First, do your messages reflect your original objectives as set during the planning process? You should ask yourself why each message has been developed. If the answer relates to accomplishing one of your objectives, then the message has succeeded at that level.

The adequacy of your selected target audience, choice of medium, and message strategy can be tested at the same time. The best approach is to test your message and medium on members of your target audience.

Focus Group Testing

Focus group testing has become a fairly common practice for those in advertising, marketing and public relations. The technique requires that you assemble a small group (usually not more than ten or so) from your target audience, present them with the message, and ask for their reactions. Your approach can be fairly formal (a written questionnaire to be filled out following the presentation), or informal (open-ended questions asked in an open discussion among the participants). The key is to design your questions in advance and to cover all the areas you need to analyze. Be sure to explore whether your message's language is appropriate to your audience. Is it difficult to follow or does it have too much jargon or too many technical terms? Does your audience understand the message? Does the message speak to them, or do they feel it is meant for someone else? Is the medium appropriate? Would your readers take time to read the message if it came to them in the mail? As an insert in their paychecks? In the corporate magazine? Answers to these questions should give you a fair idea of how your larger audience will react to your message.

The best way to set up a focus group is to hire a moderator who is experienced in asking these questions and interpreting the responses properly. Don't assume that because you are the writer, and the closest to the project, that you can interpret audience feedback clearly. In most cases, you are not the one best suited to act as the focus group's moderator. **Exhibit 1.3** describes in detail how to conduct a focus group.

Exhibit 1.3—How to Conduct a Focus Group

1.   Specify what you are trying to find out before you conduct the focus group. Don't go into a focus group without a clear idea of your objective. In fact, as with any other MBO-oriented program, you should develop a list of objectives for your focus group study. List exactly what you hope to discover from this meeting. Are you trying to find out whether your target audience will read stories about other employees? Do they react differently to different colors? Which color or combination of colors do they react most favorably to? You are trying to get your group to react to various stimuli you present to them.

2.   Decide on a moderator. It is best to hire someone who has done this before. Focus group moderators are experienced people with special skills in leading others into answering questions and reacting to stimuli without letting on what they are looking for.   Moderators moderate—that is, they lead the discussion, call on different respondents, and keep the discussion going without allowing a free-for-all to occur. If cost is a factor (and good moderators can cost a bit), you might consider conducting the focus group yourself. However, if you have never conducted a focus group or seen one conducted, you should attend a session or two before you attempt it yourself.

3.   Schedule according to your participants' needs, not yours. If members of your target audience are busiest during certain hours of the day or days of the week, don't hold your focus group during those times. Make the meeting convenient for them. This courtesy will help put them in a cooperative frame of mind. Know your audience and their special needs when you schedule. For example, if day care is an issue, perhaps you can arrange for it. If lunch is the only time you can hold your meeting, provide lunch.

4.   Select your participants properly. Develop a valid method for picking members of your target audience. In most cases, you only need a representative cross-section of your audience. For example, if 60 percent of your readers are women aged 25 to 35, make sure that 60 percent of your focus group are women with those demographics. Holding a focus group with nonrepresentative participants is self-defeating. If you are in doubt about whom to select, develop a screening questionnaire that will tell you whether the respondents are really part of your target audience.

5.   Provide for payment. Nearly all focus groups are paid. Most people won't participate for the fun of it (although some like having their opinions counted). Base what you pay on who you are interviewing. Professionals, such as physicians and attorneys, should receive around $100, while others may be happy with $20–$50 for the session. Make sure your participants know they will be paid. The screening questionnaire is a good place to mention it.

6.   Like the airlines, always over-book. If you need 10 people, book 15 or 20. Some will invariably not show up. If everyone does, just take them as they arrive, and turn away the rest once you've reached the number you need. But pay everyone, including those you don't use.

7.   Meet with your moderator and set up guidelines for the study. It is best to use your objectives as a starting point, and develop a set of procedures from them for the focus group interview. Lay out these procedures step by step so that if you conduct more than one focus group, you will be able to follow exactly the same procedures in each session.

8.   If possible, and your moderator doesn't think it will be obtrusive, you might want to sit in on the focus group as an observer. Always allow yourself to be introduced and don't interrupt or talk during the session.

9.   Provide refreshments, even if it's just coffee or juice. Most people expect some amenities in addition to the payment they receive. And it helps to put them in a better frame of mind.

10. The day of the focus group, check to make sure everything you will need for the meeting is ready and on hand. You'll be surprised how many rooms get cross-booked and you show up to find that someone else is using your room; or you count on someone else to bring the overhead projector, and they forget. Or you find you need to have pencils on hand, or paper, or wastebaskets, or any number of small items that can make or break a focus group meeting. As with everything else, it is best to make up a list of everything you will need to do or bring prior to the meeting. Then, arrive an hour early and check off your items.

11. Hold the focus group. Whether you are the moderator, or someone else, the following guidelines apply equally.

•   It is a good idea to audiotape or videotape a focus group. Many nuances of expression and voice aren't captured by simply taking notes or relying on written responses. If you use audiotape, make sure you have enough tape for the entire session, that it is good quality tape, and that your recorder will actually pick up everyone in the room. Don't rely on that tiny recorder you use to tape reminders to yourself. If you videotape, you'll need to hire a camera operator. Just positioning a stationary camera and turning it on won't do because you'll never be able to cover everyone in the room at once. And, if you do decide to tape, let your participants know in advance and remind them again when they are seated and ready to start. Don't rely completely on the tape, however. Use it as a backup and always take complete notes. If the tape fails, for whatever reason, notes may be all you have to go on. Plus, note taking makes the participants feel that you are doing your part as well.

- Always put your group at ease by telling them something about yourself, why you are conducting this study and the fact that it is entirely informal and open. Have the participants introduce themselves. Make sure they understand that you expect each one of them to play a part and that everyone's opinion counts equally. Stress that there are no right or wrong answers.

- A warm-up question that is easy to handle is a good way to get started—something fun, yet thought-provoking. For example, if part of your study is to gauge reactions to the new look of your newsletter, you might begin by asking each participant what his or her favorite color is.

- Remember a moderator moderates. Don't lose control of the group discussion. To ensure that everyone gets an opportunity to speak, try going around the table allowing each member of the group to answer each question, and don't ask a new question until everyone has answered the question on the floor. However, don't be afraid to veer from the point if an interesting side issue is raised. Just make sure everyone has a chance to respond to each issue in turn. If you find that one or two people tend to dominate the answers, focus on the quiet ones for a while, draw them out, and encourage their participation. Remind the group that everyone's opinion counts.

12. There is no set length for a focus group study. However, an hour to an hour and a half should be enough time to get what you need without tiring your participants. If you do go 90 minutes or longer, take a break midway through. When the meeting is over, thank the participants personally for their help and make sure they are paid before they leave.

13. Immediately after the focus group study is over, sit down with your notes and begin answering the questions you couched as objectives when you began this whole process. This is only the beginning, however. Don't draw hasty conclusions until you've had a chance to look at everything in context (including any tape you might have made of the meeting). Once you have a handle on the big picture, assemble all the evidence in the form of answers to your questions. Be sure to note if anything is incomplete. Perhaps you should have asked something else about reader interest in a particular area. Maybe you didn't probe deeply enough as to color preferences. Make note of these shortcomings so that if you conduct another focus group study, you can include expanded questions.

14. Draft a final report, even if it's to yourself, covering everything you found out through the focus group study. Send copies to appropriate parties and file a couple for future information. (Or for future editors of your newsletter. They'll thank you for it).

Readability Formulas

Readability formulas analyze everything from the level of education needed to understand a message to the number of personal pronouns used (a measure of the level of friendliness of the tone of your message). Two of the most common readability formulas are described here.

The Gunning Fog Index

1. Select a sample of 100 words from the middle of your message.
2. Count the number of sentences and divide 100 by that number to find an average sentence length (ASL).
3. Count the number of words consisting of three syllables or more in the 100 words. Do not include proper nouns, compound words like *typesetting*, or words that end in *ed* or *es*.
4. Add the totals from steps 2 and 3 and multiply by 0.4.

The resulting score approximates the number of years of schooling required to read the piece. College graduates usually can read at about a score of 16 while most bestsellers are written at 7-8. Obviously, if your piece is intended for vertical distribution, such as a company magazine, you will need to reach an "average" audience. Newspapers, for instance, write at about the sixth-grade level.

The Flesch Formula

1. Select a sample of 100 words from the middle of your piece.
2. Count the number of sentences; divide 100 by that number to find the average sentence length (ASL).
3. Count the number of syllables in the sample and divide this figure by 100 for the average word length (AWL).
4. Plug the resulting figures from steps 2 and 3 into the following formula:

Readability = 206.835 − (84.6 x AWL) − (1.015 x ASL)

5. Interpret the scores based on the following scale:

70–80 = very easy (romance novels)
60–65 = standard (newspapers, *Readers Digest*)
50–55 = "intellectual" magazines (*Harpers, The Atlantic*)
30 and below = scholarly journals, technical papers

This formula is based on ease of reading determined, to a large extent, by the length of words. This assumes that polysyllabic words slow down and often confuse the reader. Other formulas guage the degree of familiarity by noting personal pronouns, for instance.

This sort of evaluation is known as *preparation evaluation*. Obviously, it can only tell you if the message and the way it's packaged and presented are acceptable to your target audience. What it won't tell you is whether or not your audience will respond to your message. You'll have to wait for that.

Survey Techniques

Methods for judging the effectiveness of your communication once it is distributed range from expensive to relatively inexpensive and from complex to simple. Let's take the simplest first: readership surveys.

Readership surveys are simple questionnaires, usually included with your publication (as in a corporate magazine or newsletter), that seek to find out whether anyone out there is paying attention. A few, plainly put questions—about what interests your readers the most, the least, what they would change if they could, what they would include or leave out—will tell you a lot. Most commercial publications run an occasional readership survey just to make sure they're operating on the same wavelength as their readers.

On the more expensive level are formal, statistical surveys measuring everything from whether your readers are actually receiving your message to whether they're changing their attitudes or behaviors because of it. These surveys are best left to highly qualified specialists who will ask the right questions and properly interpret the answers. The results can be invaluable, particularly with persuasive messages. Remember, behavioral change can often be easily measured in increased sales of your new widget, attendance at the company picnic (remember to factor in the free beer as a contributing variable), more votes for your candidate, or a decrease in the number of complaint letters you receive on an issue. Attitude change, on the other hand, is more difficult to measure but, nonetheless, equally important.

Modern survey techniques, contrary to what critics say, can accurately define attitudes and measure shifts in them. Because of the complexity of the operation, however (and the need to perform both a pre- and a post-survey in order to have something to compare), you will have to pay the price. Good research isn't cheap.

The Legal Aspects of PR Writing

All those who deal in public communication are bound by certain laws. For the most part, these laws protect others. We are all familiar with the

First Amendment rights allowed the press in this country. To a certain degree, some of those rights transfer to public relations. For example, corporations now enjoy a limited First Amendment protection under what is known as *commercial speech*. Commercial speech, as defined by the Supreme Court, allows a corporation to state publicly its position on controversial issues. The Court's interpretation of this concept also allows for political activity through lobbying and political action committees.

But, as with most rights, there are concomitant obligations—chief among them is the obligation not to harm others through your communication. The most important "don't"s for public relations writers concern slander or libel (defamation), invasion of privacy, and infringement of copyrights or trademarks.

Defamation

Defamation is the area of infringement with which writers are most familiar. Although it is variously defined (each case seems to bring a new definition), defamation can be said to be any communication that holds a person up to contempt, hatred, ridicule, or scorn. One problem in defending against accusations of defamation is that there are different rules for different people. It is generally easier for private individuals to prove defamation than it is for those in the public eye. Celebrities and politicians, for example, open themselves to a certain amount of publicity, and, therefore, criticism. While a private individual suing for libel must only prove negligence, a public figure must prove malice. In order for defamation to be actionable, five elements must be present.

- There must be communication of a statement that harms a person's reputation in some way—even if it only lowers that person's esteem in another's eyes.
- The communication must have been published or communicated to a third party. The difference here is that between *slander* and *libel*. Slander is oral defamation, and might arise, for example, in a public speech. *Libel* is written defamation, though it also includes broadcast communication.
- The person defamed must have been identified in the communication, either by name or by direct inference. This is the toughest to prove if the person's name hasn't been used directly.
- The person defamed must be able to prove that the communication caused damage to his or her reputation.
- Negligence must also be shown. In other words, the source of the communication must be proved to have been negligent during

research or writing. Negligence can be the fault of poor information gathering. Public figures must prove malice—that is, the communication was made with knowing falsehood or reckless disregard for the truth.

There are defenses against defamation. The most obvious is that the communication is the truth, regardless of whether the information harmed someone's reputation or not.

The second defense is *privilege*. Privilege applies to statements made during public, official, or judicial proceedings. For example, if something normally libelous is reported accurately on the basis of a public meeting, the reporter cannot be held responsible. Privilege is a tricky concept, however, and care must be taken that privileged information be let only to those who have right to it. Public meetings are public information. Only concerned individuals have a right to privileged information released at private meetings.

The third most common defense is *fair comment*. This concept applies primarily to the right to criticize, as in theater or book critiques, and must be restricted to the public interest aspects of that which is under discussion. However, it also can be construed to apply to such communications as comparative advertising.

Privacy

Most of us are familiar with the term *invasion of privacy*. For public relations writers, infringing on privacy is a serious concern. It can happen very easily. For example, your position as editor of the house magazine doesn't automatically give you the right to use any employee picture you might have on file, or divulge personal information about an employee without their prior written permission.

Invasion of privacy falls roughly into the following categories.

- *Appropriation* is the commercial use of a person's name or picture without permission. For instance, you can't say that one of your employees supports the company's position on nuclear energy if that employee hasn't given you permission to do so— even if they do support that position and have said so to you.

  Private facts about individuals are also protected. Information about a person's lifestyle, family situation, personal health, etc., is considered to be strictly private and may not be disclosed without permission.

- *Intrusion* involves literally spying on another. Obtaining information by bugging, filming, or recording in any way another's private affairs is cause for a lawsuit.

Copyright

Most of us understand that we can't quote freely from a book without giving credit, photocopy entire publications to avoid buying copies, or reprint a cartoon strip in our corporate magazine without permission. Most forms of published communication are protected by copyright laws.

The reasons for copyright protection are fairly clear. Those who create original work, such as novels, songs, articles, and advertisements, lose the very means to their livelihood each time that novel, song, or advertisement is used without payment.

All writers need to be aware that copyrighted information is not theirs to use free of charge, without permission. Always check for copyright ownership on anything you plan to use in any way. You may want to rewrite information, or paraphrase it, and think that as long as you don't use the original wording you are exempt from copyright violation. Not so. There are prescribed guidelines for use of copyrighted information without permission. You may use a portion of copyrighted information if:

- It is not taken out of context,
- Credit is given to the source,
- Your usage doesn't affect the market for the material,
- You are using the information for scholastic or research purposes,
- The material used doesn't exceed a certain percentage of the total work.

Just remember, never use another's work without permission.

Trademarks

Trademarks are typically given for the protection of product names or, in certain instances, images, phrases or slogans. For example, several years ago, Anheuser-Busch sued a florist for calling a flower shop "This Bud's For You." The reason, of course, is that the slogan was commonly recognized as referring to Budweiser beer. The Disney studios have jealously guarded their trademarked cartoon characters for over fifty years and their trademark appears on thousands of items. Charles Schultz's Peanuts characters are also used for hundreds of purposes, all with permission. Even advertisments that mention other product names are careful to footnote trademark information.

One of the main reasons for trademark protection is to prevent someone not associated with the trademarked product, image, or slogan from using it for monetary gain without a portion of that gain (or at least recognition) going to the originator. Another important concern is that the trademarked product, image, or slogan be used correctly and under the direction of the originator. Certain trademarked names, such as *Xerox, Kleenex* and *Band-Aid,* have for years been in danger of passing into common usage as synonyms for the generic product lines of which they are part. The companies that manufacture these brand names are zealous in their efforts to ensure that others don't refer, for example, to photocopying as "xeroxing," or to facial tissue as "kleenex." In fact, one of the legal tests for determining whether a brand name has become a synonym for a generic product line is whether it is now included in dictionaries as a synonym for that product.

As harmless as it may seem, using the term "xeroxing" in a written piece to refer to photocopying, or the simple use of a cartoon character on a poster announcing a holiday party may be a trademark violation. The easiest thing to do is to check with the originator before using any trademarked element. Often, the only requirement will be either to use the true generic word (in the case of a brand name), or mention that the image, slogan, or name is a trademarked element and give the source's name. **Exhibit 1.4** defines symbols indicating protected material.

Exhibit 1.4—Symbols for Protected Material

 Copyright—Used to protect copy of any length. Can be "noticed"—or marked—either without actual federal registration (which limits protection under the law) or with registration (which expands the degree of legal protection).

 Registered Trademark—Used to protect any word, name, symbol, or device used by a manufacturer or merchant to identify and distinguish his or her goods from those of others. This mark indicates that the user has registered the item with the federal government, allowing maximum legal protection.

TM *Trademark—Similarly used, but as a "common law" notice. In other words, material marked this way is not necessarily registered with the government and thus has limited and not full legal protection.*

Learning to Adapt

One of the hallmarks of a good writer is the ability to adapt to the needs of the audience, the message, and the medium. Public relations writing, unlike many other forms of writing, requires this flexibility. In the following chapters, you will find a variety of writing styles utilized in different formats. The key to writing for public relations is to learn these formats and adapt your style to each as needed. The road to becoming a good public relations writer has many side tracks. It is quite easy to let yourself become specialized. The trick to becoming the best kind of writer is not to let that happen. The greater the variety of writing styles you can learn to use well, the better your chances of becoming an excellent writer will be.

CHAPTER 2

Media Relations
&
Placement

And do as adversaries do in law,
Strive mightily, but eat and drink as friends.

William Shakespeare

Public relations practitioners are professionals. So are journalists. Professionals, in the ideal sense, work together for the public welfare. Why, then, do public relations people see members of the media as adversaries, going out of their way to dig up the dirt? And why do reporters—whether print or broadcast—often see public relations people as "flaks," paid to run interference for their clients?

Actually, there is a little truth in either point of view and there are a number of legitimate complaints on both sides. Public relations people often are charged with covering up or stonewalling, while reporters often do seek only the negative in any issue. Obviously, this is far from a perfect relationship between professionals.

Part of the problem stems from a lack of real understanding in both camps of how the other operates. There is little you can do to make journalists find out more about PR, but you can do much to improve your own knowledge of how the media operate, what media people want from you, and what they are capable and not capable of providing.

The Stumbling Blocks

Know What News Is

The most common stumbling block to a good working relationship between public relations and media professionals is a mutually agreeable definition of the concept of *news*. Research has shown that most journalists judge news value based on at least some of the following characteristics:

- **Consequence**. Does the information have any importance to the prospective reading, listening, or viewing public? Is it something that the audience would pay to know? Remember, news value is frequently judged by what the audience is willing to pay for.

- **Interest**. Is the information unusual or entertaining? Does it have any human interest? People like to transcend the everyday world. Excitement, even vicarious excitement, often makes good news.

- **Timeliness**. Is the material current? If it isn't, is it a whole new angle on an old story? Remember, the word *news* means "new." This is one rule frequently broken by public relations practitioners. Nothing is more boring than yesterday's news.

- **Proximity**. For most public relations people seeking to connect with the media, a local angle is often the only way to do it. If it hits close to home, it stands a better chance of being reported.

- **Prominence**. Events and people of prominence frequently make the news. The problem, of course, is that your company president may not be as prominent to the media as he or she is to you.

If your story contains at least some of the above elements, it stands a chance of being viewed as news by media professionals.

Know Their Jobs

Remember the adage, "Know thine enemy"? It definitely applies to knowing the media. The media are a powerful force, and they can do a lot for you—or a lot against you. The determining factor may well be how much you know about media professionals and appreciate their jobs.

To that end, you should learn all you can about the media outlets and the individuals with whom you will be dealing on a regular basis. Having some journalism experience goes a long way toward understanding the frustrations of the job. Journalists have a tough life. I know—so do *you*. But, they are much less tolerant of people who don't understand them than you probably are. Many public relations practitioners have had prior journalistic experience or education.

Talk to journalists. Ask them for their guidelines on gathering news. Get to know how they write and what they choose to write about. Know their deadlines and keep them as if they were your own. In a way, they are. At the same time, try to let media people know what you do. Show them your style. Ask them for hints on how to make it more acceptable to their needs. Everybody likes to be asked their professional opinions.

A word needs to be said here about courting the press. Most journalists who deal in hard news don't react well to being courted. That is, they aren't likely to change anything they think or write because you invited them out to lunch. Although we've all heard stories about unethical journalists, I prefer to assume that every reporter has professional scruples. You should too. They may well go out to lunch with you, especially if you have a story that may interest them, but, they are very likely to pick up their own checks. The sole exception might be the trade press. Trade journalists are used to receiving samples of products that they are writing about. The editor of a plastics industry trade journal might have a desk full of everything from pieces of new plastic to lengths of rubber hose, or actual products made from new compounds. They usually look at these, not as gifts, but rather as evidence of the application or existence of new products. In fact, one of the stages product publicity goes through involves having the trade media "test" new products. The results usually end up in what are known as "roundups"—articles written in the trade media on a number of similar products, contrasting their pros and cons. Everything from small parts to expensive equipment is loaned out to the various trade publications for these purposes. These products are normally sent on a 90-day loan and returned after the testing is completed. For most media, though, the golden rule of media relations is, "Let them know you by your work, not by your checkbook."

Working with Media People

Finally, there are a few basic rules of thumb that will help you in dealing with the media.

- Always be honest. It takes a lot of hard work to build credibility, and nothing builds credibility like honesty. It only takes one mistake to ruin months of credibility building. If you are honest with the media, they will be fair to you. But, remember, fair to them means balanced and objective. They will tell all sides of a story, even the negative. You should be willing to do the same.

- Give media people what they want, not what you want. Ideally, they can be the same thing. The key, of course, is to make your information newsworthy, following the criteria listed earlier.

- Along the same lines, don't bombard journalists with a daily barrage of press releases. Nothing that happens that often is newsworthy. The reporters and editors who receive your releases know this and are very likely to stop reading your information.

- Don't plead your case or follow up on stories. The nature of publicity is to let the media handle it once you have released it. If you want more control than that, take out an ad.

Media Placement

Knowing the media will enhance your chances of placing valuable information with them. But, you can't rely on personal contact for everything. Placing PR materials with the media requires up-to-date information on all of the possible outlets for your materials. Naturally, the number and type of media outlets will depend on your business. If you are in the automotive industry, trade journals will be a vital link between you and your publics. If you work for an organization that is strictly local, then your media contacts will be limited to the local media. Local interest news will be important, too, within the communities in which your plants or offices are located. If you work for a regional or even a national operation, then your contacts will expand accordingly. Whatever media you deal with, it is important to keep updated lists and directories that meet your particular needs with the least amount of waste information.

Directories and Media Lists

A good directory is an indispensable tool for the media relations specialist. Directories come in all sizes and address almost every industry. Publishers of directories offer formats ranging from global *checkers* that include a variety of sources in every medium, to specialized directories dealing with a single medium.

There are a number of excellent directories for media placement. Here are some of the major ones.

- *Bacon PR and Media Information Systems.* A series including *Bacon's Publicity Checker* (two volumes covering editorial contacts in the US and Canada, magazines organized by industry, daily and weekly newspapers, and all multiple publisher groups); *Bacon's Media Alerts* (a directory of editorial profiles covering editorial features and special issues, often planned months in advance, for both magazines and newspapers); *Bacon's Radio/ TV Directory* (a listing of every TV and radio station in the US, listed geographically); and *Bacon's International Publicity Checker* (editorial contact information on magazines and newspapers in 15 Western European countries).

- *Burrelle's Media Directory*, organized similarly to Bacon's and published on a similar schedule. Both *Bacon*'s and *Burrelle*'s also provide clipping services separate from their directories.

- A series published by Larrison Communications that includes *Medical and Science News Media; Travel, Leisure and Entertainment News Media;* and *Business and Financial News Media.*

- *Editor & Publisher.* Several media guides, including the well-used *Editor & Publisher International Yearbook* (a collection of newspapers divided into dailies and weeklies and covering everything from local and national publications to house organs and college papers).

- *Standard Rate and Data Service* (SRDS), used primarily by advertisers, this multivolume set is one of the most exhaustive around for shear inclusion. If you are looking for every magazine published in the United States, in every category imaginable, this is your directory. SRDS also provides information on electronic media and newspapers as well.

Because the prices of these directories can range into the hundreds of dollars, you will need to be fairly selective.

When choosing a directory, keep the following key points in mind:

1. The directory should be current. If it is not updated at least once a year, its uses are limited.

2. The directory should cover the geographic area in which you operate and in which you want your organization's message to go out. You may not need a national directory if your operation is strictly local or statewide. Many states publish directories of all kinds of information, such as almanacs, that include media addresses.

3. If your primary target is trade publications, then you need to choose a directory that lists them. Standard Rate and Data Service, for instance, publishes a constant stream of listings, including business and industry directories.

4. If you are a heavy user of broadcast media, your directory should include broadcast listings.

5. The directory should list names of editors, news directors, and so on, and their addresses. Make sure these are current. Nothing is more embarrassing to you and more infuriating to them than to receive a press release addressed to the previous editor.

6. Make sure circulation is listed for print publications and listening/viewing audience for broadcast outlets. You don't want to waste an excellent story on a tiny circulation trade when you might have reached a much larger audience.

Directories are essential, but they are not the only tools you will need to keep up to date with media relations. Media lists are vital to your job. They are a more personal tool than directories because they contain details about local contacts and all the information you need to conduct business in your community. Media lists may include regional and even nationwide contacts depending on the scope of your operation. A media list, once compiled, has to updated by hand at least once a month. This job can usually be handled efficiently by clerical staff once the list is compiled. It only takes a 30-second phone call to each of the media outlets on your list to verify names and addresses. In the long run, the routine of updating will pay off.

In compiling a media list, you will need to include most of the following items.

1. Name of the publication, radio/TV station, particular show (for talk shows), and so on.

2. Names of editors, reporters, news directors, etc.

3. Addresses, including mailing and street addresses if they are different. You may need to hand deliver a press release on occasion, and this can be difficult if all you have is a P.O. box number.

4. Telephone and FAX numbers for the media outlets as well as for each of the people you have on your list. Many media outlets can now accept computer-generated press releases through normal telephone lines or satellite-transmitted video or audio actualities. Include details in your media list.

5. Any important editorial information such as style guidelines, deadlines, times of editions (morning/evening), dates of publication for magazines, times of broadcasts, use of actualities, photo requirements, use of facsimile or electronic transmission (and applicable phone numbers).

A computer is a great way to compile and maintain a media list. Computer software designed specifically for media lists (such as *PR Works* for the Macintosh) is available.

Placement Agencies

Placement agencies are outfits that will take your information, such as a press release, and send it out to a great many media outlets using their regularly updated media lists and computerized mailing services. Many of these firms mail out hundreds of releases for you—at a tidy cost.

Placement agencies will provide you with a great many more mailings than you might have gotten from your personal mailing list, but much of what is mailed out is not correctly targeted and ends up as waste coverage. As any business editor will tell you, the majority of press releases received are not relevant to the publication, and many originated from placement agencies in other states. You are often better off targeting those media with which you are most familiar and who you know are at least interested in your information.

The sole exception might be the newer, computerized firms such as PR Newswire. Organizations such as this send out your release electronically, over a newswire—just like the Associated Press. Media outlets can subscribe (free of charge) to the service and will receive your release—along with hundreds of others—sorted by subject and other descriptors. They can scan by subject, look at the lead only, or pull up the whole release. This method substantially reduces the amount of paper they have to plow through and guarantees at least subjects of interest to them. Your advantage is that you can target locally, regionally, or nationally. Of course, the price of placing the release increases with its coverage.

Fitting Your Information to Your Outlet

It is essential to know as much as possible about the media outlet to which you are sending your information. Never submit information blindly to publications or stations you've never read, watched, or listened to. Picking a trade publication out of *Standard Rate and Data* just because it has a large circulation doesn't ensure that it is the type of publication in which you want to see your story.

The key, of course, is to read the publication, watch the TV station, or listen to the radio station first. By doing so, you also will learn about the outlet's style and will be able to tailor your release accordingly.

If you are writing for a trade journal, don't automatically assume that the one you have chosen is similar in style to others in the industry. Remember that publications are often differentiated by their styles when they deal with similar subject matter.

Understanding Radio and Television

Before placing information on the radio, you will need to understand the concept of format. Whereas placement of your message on television requires a familiarity with the various program offerings of the stations you are dealing with, placement on radio is usually determined by the format of the station—usually designed around the type of music it plays or information it provides. For example, some stations play only Top-40 hits. These stations usually cater to a teenage audience. If a teen audience is your target public, then you might want to consider sending your information to a Top-40 station. Other stations might provide a news-only format, or a jazz format, or a classical music format.

Determining what radio station you place your message on depends on what your target audience listens to, and that is determined through audience research. If, for instance, your target audience regularly listens to jazz, then you would be best served to place your message on a station using a jazz format. Examine the formats and styles of all publications or broadcast shows you would like to accept your information. Prepare your material in a style as close to theirs as you can. For example, if you are prerecording PSAs (public service announcements) for use on various stations, you might want to put a different music track on each spot depending on the format of the station with which it will be placed. Nothing is quite so jarring to listeners of a classical music station as to have their entertainment interrupted with a message surrounded by a rock music background. Although a rock music station might carry a spot with a classical music background, the opposite is probably not true.

Any radio sales manager will be able (and quite willing) to provide you with detailed analyses of the station's listening audience. All you have to do is to match your target audience profile with its listener profile.

Television is much easier to figure out. It is the medium that reaches the broadest segment of the population. Rather than depending on formatting to attract a single audience, television depends on different programs and times of day to attract different audiences.

To determine which television station to use, you will first need to know how far its signal reaches (commonly referred to as *reach*). Just like radio, a TV sales manager will be able to give you detailed statistics on viewing audiences by time of day and program.

You will need to consider the following questions before you write for either radio or television.

1. If radio, what format does the station use? If television, what programs are appropriate to your message?

2. Will the station take taped actualities (for interviews or reactions)? If so, what kind of tape? Reel-to-reel? Cassette? If it is video for television, will the station want one-inch tape, or three-quarter- or half-inch cassette? Can they use slides? How about slide-tape?

3. What length spot will the station use? 10-, 20-, 30-, or 60-second spots?

4. Who will write the copy? Will you write and submit it or will you simply give the station the information? Will the station use scripts you have written for its announcers to read?

5. Will the station provide production services or will you have to have your message prerecorded?

6. How much lead time does the station need? For production? For placement?

All of these considerations, and probably a few more, will have to be taken into account before you can work successfully with the broadcast media. Note that all this information should be included in your media list.

Broadcast Cover Letter

Before you send any information to a radio or television in station in the form of a "spot" (a written script or prerecorded message designed specifically for broadcast), make sure it is accompanied by a cover letter explaining the content and a mail-back card of some kind through which the station can let you know when and if your spot was aired. **Exhibit 2.1** is a generic example of such information.

Cooperation Is the Key

Whether your message is delivered to your target audience depends a great deal on the cooperation of the mass media. It is in your best interest to foster a professional relationship with those media representatives with whom you deal regularly. If they respect your professionalism in meeting their (and by inference, their audiences') needs, you will be rewarded with cooperation—and that is a major step in the right direction.

Exhibit 2.1—Cover Letter and Mail-back Card

The American Tuberculosis Foundation
1212 Folger Street
New York, New York 00912

Dear Program Director:

Smoking and lung disease are issues that affect all of us in some way. The recent concern over second-hand smoke has resulted in considerable debate. In an effort to help "clear the air," the American Tuberculosis Foundation hopes you will run the enclosed radio/TV spots for the education of your listening/viewing audience.

Since our campaign started in January, over 300 radio/TV stations around the country have responded by airing the "Your Good Health" spots. We hope that you will join them in serving your listening/viewing audience.

For your convenience, we have provided you with a mail-back card. By filling out this important evaluation, you will help us to better serve our common interests in the future.

Thank you,

MAIL-BACK CARD: "YOUR GOOD HEALTH"

I have aired or intend to air the following spots: (circle appropriate length).

10 sec.   20 sec.   30 sec.   60 sec.

Radio   Television

The spots aired the following times and dates:

Day	Times

CHAPTER 3

Press Releases
&
Backgrounders

Though it be honest, it is never good to bring bad news...

William Shakespeare

T he press release has been called the workhorse of public relations. Every day, thousands of press releases are sent out all over the country to newspapers, magazines, and radio and television stations. Some newspaper editors receive as many as a thousand a month. Of these, only a minuscule number are ever used, and most of these are severely edited. Why, then, do public relations professionals, and the people who employ them, continue to use press releases? Because they are still effective. They are still used by newspapers and trade journals to pass along information about events and occurrences that reporters might not otherwise have the time or the inclination to cover.

The key to effective press releases is not so much in the writing, although we will concentrate on that, but in the placement. As we saw in the previous chapter, knowing when something is newsworthy and when it is not, and knowing your contacts in the media and their schedules and guidelines, are the most important elements of press release writing.

As a writer of press releases, you will become a reporter. It is essential that you understand journalistic style in order to present your releases in the proper format. Remember that reporters and editors are used to seeing one style of writing on a daily basis. That style fits their papers and they are unlikely to print anything that doesn't conform. Remember, too, that although the reporter is responsible only to his or her editor, you are responsible to both the editor and the people you work for. This means that you must accommodate both the style of the newspaper and the needs of your employer. It is not an easy fence to walk, but as a public relations practitioner, you have to try to keep your balance.

What Is a Press Release?

A press release is information that you wish released to the press, usually the print media. Although all press releases have format in common, there are different emphases.

- Basic **publicity releases** cover any information occurring within an organization that might have some news value to local, regional, or even national media.
- **Product releases** deal with specific products or product lines. These are usually targeted to trade publications within individual industries. They can deal with the product itself, consumer use of the product, or a particular business or marketing angle.
- **Financial releases** are used primarily in shareholder relations; however, they are also of interest to financial media and many local, regional, and national general media have financial highlights sections.

Writing a Press Release

The style of the press release is that of the straight news story: it begins with a lead, expands on the lead, and proceeds to present information in decreasing order of importance. This "inverted pyramid" style allows an editor to perform his or her job—that is, edit—from the bottom up.

The Lead

The lead is all important. You are competing for the editor's attention with scores of other press releases. A quick glance at the lead should tell the editor whether he or she can use your release or not. Note, however, that a publicist's lead is likely to differ from one written by a newspaper reporter. The following examples, written for a local newspaper, will serve to explain the difference.

Publicist's Lead:
Francis Langly, former Director of Research and Development at Rogers Experimental Plastics Company, will be
awarded the prestigious Goodyear Medal on June 6 in
Indianapolis at a banquet held in his honor. Awarded by the
American Chemical Society, the Goodyear Medal is the
premier award for work in the field of specialty elastomers.

Reporter's Lead:
Francis Langly, 24 Cedar Crest Drive, will receive the
Goodyear Medal at the annual meeting of the American
Chemical Society. The conference is being held in India-
napolis on June 6.

Although neither of these examples is particularly original—public
relations releases rarely are—there are still reasons for the differences
in content and style. Consider these questions.

    1. Why is the address left out in the publicist's lead?
    2. Why is Langly's title included in the publicist's lead?
    3. What is the difference between the phrases "will receive" and
       "will be awarded"?
    4. What is the significance for the publicist in pointing out that the
       Goodyear medal is the premier award in the field?

Answers to these questions illustrate the differences between hard news
and publicity and between the publicist's and the journalist's objectives.

As every journalist knows, the lead is the hook that entices the
reader into your story. For the public relations practitioner, too, the lead
is a hook to entice the editor into running your release. Don't ever get
the notion that any press release you send out will automatically be
printed or that it will even be printed the way you wrote it. The fact is,
that even if you have written the most appealing press release ever seen
at the *Daily Planet*, editors feel an obligation to edit. You will be lucky
to have the information in your release placed. This should not deter you
from writing a good lead, however, and a good release. First, you have
to sell the editor before your release will ever be seen by anyone else.

Editors often take less than 30 seconds to peruse a press release. A
lot depends on how you present yourself in the headline (title) and the
lead. Most editors use several measures to determine whether your
release will be used. Who you are, as regards your past record of
providing only legitimate news, is the first important consideration.
Once past that, your headline or title should tell them whether your

release is important to them or not (more on this later). Finally, your lead should summarize the relevancy of your story.

The *summary lead* is by far the most common type. A good summary lead will answer the key questions—who, what, when, where, why, and how. The delayed lead is used to add drama to a news story; however, this type of lead is usually reserved for feature stories and is not appropriate for straight news.

Before you write the lead, you must first decide on a theme. Try to determine what is unique about the event covered by your release. Although press releases should generally be considered as straight news stories, and must be informative, they don't have to be boring. To illustrate, look at the lead from a release distributed by the Electronic Products Producers Association.

> "The present condition of the software market is such that companies involved in software development should be able to capitalize on current economic trends. This means that new product development should allow the earliest investors a significant niche in the market." This statement was made by Mr. James L. Sutton, President of Associated Products Corporation, during a speech at the Fall convention of the Electronic Products Producers Association held in Syracuse, New York.

Now consider this revised version of the same lead.

> A leading electronics industry executive declared today (October 21) that the computer software market is wide open to new investors.
>
> "The present condition of the software market is such that companies involved in software development should be able to capitalize on current trends," said James L. Sutton, president of Associated Products Corporation. "This means that new product development should allow the earliest investors a significant niche in the market."
>
> Sutton's prediction of a dynamic market was made in a speech given at the Fall convention of the Electronic Products Producers Association in Syracuse, New York.

Notice how the second lead has broken up the quote and used the proper journalistic form for attribution. The opening paragraph has been rewritten to include most of the pertinent information:

Who? A leading electronics industry executive.

What? Declared a wide-open computer software market.

When? Today (October 21). Notice the inclusion of the actual date in parentheses. This is to let the editor know that the "today" you are speaking of is October 21. If the paper receives the release on October 20 but doesn't publish the information until October 22, they will need to correct the copy to read "yesterday."

Where? Left until the final paragraph. (It isn't always necessary to squeeze all of the information into the first paragraph.)

Why? Included in the explanatory paragraph following the lead. Of all the information, "why" is the most likely to be left out of the lead because it usually takes the most explanation and invites the interested reader to look further.

How? In a speech. Also left for the final paragraph.

The thing to remember is that you are responsible for the ordering of points in your lead and in your press release. The more interesting you can make the information by order of presentation, the better it will read. Notice also how much shorter the sentences *seem* in the revised version. In fact, there is only one more sentence than in the original, but because the quote is broken up and the attribution placed in the middle, the sentences seem much shorter. Although it is wise to present most of the key information early in the release, only the most important elements need appear in the lead. The rest can follow in logical order.

Using Quotations

Quotations add interest to your press release. It is always good to obtain usable quotations and then to place them at appropriate spots throughout the release. Note that it is never a good idea to begin a press release with a quote. Because press releases are considered straight news stories, a quote fails to come to the point soon enough. As was seen above, quotes need not be written as complete sentences, followed by the attribution; they can be broken up by the attribution. You don't need to follow every quotation by an attribution, especially if it is understood that the same person quoted earlier is still being quoted. A good rule of thumb is to repeat an attribution if more than one paragraph has elapsed since it was last given. Of course, if you change the source of the quotation, you will need to designate the change by a new attribution. Don't be afraid to work with the form of attribution, and don't use the same form each time. Consider the following:

> Johnson, a long-time trucker, doesn't like the strike. "This layoff has really affected my family," *he said.* The strike has

> been in effect for three months. "We're down to eating beans
> out of a can," *he said.* Johnson has three small children
> and a $500 a month house payment. "I don't know what I'm
> going to do about my bills," *he said.*

The form of attribution (*he said*) is correct but its repetition is monotonous. There are a number of ways of attributing a quotation that can add variety to releases. For example, you can simply paraphrase points of the quote, combine quotes, or simply use one attribution between two quotes. Look at this revised version.

> Johnson, a long-time trucker, doesn't like the three-month-
> long strike. "This layoff has really affected my family," he
> says. "We're down to eating beans out of a can."
> Johnson, who has three small children and a $500 a
> month house payment, says he doesn't know what he's
> going to do about his bills.

Notice that the tense of the attribution has also been changed to the present. Press releases need to sound as timely as possible, which includes using the present tense in attributions if possible. If you are dealing with a story that is obviously past, then attribution must reflect this.

Most newswriting classes and most journalists adhere to the rule of using only the last name in an attribution. Press releases, on the other hand, must follow the conventions set up by the originating organization. In most cases, even if you do insist on attributing a quotation to "Mr. Jones" or "President Smith," the news editor will delete the honorific. You will have done your job by using the conventions of your employer. In the long run, that is all you are expected to do.

Accuracy

The accuracy of quotations is obviously important, but while public relations writers can have some leeway, reporters must be absolutely accurate. An illustration will help explain. Suppose you work for Rogers Experimental Plastics Company. You are writing a release on a new product line and are quoting the company president. You have interviewed the president and he knows you are writing the release. He is also aware of what he said. However, because he will probably be reviewing the release before it is sent out, he will correct anything he doesn't like. As a writer and an employee, you have the creative ability and leeway to "invent" a quotation as long as he approves it. No employer will fault you for putting well written words in his mouth. Suppose the president had said:

> I don't think anything like this new plastic has ever been seen—at least not around this area of the world. It may be the greatest thing since sliced bread and who knows how much money we'll make from it.

You may actually write in your release:

> Paul Johnson, President of REPC, is excited about the new product. "We've come up with a totally new concept in plastic," he says. "I expect that the market for 'Plagets' in the West will be tremendous."

All you've done is tidy up the quotation and make it more interesting. Remember that you may "doctor" only quotations that will be checked for accuracy and approved by the party to whom they are attributed. It is a good rule to make sure that anyone you interview receives a copy of the finished release before it is distributed. There is nothing like a libel suit for sobering up a writer. Of course, one legitimate way of presenting unclear or clumsy quotations is to paraphrase or use indirect attribution. This is fine for news stories written by reporters, but press releases can benefit a great deal from well-written quotations.

Press Release Format

Although public relations practitioners often incorporate the conventions of their organization into their press releases, there is a standard press release format (see **Exhibit 3.1**).

1. Press releases are typically written on plain, white bond paper with no decorative border.
2. Margins are one to one-and-a-half inches on all sides.
3. The address of the sender is placed in the upper left-hand corner of the first page. This identifying block should include the complete address, name of the contact person (usually the person who wrote the release), and a telephone number. It is especially important to include a night telephone number as well as a daytime number. Remember, newspapers don't shut down at night and if an editor wants to use your release but needs further or clarifying information and can't reach you, the release may get dumped.

4. The release date appears on the right margin, slightly lower than the bottom of the address block. This portion provides the editor with exact information concerning the appropriate timing for the release. More about release dates later.

5. The body of the release begins about one-third of the way down the page, allowing some white space for comments or notes from the editor. If there is to be a title—and titles are entirely optional—it should come between the address block and the body of the release, flush left. Typically, the title does not extend beyond the address block by more than a few characters, which usually means that it will be stacked (broken into two lines on top of each other). The title should be in all caps, single spaced, with the last line underlined.

6. The body of the press release is double spaced. Never single-space a press release. Paragraphs are usually indented with normal spacing between paragraphs. Some companies prefer no indention and triple-spacing between paragraphs but the standard is indented.

7. If the release runs more than a page, the word "more" is placed in brackets or within dashes at the bottom of the page.

8. Following pages are identified by a slug-line followed by several dashes and the page number at the top of the page, usually either flush left or flush right.

9. The end of the release is designated in one of several ways. Use the word "end" or the number "30" either in quotation marks or within dashes, or the symbol # # # # #.

Timing and Dating Releases

When do you want your release to be published or broadcast? If you have just written a release about an important meeting that will be held tomorrow (January 23) but you don't want the information that will be presented at that meeting to reach the public prior to the meeting, you will have to say so on your release. Although it is wise not to send out releases too far in advance of an event, it is also wise to be as timely as possible—which means getting your release to the paper beforehand.

There are a number of ways of designating release dates and times, and all of them belong below the address block, flush right.

Exhibit 3.1—Press Release Format

Company or Client Name
and Address Here
Contact: (Your Name)
Day Phone:
Night Phone:

Release Date and Time

THE TITLE GOES HERE, ALL UPPER
CASE AND UNDERLINED LIKE THIS

The Point of Origin Dateline Goes Here -- The body of the release should begin one-third of the way down the page to leave enough room for the editor or copy person to write remarks.The release proper should be all double spaced for ease of readability and editing.

Be sure to use normal indents and consistent spacing between paragraphs. It is not necessary to triple space between paragraphs. All information should be presented in descending order of importance, ending with the least important items in case last-minute editing results in the bottom of your release being lopped off.

Remember to leave at least one-inch margins all around, but resist the urge to leave huge right-hand margins in order to stretch your information.

When you arrive at the bottom of the first page, leave at least a one-inch margin and indicate either the end of your release (-30-) or that more information follows (-more-). If more information follows, try not to break paragraphs or sentences in the middle. Never break a word and complete it on the next page.

-30-

1. **Release with no specific time frame.** By far the most common type of release and usually designated by *For Immediate Release*. Other phrases include *For Release on Receipt* or *For Release at Will*. It is unnecessary to add a date to this type of release statement.

2. **Release with specific date.** An example would be *For Release January 23 or Thereafter*, or if you need to be even more specific, *For Release January 23, 10:00 p.m. or Thereafter*. Other options are *Hold for Release, Friday, January 23, 10 a.m.,* or *For Release after 10:00 a.m., Friday, January 23*. This type of release statement could be used, for instance, if you want all the media to carry it at one time; or if the event is actually occurring at a future date but you want to release the information early.

Datelines

Datelines are used to indicate the point of origin of your press release if, for some reason, that is important. Datelines are important to foreign correspondents to enable readers to appreciate that a story originated at the location where it happened. For public relations practitioners, a dateline may serve the same purpose. It alerts the editor to the fact that your release concerns an event either reported from or happening at a certain geographical location. Datelines should be placed immediately preceding the opening of your release proper, on the same line.

> Springfield, OH—Rogers Experimental Plastics Company (REPC) has announced the development of a versatile new plastic widget that has the potential for use in a number of industries from automotives to electronics.

Note that if the city is well known, there is no need to include the name of the state (New York, Los Angeles, etc.). In the case of a city whose name may be popular in a number of states, you would want to designate the state, (as in the example above to differentiate Springfield, OH, from Springfield, OR, or Springfield, KY, or any number of Springfields). However, if the release is intended for a statewide press only, you can get by with just the name of the city. If there is any possibility that confusion might arise from use of the city name only, include the state (Moscow, Idaho or Moscow, Russia?).

Exclusives and Specials

If your release is an exclusive (intended for only one paper) make sure the editor knows it. Remember that an exclusive can only be sent to one publication. A special, on the other hand, is a release written in a certain style, intended for a specific publication, but being released elsewhere as well. (See **Exhibit 3.2.**) Both designations should be noted immediately below the release information as follows:

> For Immediate Release Exclusive to the <u>Daily Planet</u>
>
> For Release February 24 or Thereafter Special to the <u>Daily Planet</u>

Exhibit 3.2—Exclusives and Specials

Deer Point Development, Inc.
Box 1387
Deer Point, Michigan 72493
Contact: Warren Bailey
Day Phone: (714) 555-6635
Night Phone: (714) 555-1765

For Immediate Release
Special to the Deer Point Sentinel

<u>NEW PLANT TO OPEN IN DEER POINT</u>

 A new plant designed to manufacture high tech components for automobiles is scheduled to be opened in late July according to Eleanor Maston, president of Deer Point Development, Inc. (DPD).The two-building facility will encompass over 55,000 square feet and be housed on a five-acre plot near the Doe River. Maston's company was instrumental in the planning, acquisition of land, and contracting of firms for the construction of the new plant. The plant will be owned and operated by Auto-Tech, Inc. of Albatross, Maine—a long-time member of the automotive peripherals industry.

 Maston predicts that over 800 new jobs will be created by the plant's construction. "Auto-Tech has assured us that they intend to

-more-

New Plant—2

hire the majority of their plant workers from the local community," she says. "They plan to bring in only a bare-bones management crew from the outside to begin with, and train local people
from the ground up."

According to Maston, DPD first learned of the scheme last
December when Auto-Tech president Wilson Klatchki contacted
her. The New England-based company was seeking to expand
into the high-tech industry and needed a plant close to the major
automobile manufacturers in Detroit. Deer Point seemed like the
perfect solution.

"Auto-Tech felt that our proximity to Detroit was ideal," Maston
says. "They wanted to be close without having to build in the city
itself."

The site was chosen for its availability and scenic location,
according to Maston. "Because high tech is basically a 'clean'
industry, being located near Doe River poses no environmental
problems," she says.

Construction of the plant began in February and is expected to
continue through the summer.

-30-

Local Interest

Local media outlets like local stories. For most public relations writers,
press releases can almost always be oriented to a local audience. The
real problem is finding just the right local angle—the one that will
entice the newspaper into running the story. Some basic rules of thumb
will help you in your placement:

1. If you are releasing a story with national as well as local interest,
    try to construct your release so that any local information is
    interspersed throughout the release. This way, it will be difficult
    to cut out the national information, which might not be of
    interest to a local editor, without harming the local angle.

2. Avoid commercial plugs. Editors recognize advertising instantly and will simply round-file (trash) your release. Keep your local angle newsworthy.

3. If you are sending only to local media and you reference a local city in your release, omit the name of the state.

4. Above all, don't strain to find a local angle where there is none.

Suppose that you are assigned to write a release that has national importance and you want to target it for a local paper, the *Seattle Times*. You know from your interview with William J. Hoffman, chief systems engineer of Associated Products Corporation of Syracuse, N.Y. that he went to high school and college in Seattle. Based only on this little bit of knowledge, the piece can be localized. In addition, you could try to place a version of the release in the *Lincoln High Review* and another version in the University of Washington *Husky* (the alumni paper). Your leads might look like this:

> For the *Seattle Times*
> William J. Hoffman, Seattle native and Chief Systems Engineer for Associated Products Corporation (APC) of Syracuse, N.Y., has been credited with developing a revolutionary educational software line.

> For the *Lincoln High Review*
> William J. Hoffman, a Lincoln High School graduate and former president of the LHS Electronics Club, has been credited with developing a revolutionary educational software line.

> For the *University of Washington Husky*
> William J. Hoffman, a University of Washington graduate with honors in Engineering, has been credited with developing a revolutionary educational software line.

You might think that the Lincoln High School angle is too much of a strain. If you do, don't use it. Every angle, however, is worth at least some consideration. You'll be surprised how your placements can multiply if you ask the right questions in your interviews and construct the right angles from the answers.

Remember, though, that the focus of your release isn't always the local angle. That is only the hook. Don't slight your real story in favor of the local angle, no matter how interesting it is. In the samples above, for instance, Hoffman is the angle, but the software is the story. The trick is to lead with the angle, move to the story, and keep the two so intertwined that any editor will have difficulty separating them.

Product Press Releases

Product publicity often has little or nothing to do with advertising. In its strictest sense, advertising refers only to the purchasing of time or space in which to run a message. Product publicity is not paid for. It is a far more subtle art. You must be able to construct informative passages concerning a given product without actually "pitching" the product. This is not an easy task. The minute an editor detects a sales pitch, the release gets pitched.

Most product publicity goes through several stages: product introduction (usually via press releases to trade media), articles in which the product is reviewed after testing (written by the trade publications themselves), and "user articles" (submitted by the public relations writer focusing on actual users of the new product). This section covers only product introduction releases.

Product releases serve a multitude of purposes, from pure information about a single product, to publicity for other companies and other products. It is quite common to mention contributing manufacturers in a product release. For example, if you develop a basic plastic that is then used by a leading headphone manufacturer in their product design, it is usually acceptable to mention their use of your product. There is always the chance that the headphone manufacturer will reciprocate. In fact, many such joint arrangements are formalized when products are publicized. Consider the release in **Exhibit 3.3** about a new water cooler.

Exhibit 3.3—Product Press Release

Tall Drink of Water, Inc.
435 Lasado Circle
Watertown, NY 10056
Contact: Myrna Hofman
Phone: (121) 555-1222   For Immediate Release

NEW FOUNTAIN DISPENSES
COLD, HOT, AND ICE WATER

Watertown, NY—A new water fountain that dispenses cold water, hot water, and ice has been marketed by Tall Drink of Water,Inc. (TDW) of Watertown, NY. The new fountain, which already is appearing in offices across the country, operates on an entirely new system for compartmentalizing water supplies.

-more-

Fountain—2

According to TDW president and co-founder, Willis Reed, the new fountain represents four years of hard work. "We spent a lot of time on this new fountain," he says. "It's a whole new concept in water fountains. We did some initial research on office water consumers and found that they wanted not only cold water, but also hot and iced water as well."

The new fountain uses a system of valves that pass the water from the building plumbing system through the fountain in a series of stages. The incoming water is captured first in a central reservoir. From this central pool, the liquid is siphoned off to the cold water tank. This tank feeds the main drinking spout for normal water needs. Ice is produced in a refrigerated tank located next to the cold water reservoir and dispensed through a separate opening in the side of the fountain. On the opposite side of the fountain is the hot water dispenser, which feeds off a heater tank located above the main reservoir.

"It's the addition of the ice maker that makes our fountain unique," says Reed. "We use a Handy-Ice III manufactured by FREON, Inc. in Asbury Park, NJ," he says. "The Handy Ice III produces ice at a rate that far exceeds anything else on the market today. A number of other manufacturers already make dual purpose fountains, but ours covers the entire range of drinking needs."

Reed indicates that the new fountain will probably be marketed in areas with noticeable seasonal shifts. "We expect that areas that have pronounced seasonal temperature fluctuations will have the greatest need for our fountain," he says. "But almost any office where people have different tastes in beverages is a potential market." Reed explains that in any given office environment, 75 percent of the staff will be satisfied with just plain water; however, the other 25 percent will use a fountain for making hot drinks such as tea and soup in the winter and iced drinks in the hot months. He also expects that the very availability of such a fountain will increase its usage.

# # # # #

Can you tell who the publicity is for? From the address block you learn that the company which manufactures the fountain is sending out the release; however, a second company is also mentioned. The manufacturer of the ice maker is given some free publicity. In many cases, this is a good thing to do. Obviously, you don't want to give your competition a helping hand, but it never hurts to help your friends. Often, it's difficult to tell what the real publicity point is in a product release. If the above release had been written and distributed by an agency or by FREON, Inc., then the "bottom line" publicity would actually be for the ice maker, through publicity for the fountain. This is not an uncommon approach in product publicity and is not normally considered unethical.

Product press releases are arranged slightly differently from other releases. Although they certainly follow the normal inverted pyramid style of decreasing order of importance, they are quite obvious in their inductive approach to the product definition. In other words, product releases normally proceed from a general statement concerning the product (often an announcement that the product is on the market) to specific information about the product's attributes, characteristics, and applications. The end of the release is usually reserved for company background—full name, relationship to parent or subsidiary companies, and branch locations or the location at which the specific product is made. The release in **Exhibit 3.4** reflects this pattern of organization.

Writing News Releases for Broadcast

Radio is meant to be heard and television is made to be seen and heard. That means you have to write for the ear or for the ear and eye. Simplification is the key to broadcast writing. Because it is harder to absorb the spoken word than the written word, concepts need to be pared down to the bare bones. Sentences must be shorter, speech more colloquial, and complex issues distilled to their essence. One of the major advantages of using broadcast media is repeatability. Listeners may hear or see a message many times in the course of a single day or a single week. Even so, you must learn to write as though your audience will only hear or see your message one time.

Consider the differences between the following leads written for two different releases—one meant for print, the other for radio.

Print:
INDIANAPOLIS, June 6—Francis Langly, former Director of Research and Development for Associated Products Corpo-

Exhibit 3.4—Product Press Release

1800 Avenue of the Americas
Syracuse, NY 10025-1234

Contact: Mark Spanger
Day telephone: (315) 555-9836
Night telephone: (315) 555-5467

For Immediate Release

VERSATILE NEW ELASTOMER
HAS INDUSTRY-WIDE APPLICATIONS

Associated Products Corporation (APC) has announced the development of a versatile new elastomer with the potential for use in a number of industries from automotives to electronics. The new compound, dubbed "PLIENT," is a vacuum-molded elastomer product displaying characteristics of both plastic and rubber.

"We've worked for almost five years on this product,"says Raoul Simpson, materials engineer for APC. "We think 'PLIENT' will revolutionize the way designers think about certain applications from now on." Simpson led the team that developed "PLIENT" and has already begun experiments designed to test its broad range of applications. "We already know it can be used in the automotive industry replacing the heavy two-piece metal widgets now being used," he says. "We suspect that it will be useful in a number of related and unrelated industries including electronics as a more cost-effective replacement for fiberoptics."

The key element to the success of "PLIENT" is its ability to withstand temperature extremes and its resistance to oil and abrasive chemicals. And because of its characteristic conductive nature, it has the potential for a number of applications in the electronics industry.

Paul Johnson, Vice President of the Elastomers Division of APC, is excited about the new product."We've come up with a totally new concept in versatility," he says. "I expect that the market for 'PLIENT' in the West will be tremendous."

Associated Products Corporation has been developing plastics products for uses in industry since its founding in 1979. Its Elastomers Division is located in Springfield, N.Y., with a subsidiary in Cleveland, Ohio.

# # # # #

ration (APC), today received the American Chemical Society's (ACS) Goodyear Medal—ACS's most prestigious award—for his work in the field of specialty elastomers.

Radio:
At an awards luncheon in Indianapolis today, a Wilmington native received the highest honor of the American Chemical Society. The prestigious Goodyear Medal—awarded for work in the field of specialty elastomers—went to Francis Langly, former Director of Research and Development for Associated Products Corporation.

Although both releases are of approximately the same length, there are some noticeable differences that raise some interesting questions:

1. Why doesn't the broadcast release start with a dateline?

2. Why not use the abbreviations ACS and APC in the broadcast release?

3. What is the reason for beginning the broadcast release with the location rather than the name as in the print release?

Datelines are not needed in broadcast releases because they won't be read. The point of origin usually becomes clear through the narrative. Abbreviations are too confusing when heard on the air. It is always advisable to use the entire name, unless the abbreviation has become commonplace usage. Finally, beginning with location in broadcast helps set the scene. This is peculiar to broadcasting and is a carryover from drama, in which a scene is set prior to any dialogue.

Use the medium to your advantage. If you are using radio, set the scene first, then populate it with real people and easy-to-understand facts. Remember, a news release for radio or television is just that—news. It is intended for the same purpose as a press release—to be used as news. The closer to acceptable news style it is, the better your chances of getting it broadcast. Prepare your releases for broadcast media using the same format you would use for a print release. **Exhibit 3.5** illustrates this.

After reading the broadcast release in **Exhibit 3.5**, ask yourself some questions.

• Why is paraphrase used instead of direct quotation in this release?

• Does the lead establish a sense of place prior to coming to the point?

• Can you locate all the elements of a lead within the release?

Exhibit 3.5—Broadcast Release

Society for Needy Children
4240 Welxton Avenue
Newhope, MN 78940
Contact: Lucille Bevard
Day Phone: 555-8743
Night Phone: 555-9745

For Immediate Release

A little girl stood for the first time today to receive a new teddy bear and a check for $75,000 from the Society for Needy Children. Eight-year-old Mary Patterson accepted the check on behalf of the children at the St. Mary Martha's Children's Hospital. The money represents the culmination of a year-long fund-raising drive by the Society.

The money is earmarked for a new ward to be devoted exclusively to the treatment of crippling diseases in children. One of the first beneficiaries will undoubtedly be little Mary, who has been disabled by congenital arthritis since birth. Along with her new teddy bear, Mary and the other children at the hospital will be using a new physical therapy center donated through a matching grant from the Friends of St. Mary Martha's.

Hospital Administrator Lois Shelcroft says that the check and the new therapy center are just the first step, and that the Society for Needy Children has promised to continue their fundraising efforts on the hospital's behalf in the coming year. Society spokesperson Jane Alexander says that the next fund-raising drive, scheduled to begin in September, will provide funding for a new lab.

# # # # #

- Are they where they should be in order of importance?
- If you were a news announcer, what additional information would you want to have before you ran this story?

Remember, no matter what the type of press release, it is still information you will lose control over once it is sent out to the media. They are your primary audience. You must learn to write for them first. To the extent that you do this, your releases will have a greater chance of reaching any other audience.

Backgrounders

Backgrounders are in-depth information pieces. As the name implies, they provide background information for anyone wishing it—reporters, ad copywriters, speech writers, and editors. Backgrounders are almost always prepared by the public relations staff. A good backgrounder is comprehensive yet concise. It should never be used to espouse company policy or philosophy. That is reserved for controlled media, such as ads, and editorials.

Backgrounders frequently accompany press releases in press kits. They usually supply enough information to fill in any gaps left by the release. Often, they are just insurance against getting called in the middle of the night by a reporter who is editing your press release and in the need of some "background." Other times, they are important "sales pieces," setting up an historical need for a new product. In order to make a backgrounder comprehensive, the public relations writer must research as many sources as possible, including old articles, brochures, reports, press releases and materials published outside the organization. Backgrounders can also benefit from personal interviews. As with press releases, backgrounders are more readable if they contain firsthand information.

A backgrounder should begin with a statement of the issue being addressed. Because it is not a news story or press release, it need not be presented as a lead nor need it follow the inverted pyramid style. Most backgrounders, however, do follow a basic pattern.

1. Open with a concise statement of the issue or subject on which the accompanying press release is based. Try to make it as interesting as possible. This opening statement should lead logically into the next section.

2. Follow the opening with an historical overview of the issue. You should trace its evolution—how it came to be—and the major events leading up to it. It is permissible here to use outside information. For instance, if you were writing a backgrounder on a new surgical technique, you would want to trace briefly the history of the technique's development and tie this in with information on techniques that had been used in the past. It is advisable to name your sources in the body of the text when appropriate. Readers of backgrounders want to know where you got your information.

3. Work your way to the present. This is the meat of your backgrounder. You want to explain the issue you opened with and its significance. Be factual. Remember, a backgrounder is an information piece, not an advertisement, or the place to sell your company's philosophy.

4. Present the implications of the issue being discussed and point the direction for future applications. Even though a backgrounder is a public relations piece, it needs to be carefully couched in fact-based information.

5. Use subheads where appropriate. Subheads negate the need for elaborate transitions and allow you to order your information logically. Subheads need to be carefully chosen and should contribute to understanding.

6. Most backgrounders are four or five pages in length. Let your information dictate your length; however, don't become long winded or pad your document. Editors will recognize fluff immediately. The object of a backgrounder is to provide information and answer anticipated questions, nothing more.

The backgrounder in **Exhibit 3.6** was used as an accompanying piece to a press release touting the advantages of a fire-resistant latex foam for use in upholstered furniture and mattresses.

- How does it follow the recommendations for writing a backgrounder?
- How does it differ?
- Does it trace the history of the issue adequately?
- Does it bring the reader up to the present and cover the current status of the issue?

Can you tell from reading this backgrounder that it was meant to sell a product? Probably not, unless you knew in advance that it was part of a product-related press kit. The object of a backgrounder is to provide background, not to "sell" anything. In the case of this particular backgrounder, information is provided concerning fire safety and the need for purchasers of upholstered furniture to be aware of the dangers of fire.

The next step is to present the readers with a suggested action. This can, and often does, come in the accompanying product press release. Thus, the trick to writing backgrounders is to make them relate to your subject without actually "pushing" your product, philosophy, or service.

Exhibit 3.6—Backgrounder

Contents, Not Structure, Pose the Most Fire Hazards

Losses to fires are costing billions of dollars and claiming thousands of lives each year in the United States. The National Fire Protection Association handbook states: "Fire resistive construction is an important life-safety measure. However, severe fires may occur in the contents of fire resistive buildings, and highly combustible decorations and interior finish materials may more than offset the value of noncombustible structurals." In fact, of all the contents common to residential, commercial, and institutional occupancies, the most often underestimated is the hazard from burning upholstered chairs and mattresses.

Although the many desirable features of a fire resistive building cannot be overlooked, there is no such thing as a "fireproof" building. Regardless of the construction type, there are always combustibles within the building. Generally, contents fires present a greater life safety hazard to building occupants than the eventual ignition of the structure. In fact, the cause and early stages of fires are related to the building contents and interior finish materials and not the structure.

No matter what the construction type, the contents fire must be controlled in order to achieve life safety. A parallel may be drawn between a contents fire in a fire resistive building and a fire in a furnace. The contents are the fuel and the building is the furnace.

Statistics Show Furniture Fires on the Rise

The Consumer Products Safety Commission recently stated that last year there were about 62,000 bedding fires which caused 930

-more-

fatalities. Another 35,000 fires in upholstered furniture took 1,400 lives, prompting the Commission to declare that these materials are the "biggest killer of all the products under the jurisdiction of the agency."

The National Bureau of Standards had earlier reported that mattresses, bedding, and upholstered furniture were involved in 45 percent of the fatal fires they reviewed where the materials first ignited could be identified. They concluded that "any inroads that can be made into the furniture problem promises greater fire-death reduction than any other type of strategy."

Building Design Not the Answer

As for building design, recent well-publicized fires have resulted in new provisions to building fire codes; however, over 90 percent of the buildings that will be in use in the year 2000 have already been built. Reliance on these new fire codes for personal safety may, in fact, be unwarranted.

Although building design and fire protection devices are important, they do not guarantee the safety of the occupants. Many fires develop too rapidly for fire systems, such as sprinklers, to control. Fires can spread past a sprinkler head to another area before the sprinkler head operates. Another fire might smolder for hours, producing deadly smoke and gases but not enough heat to cause operation for the sprinkler system. In addition, property loss is most closely related to fire-resistant building materials which would have to be incorporated into future structures. Building contents most strongly affect human safety.

Fire Reduction Not Yet a Reality

A decade ago, the National Commission on Fire Prevention and Control reported that fire was a major national problem, ranking between crime and product safety in annual cost. They were appalled to find "that the richest nation in the world leads all the major industrialized countries in per capita deaths and property loss from fire." The efforts of this commission focused attention on fires and resulted in the establishment of a goal to reduce the nation's fire losses by 50 percent in the next decade. That goal has not be realized.

Recent fire loss data from the National Fire Prevention Association suggests that we have performed poorly in our efforts to reduce the nation's fire losses. Multiple death fires, killing three or more people, have increased 70 percent in the past decade. In fact, fatalities in this group rose 37 percent between 1972 and 1980, and fires in this category are increasing at an average rate of 7.5 percent a year.

-more-

The estimated property loss from just building fires in the United States last year was about $6 billion, an increase of almost 7 percent from the year before. Further analysis of the estimate for fire loss data this year shows that:

— Educational facilities lost $184 million, an increase of 82.2 percent over last year's figures.

— Institutional facilities lost $38 million, up 52 percent.

— Areas of public assembly lost $356 million, up 9.2 percent.

— And residential occupancies, such as hotels, motels, and apartments, lost $3.3 billion, up 7.1 percent from last year.

Judging from this data, it is apparent that the goal of reducing fire losses by 50 percent has not been met. In fact, fire losses are steadily increasing in most cases. Why? In answering this question, some important points must be taken into consideration:

— Contents may more than offset the value of noncombustible building materials, and

— The flammability properties of the contents are critical to life safety.

Although most new buildings are constructed in accordance with a national building code such as the National Fire Protection Agency (NFPA) 101 Life Safety Code or a similar code, no national code regulates upholstered seating or mattresses. And although a Federal mattress flammability standard exists, its effectiveness has been questioned by both the Consumer Products Safety Commission and the National Bureau of Standards. As a result, a concrete fortress could be built according to code and filled with furniture that burns like gasoline. Larger buildings can contain tons of such furniture.

The Burden of Safety Is on the Buyer

In the absence of codes specifically meant for furniture, the burden of safety falls on the person selecting furniture for a residence, commercial structure, or installation. Greater care must be taken to select the most fire-resistant furniture available for a particular need. In judging these needs, the hazards to which the furniture might be exposed should be considered, such as the likelihood of cigarette burns, open flames, proximity of fuel or other combustibles, and population density. For example, in areas with a high level of vandalism, materials with a good open flame resistance might be needed, while furniture prone to accidental ignition may only need to be cigarette resistant.

-more-

The ultimate test of any furniture is, of course, how it will perform in an actual fire. It is obvious that fire-resistant structures are not enough to ensure life safety. If the nation's fire losses are to be reduced, then the potential hazards of furnishings must be considered.

# # # # #

Fact Sheets

Fact sheets contain just that—facts—and nothing more. If you have a lot of figures, for example, or a few charts that help explain your topic more easily, or simply a few itemized points you want to make, then a fact sheet is the form to use. A fact sheet is usually only one page, sometimes printed on both sides. It should elaborate on already presented information, such as a press release, and not merely repeat what has already been said.

For example, if you have written a press release about the relocation of a facility to a new site, a press release will disclose the newsworthiness of the event with particulars on when the move is to take place, for what reasons, etc. A fact sheet, however, can elaborate in interesting ways. For example, you might want to itemize costs, or break out major donations made toward the move, or elaborate on size of facility with square foot comparisons.

Take a look at **Exhibits 3.7** and **3.8** . These fact sheets are slightly different, but each contributes to forming a more complete story. The first fills in the numbers on a museum move, and the second supports a product press kit for a line of vitamins.

Exhibit 3.7—Museum Fact Sheet

University of Northern Washington
2900 Provender Drive
Alderdale, Washington 99304
Contact: Richard Lawson, (206) 555-1234

<u>Museum of Natural History Fact Sheet</u>

The University of Northern Washington Museum of Natural History will move into a new building on the east side of campus by March of 1996. The museum is being relocated as part of the university's $45 million project to expand and modernize its science facilities.

-more-

Museum Fact Sheet – 2

Future Location:
On the northwest end of a university-owned parking lot on East 23rd
Avenue, between Renton and Box Streets. The parking lot is being
redesigned so that no parking spaces will be lost as a result of the new
building.

Construction timeline:
Five months, beginning in late summer.

Cost:
$635,000

Fund-raising goal:
$150,000 to complete and equip the building.

Balance left to be raised by mid-August:
$72,500

Pledges to date: $77,000

- $32,500 from former UNW football coach Arlyss Thompson to
  build the storage area for the geology collection.

- $22,500 on a one-to-two challenge match pledged by
  Thompson for construction costs.

- $22,500 from Seattle philanthropist Frazier Crane, to match half
  of the Thompson challenge, on the condition that the rest of the
  money be raised from other sources.

Other funding sources:
$485,000 allocated by the university from the $8.1 million Department
of Energy grant for the first phase of the capital construction program to
build modern science facilities on campus.

Square feet:
11,000 with a 9,100 square-foot courtyard. Total square footage of
existing building is 10,689.

Special features:
Air-conditioned and climate-controlled to protect the highly fragile
collections.

Advantages:
Improved public access and increased public parking.

# # # # #

Exhibit 3.8—Weight Control Fact Sheet

VITAMIX VITALSTATS

Vitamix International
P.O. Box 9234
Westphalen, Ohio 76456

Vitamix Vital Statistics

- About 2/3 of U.S. households reported making dietary changes in the past survey year for reasons of health or nutrition. Of these, 43% cited weight control as the primary reason for the changes.

- 53% of the adult population surveyed have tried to control weight during the past year by "staying away from fattening foods and/or eating less"—up from 48% the year before.

- 18% of the adult population surveyed this year reported the use of "low-fat" food/beverage options as part of weight control strategy.

Population Overweight/Obese

- According to the data collected in the most recent Health and Weight Loss Survey (HWLS), 32% of the men and 36% of the women aged 20-27 were 10 percent or more above their desirable weight.

- 14% of the men and 24% of the women were 20 percent or more above their desirable weight in the same HWLS survey.

- 7 million Americans are classified as extremely obese.

- 30% of all males and 49% of all females surveyed by the National Center for Vital Statistics said they considered themselves overweight.

- More than half of those surveyed in a recent Aerobic 4 National Fitness Survey said "it would be beneficial to lose weight."

-more-

<u>Weight Control Diets</u>

- At any given time, at least 20% of the population are on some kind of weight-loss diet.

- 33% of those surveyed in the Aerobic 4 National Fitness Survey said they are dieting either to lose or maintain weight.

- 56% of women aged 25-34 said they were dieting in a recent Nielsen Survey.

# # # # #

The Press Kit

One of the most common methods of distributing brochures and other collateral information pieces is via the press kit. Press kits are produced and used for a wide variety of public relations purposes. They are handed out at product promotion presentations and press conferences; they are used as promotional packages by regional or local distributors or agencies; and they are part of the never-ending stream of information provided by organizations to get their messages out. When a press kit, or press packet, is used properly, it can effectively aid message dissemination by adding the right amount of unduplicated information to the media mix.

The press kit (also called the media kit or information kit) is usually composed of a number of information pieces enclosed within a folder. (See **Exhibit 3.9.**) The cover usually indicates who is providing the kit and its purpose. A press kit should include the following at the bare minimum:

- A table of contents;
- A press release;
- A backgrounder or a fact sheet;
- One or two other information pieces such as:
    —Already-printed brochures
    —Company magazines or newsletters
    —An annual report
    —A feature story or sidebar, if appropriate to the subject matter
    —A biography (or biographies) and accompanying photos

Anything fewer than these items is a waste of folder space. If you have only a few items to disseminate and wish to avoid the cost of producing folders, use plain, manuscript-sized envelopes. They are cheaper than folders; you might already have them in stock with your address printed on them; and they are ready for mailing.

The contents of a press kit can vary greatly depending on the intent of the kit. For example, the contents of a *media kit* distributed by the American Lung Association to its regional offices contained the following items:

- Cover letter
- Table of contents
- Clipsheet (photos and logos for newspaper placement)
- Magazine ad folder with sample return order card
- Magazine drop-in ad instructions
- Suggested cover letter for magazine ad folder
- Newspaper clipsheet instructions
- Captioned photo
- Direction sheets titled "How to get the best use of TV PSAs" and "How to get local ID on TV spots"
- Radio scripts (tapes sent with kit)
- Radio usage report and cover letter
- Report of use card
- Radio station phone call (scripted inquiry used to contact radio station program directors)
- Radio PSA distribution report card
- Television scripts (tapes sent with kit)
- Storyboard for TV spot
- Cover letter for TV stations
- TV PSA delivery report card
- Report of use card for TV PSAs
- Supply service memo and order form for more of any of these items

In contrast, a *press kit* for a corporate product introduction briefing included these items:

- Press release on the new product
- Color photo and cutline (caption)
- Press release on the product content (the material used to manufacture the product)
- Black and white photo and cutline of other products made from the manufactured material
- Press release describing another application of the material

- Black and white and color photos of that application
- Backgrounder on the material
- In-house magazine article tear sheet on the material
- Color brochure on the material and its uses
- Press release on new materials being developed
- Hard copy of the product presentation speeches

Press kits can serve many purposes and should include enough information to meet the needs of their audiences. The key to assembling a useful kit is to keep in mind the needs of those receiving the information.

If you are providing a press kit to the media for a press conference, it should include some of the following items:

- A cover letter explaining the kit and a table of contents listing each item in the kit, with each item listed as appearing on the right or left side of the folder.
- A basic facts sheet outlining the participants at the press conference, the relevant dates, and any facts or figures that might be unclear.
- A backgrounder explaining the relevance of the current topic in an historical context.
- Press releases of about one and one-half pages for both print and broadcast media. Give both releases to each reporter.
- Any feature stories or sidebar-type information that might be of interest to reporters. Be sure it is relevant.
- Any photos or other visual materials that might add to the stories. Include cutlines.
- If any individuals play an important part in the event the press conference covers, include biographies on them as well as photos.
- Include any, already produced information pieces that might be of interest to the media, such as brochures, in-house publications, etc.

Once you have assembled a press kit, make sure that all of the media get a copy, even those reporters who do not attend the event your press kit is designed to cover. Press kits are most effective when used with a good, up-to-date media list. By labeling your press kits with the name of the various media outlets prior to your event, you will know immediately after the event who showed up and who didn't. You can then mail the remaining kits to the prodigal media.

Exhibit 3.9—Press Kit

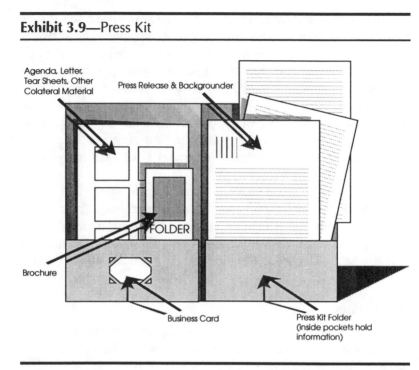

Agenda, Letter, Tear Sheets, Other Colateral Material

Press Release & Backgrounder

FOLDER

Brochure

Business Card

Press Kit Folder (inside pockets hold information)

Case Study: Associated Products Corporation

The following information pertains to a mythical company. Additional information will be presented in subsequent chapters. Use this and the additional information to complete all assignments.

Background

You work in the Public Relations Department of the Marketing Division of Associated Products Corporation (APC), located in Syracuse, New York. APC is a large company with several divisions, each manufacturing a different product. The Marketing Division handles all the marketing for all of the products company wide. As part of the Marketing Division, the Public Relations Department is charged with handling the company's image with its various publics including consumers.

The Electronics Division of APC has just developed a new line of educational software for both IBM and Apple computers. The software, called InfoQuick or IQ, is a series of programs designed as teaching aids for a variety of curricula from first grade through high school.

The development of the IQ series was an ambitious undertaking costing millions of dollars. Not only were educators in a number of fields consulted, but the best programmers available were hired to develop the software. At this point, the first programs have been developed in history and science for grades 1–12 , and in math for grades 9–12.

Advertising is being handled by an outside agency. The new software line will be marketed under a blanket educational "road show" demonstrating its uses in schools, shopping malls, and trade shows, in addition to the agency advertising. The road show will all be handled in-house by the Marketing Division and the Public Relations Department.

The Product

Since the advent of the personal computer a major market has developed in software. Companies ranging from the manufacturers of the personal computers on which the software is to be run to independent companies whose sole product is software have entered this very lucrative market. Each year in the U.S., over $10 billion in software is purchased by owners of business and personal computers. Of that $10 billion, some $2 billion is spent on educational software. The major buyers are individuals who purchase the software for their children. Schools account for roughly four percent of purchases.

The range of software available includes game-oriented programs designed to stimulate the otherwise reticent learner. Recent studies conducted at California University have shown that problem learners have benefited the most from this type of program. The increasing popularity of video games has added impetus to the market by providing a vehicle for learning. Many programs have already been developed utilizing the video game approach to learning. It has been found that students become more involved and acquire knowledge faster when the learning process is interactive.

The major thrust at this time appears to be the development of cohesive and comprehensive software packages which can be used by a varied age group at different levels of education. As part of a major study carried out last year by California Research Institute (CRI), teachers in grades 1–12 were questioned as to the educational needs of their students. Forty-five percent stressed the need for more student-teacher interaction, given large class sizes and brief class periods. Among the 1,200 respondents in the CRI study, 35 percent knew something about computers, 25 percent owned their own personal computers, and 40 percent rated themselves as having little or no knowledge of computers. However, even among those who expressed no knowledge of computers, there was a strong willingness to accept computer technology as a suggested solution to the student-teacher interaction problem.

Name of software package: InfoQuick or IQ
Areas developed to date:
>History programs, grades 1–12
>Science programs, grades 1–12
>Math programs, grades 9–12

Sample software programs
History
1. Famous Historical Personalities Series
>*Meet Mr. Franklin*
>*Meet Mr. Lincoln*

These programs explore historical figures as if they were living people. The students must interact with them in simulated computer conversations. By learning about the characters, the students will learn something about the period in which they lived and the policies they helped develop and influence.

2. Famous Documents Series
>*Writing the Constitution*
>*Mapping the Way West*

These programs require the student to write or create a map while exploring the reasons behind specific historical events. For instance, a student might be asked to write what he or she might include in the constitution if it were to be written today. The Way West program teaches basic mapping skills while students learn the historical significance of the westward expansion. Students will read and work with the treaties that created our country piece by piece.

Science
>1. *Big Bones*—All about dinosaurs, with special computer graphics of dinosaurs and their skeletal structures.

2. *Small World*—All about the inside of the atom, with special computer graphics of atomic structure.

3. *Guts*—All about human biology, including skeletal structure, digestive system, circulatory system, and muscles.

For High School:
Advanced programs in all Math, Science, and Social Studies areas such as *Algebra IQ, Chemistry IQ, Geometry IQ.*

Software development is continuing and a complete series is expected in all grade levels within two years.

Market Testing

During the concept and development of InfoQuick (IQ), the proposed product was field tested through a series of programs in target schools. The educators who were hired initially to work in the concept stages of development were also utilized in the premarketing test stages. Three schools were chosen for the test: one each on the East Coast, in the Midwest, and on the West Coast. The schools were selected as reflective of the national average for student enrollment, socio-economic stratum, and cultural balance.

Although it was impossible to select a perfectly "average" school or group of schools, the aim was to test the marketability of IQ on the type of student and school that would be most likely to use the finished product. A high school, junior high, and elementary school were chosen and one complete curriculum package was tested in each school as follows:

Location	Grade	Program
East Coast	4	*Big Bones*
Midwest	7	*Meet Mr. Lincoln*
West Coast	11	*Algebra IQ*

The results were analyzed and the programs were moderately revised to adjust to recommendations from teachers and students. The remainder of the programs were designed along the guidelines resulting from these test situations.

The Project

The company realizes that to sell educational software, there must be a demand. To help generate increased demand, and to enhance its status as a corporate good citizen, APC has contacted the National Education Association (NEA) and arranged to work with them on a project that will introduce children to computers. The proposed APC/NEA project will emphasize learning problems, computer skills, and the importance of new technology to education. The emphasis will be on both the learning of computer skills and learning from computers. APC has donated $1 million to NEA as seed money to get the project underway. Although the public relations aspects of promoting the company through the NEA project and marketing aspects of launching the new IQ line are somewhat separate, there is some overlap.

In addition to the advertising, APC will be working closely with the NEA in developing and releasing information and organizing special events to educate the public about computers (and by extension, IQ). The NEA proposes to develop a speaker's bureau composed of computer trained educators who will be available nationwide as tutors for other educators and for students. The idea is to set up workshops for educators first, followed by basic demonstrations for students. Part of the APC seed money will go toward supplying computers for the training sessions. Another portion will go into an NEA fund that will help defray the cost of a school or school district's purchase of a computer system.

Some facts:
- More than 2,000 school districts in the U.S. have access to or own their own computer system.

- Statistics show that high school graduates with computer skills are likely to obtain higher-paying jobs than those without.

- The National Institute for Scholastic Testing has released a study showing that students between the ages of 7 and 14 have the ability to acquire computer skills readily and absorb information more quickly when it is embedded in a fun-oriented, interactive format such as a computer program.

The NEA

The National Education Association (NEA) is an organization of professional educators in the United States, with more than one million members. The NEA was founded in 1857 as the National Teachers Association and was chartered by Congress in 1906. It is composed of four departments, 16 national affiliates, and 11 associated organizations, each representing an area of specialized interest. Its general aim is to promote the welfare of all professional educators, including both teachers and administrators; however, it has also been a leader in educational innovation and reform.

Utilizing the $1 million APC grant, the NEA has assembled a number of speaker-instructors to augment their new program of educating teachers and students in the use of computers as a learning tool. The services of the group, called "Byte of the Apple," are available nationwide by writing care of the National Education Association, Box 1776, Washington, DC 00716.

A speaker-instructor will come to the school, present a training session to the teachers and students who will be using the computers, and provide the school or school district with information on setting up a computer teaching facility of their own. Computers for the NEA/APC sessions will be provided for by the APC grant. The training sessions can be adapted to individual needs. The workshop normally includes one four-hour session for teachers only. The next day (or that afternoon if a one-day workshop is desired) another four-hour session will be held involving selected students, allowing teacher-student interaction. Included in the training sessions will be an explanation of how computers work, how they fit into the various curricula, how to teach with a computer, and selected software recommendations for future reference. Initial handouts will include a pamphlet presenting an overview of what the speaker-instructor will be talking about.

Should the school adopt the new computer learning program and wish to set up a computer learning center of its own, it will also receive complete print support in the form of workbooks, instruction manuals, and posters concerning computers and software.

The Company

Associated Products Corporation was founded in 1966 as Apex Frozen Foods. In 1970, the company purchased Traxton Electronics and changed its name to Associated Products Company. Since that time, APC has acquired four more concerns: Johnson Paper Company in 1972, LLD Packaging in 1975, Trading Post Textiles in 1975, and Philcronics Electronics in 1970. The current president, James Sutton, took over from the company founder, Alex Cordel, in 1985. Cordel is now Chairman of the Board for APC. Under Sutton, APC has developed several new products including IQ software, a new line of facial tissues, and a new stereo headphone that folds up to fit in the palm of your hand. It has also developed innovative packaging designs for perishable items such as milk, other dairy products, and fresh fruit juices.

Currently, APC is in the midst of negotiating a deal to purchase Value Rent-a-Car. Since its founding in 1966, APC has grown to a position as one of the top 500 corporations in the country. Its total profit last year was $456 million, up 24 percent from the previous year. Its stock has been consistently strong. At the present time, Alex Cordel holds 43 percent of the company stock with the rest divided among about 4,500 investors.

The People

William J. Hoffman, chief systems engineer, heads the research team that developed the new IQ software. Hoffman has been chief systems engineer at APC for 10 years and is a native of Seattle, Washington where he attended Lincoln High School and the University of Washington. While at Lincoln High, he was the president of the electronics club and the chess club. At the University of Washington, he majored in engineering and graduated with honors in 1976. Hoffman has worked for APC since 1977 and was promoted to chief systems engineer in 1984. Here is a sampling of his statements made in a recent interview concerning the development of the new software.

> "We've been working on IQ for about five years now. Me and the others on the team think we've got something big here."

> "This package is designed to cover an entire educational career, from first grade through high school. It took a lot of sweat to come up with program ideas and information enough to cover that amount of time, skill levels, and grade levels."

> "I got to work with pretty smart people outside the computer field for a change, and I think we all learned a lot in the process."

> "I think I always knew that this is what I would do. Even in high school, before computers were everyday things, I was interested in the concept of computers and programming."

> "This kind of creative engineering is what I like to do the most. I could easily do this for the rest of my life."

James Sutton has been president of APC since 1985, when he was promoted from senior vice president of marketing. Sutton is a native of Deerborn, Ohio, and graduated from Ohio State University in 1979 with a business degree. He was instrumental in coming up with the idea for a new software line and has developed successfully other product lines for the various divisions of APC since he assumed the presidency. Here is a transcript of a recent interview.

Interviewer: Mr. Sutton, I understand that this new educational software, InfoQuick, that APC has developed is an entirely new concept. How so?

Sutton: Well, it's new in that it is so expansive. That is, it covers so many subjects over so many grade levels. We designed it to be used with children all the way from the first grade through high school. Educational software isn't exactly new, but IQ is like a textbook company providing all the textbooks needed for a child's entire educational career. We cover everything from spelling to higher math, including calculus and algebra. Our programs also have the advantage of being interrelated because they're produced by a single company.

Interviewer: Do you see that interrelatedness as being a problem? I mean, doesn't that amount of interrelatedness lead to a sort of tunnel vision—like being taught the same courses by the same teacher all your life. Wouldn't you tend to see only one side of everything?

Sutton: Not really. What we've done is to hire the top programmers and educators in the area of software curriculum development to work on our project. Each discipline—history, math, science, etc.—is covered by a number of experts in the field, not a single person. What I'm talking about when I speak of interrelatedness is our ability to reference across a number of courses by computer. In other words, the student using one program of the IQ series will be guided to related topics in other subject areas much the same way you are guided by cross-references in the library card catalog.

Interviewer: You've obviously spent a lot of time and money on this project. Why do you think it will be successful— especially in the light of the recent drop-off of interest in video games?

Sutton: Part of the reason is that we are "selling" (if that's the right word) our curriculum to schools and educators. We have to first convince them that the IQ system of learning is easy and fun. Which brings me to another point. One of the reasons for developing IQ in the first place is to take some of the load off the teacher.

We have statistics showing that an average teacher in a, say fourth-grade class of 30 students, spends approximately only 10 minutes a day with each student individually. Students who need more than that 10 minutes either have to take up time outside of class or try to get the needed in-depth information from their textbooks—or their parents.

IQ helps provide that needed personal attention because of its interactive format. Look at it this way: what is the reason for questions at the end of a chapter in a standard textbook? They're supposed to stimulate the student to "interact" in a sense, with the book. But the book doesn't really respond in the truest sense of the word. It merely houses the answers to the questions while the student carries out any action that is taken.

On the other hand, when a student works with a computer loaded with an IQ program, she is interacting with it. The computer not only asks questions, it provides the student with hints, advice, and guidance. IQ programs explore various facets of each subject by quickly leading the student through an assignment, for instance. It can actually teach, ask questions, and guide the student in her search for the answers.

Interviewer: Could you give me a concrete example of what you mean?

Sutton: Sure. We have a program already developed called *Meet Mr. Franklin,* in which the student will actually carry on a computer-initiated conversation with Benjamin Franklin.

Interviewer: You mean, they actually hear Ben Franklin talk?

Sutton: No. What happens is that the computer introduces Franklin to the student as if it were the person himself. The program is designed for younger students, fourth to sixth grade, and makes heavy use of computer graphics. Graphics have become very sophisticated today. The Franklin program opens with a picture of Ben Franklin who introduces himself on the screen. From that point on, the student is actually involved in a conversation with him.

Franklin tells him about his life and the times in which he lived, punctuated with graphic displays of objects, maps, and documents of the period. At certain points throughout the lesson, the student is prompted to ask questions of Franklin. Depending on the question selected, from a list on the computer screen, Franklin will then respond.

Again, what's most exciting about the entire package is its interrelatedness. On the Franklin program, for instance, the student will be referred to other programs in the history series for that age group. You can go from the Franklin program to one on Washington, or Jefferson, or Adams and begin to get different perspectives on the same historical era.

Interviewer: To change the subject slightly—I understand that APC is now involved with the National Education Association in a joint project concerning computers.

Sutton: Yes, and again, we're very excited by the prospects of working with such a large and important group. As I've said many times before, we're strong on education here at APC—and that's not just PR talk. I wouldn't be where I am today without my education, and I want to do everything I can to see to it that other children get the chance to get the best education possible.

We've given the NEA a rather large grant to get them started on a program of teaching seminars all over the country. They'll set up a speaker's bureau of educators in the area of computer learning who will travel to requesting schools and explain the benefits of computer education.

They'll hold workshops for teachers and students and provide information for schools on how to begin computerization of their own classrooms.

Interviewer: Is this tied in with your software marketing effort?

Sutton: Not directly, no. But, of course, they're related. I'd look like a fool if I told you that they're not. But the money APC's donated to the NEA is a no-strings-attached grant. We're not requiring that they use our software or even mention it in any way. The money is a gift. We're not even asking for sponsorship identification.

Interviewer: Why this sudden push by APC in education, especially computer education?

Sutton: Because we live in a different age than we did when I grew up. Kids today need to know how to cope with the "information age." They need to know how to work with computers. I don't want this generation to be replaced by these machines—I want them to learn to master them.

I believe our joint project with the NEA will give them that chance. I also believe our new software will teach them the same basics I learned as a kid while showing them the wave of the future. We're committed to this course. We've pumped a lot of time and money into it, and we all want to see it work.

Assignments: Press Releases and Backgrounders

Assignment 3-1: Press Release

Write a press release on APC's involvement with NEA and its proposed program to educate children through computers. This is to be a jointly-approved release and cannot mention APC's new software line. The proposed publics are educators, parents, and students. The release will be distributed by the NEA placement service to newspapers, educational publications, and school districts around the U.S. Your address is: Associated Products Corporation, 1800 Avenue of the Americas, Syracuse, NY 10025 Contact: (your name); Day telephone: (315) 555-9836; Night telephone: (315) 555-5467.

Before you begin, develop several different leads—One emphasizing APC; one emphasizing the NEA; and one emphasizing the APC grant.

Read the background materials thoroughly then list items you would include in your release in the order in which they would appear in your release. Do this for each of the leads you have prepared. Remember to use an inverted pyramid style in which the least important information will appear at the end of your release. Arrange your information in the form of an outline.

Using your outline as a guide to organization, write the release.

Assignment 3-2: Press Release

Write a second release on the development of the product itself. The company needs to get some mileage out of the personal angle. Although development and description of the software is the focus of the second release, the angle should be the people who were in charge of development. Prepare one release for the *Seattle Times* and another for the *Deerborn Sentinel*.

Remember, the story is the software; the angle is the person you are using for human interest. Naturally, the leads for the two releases will have to be localized. Consider such approaches as using a dateline, leading with the name, leading with the software, or leading with a piece of local information (from the biographies). Develop one lead for each of these possibilities.

Develop an outline for each lead as you did in **Assignment 3-1**.

Assignment 3-3: Backgrounder

Prepare a backgrounder of no more than three pages explaining the current marketing strategy of APC. Try to couch the "sales pitch" in the light of software development in general. In addition, try to utilize previous information about the company and the people involved to help "flesh out" your backgrounder. Remember, this is a background piece and will probably be used to fill gaps in editors' knowledge about the company and the market in general. Remember also, that backgrounders need to follow a logical pattern in development. It is not sufficient simply to string information together.

The strength of a backgrounder is in its organization. Before you begin your backgrounder, develop an outline, including a thesis statement in the form of an interesting lead.

Assignment 3-4: Press kits

Assume that you are charged with assembling a press kit for InfoQuick, to be distributed at a product press conference announcing the new software. The press conference is to be held at the Downtown Hotel in the Sheridan Room at 10:00 a.m. on Tuesday, November 17. Attending will be APC President James Sutton and project head William Hoffman. Both will give short talks and take questions from the trade media present.

Make a list of items you would include in this kit, including any you may have already produced and any you would recommend be produced specifically for the kit. In addition, write a cover letter, to be included in the press kit, explaining the purpose of the press conference. Also, put together a table of contents for your press kit, listing the items in the kit in the order in which they are to be placed in the kit.

## CHAPTER 4

Brochures
&
Flyers

I've got a million of 'em
Jimmy Durante

W hat most people refer to as brochures are technically called folders, but because the term "brochure" has come into common usage, we'll stick with it here. Brochures are usually formed of a single sheet of paper folded one or more times. The folded brochure may be pocket sized; however, it doesn't have to be. Part of the fun of designing a brochure is choosing its size and number of folds. Although writing for a brochure implies that you already know what size and shape the finished product will be, you can also write first and then determine the size and shape that fits your copy. As with any in-house publication, you can work it either way, fitting copy to design or design to copy. You should take the approach that works best for you, though you may need to cut costs by trimming your copy, or accommodate mandatory information by expanding it. Longer copy is best suited to other formats such as booklets or pamphlets. In any event, brochure copy is usually abbreviated. Also be aware that odd-sized brochures will probably be more expensive to produce since printers will have to make special adjustments to their equipment to accommodate you.

Exactly how abbreviated, no one seems to know, for the length of a brochure varies enormously. Information is the key. Most brochures are used to arouse interest, answer questions, and provide sources for further information. Even when used as part of a persuasive campaign, brochures are seldom persuasive in themselves; they are support pieces or part of a larger media mix. Brochures can serve as stand-alone display rack literature, as a component of a press kit, or as part of a direct-mail packet. They can vary in size as well as length and are usually limited only by budget, talent, and imagination.

Before you begin to write, you need to determine exactly what your message is. Are you trying to inform or persuade? Is a brochure the best medium for your message? Who is your intended audience? Your format and your style must match your audience's expectations and tastes.

Before You Write

Know Your Intended Audience

You can refer to **Chapter 1** for detailed information on target audiences. But you can begin by assuming that your audience will be seeking or processing an abbreviated amount of information. Most readers understand that brochures aren't intended to provide long, involved explanations.

There are several audience-centered considerations you should make before you begin writing.

- Is your audience specialized or general? If it is specialized and familiar with your subject, you can use the trade language or jargon familiar to them, no matter how technical it might be. For example, in a brochure on a new chemical product (a copolyester, let's say) you can deal with durometer hardness, temperature-related attributes, resistance to pollutants and weather, and stress characteristics. None of these concepts should be new or surprising to a specialized audience of chemical engineers or designers who use polymers. On the other hand, if your audience is a lay audience, you will have to deal in generalities.

  Here are two examples of a piece on an imaginary copolyester—one for a technical audience (engineers) and one for a less specialized audience (retailers of a manufactured product made from the raw product).

  Technical:
  The results of laboratory testing indicate AXON II® polyester elastomer is resistant to a wide variety of fuels including leaded and unleaded gasoline, Gasohol, kerosene, and diesel fuel. With a hardness range of 92A to 72D durometer, tests show the most fuel-resistant type of copolyester to be the 72D durometer with the other family types also showing an impressive amount of fuel resistance.

  General:
  AXON II® polyester elastomer offers design potential plus for applications in a variety of industries. On the toughest

jobs, AXON II® is proving to be the design material of the future. Its unique properties and flexibility in processing make it applicable in areas previously dependent on a range of other, more expensive, products.

- Are you persuading or informing? If you are persuading your audience, you can use the standard persuasive techniques covered in **Chapter 1** including emotional language, appeal to logic, and association of your idea with another familiar concept. As with print advertising, the tone of the brochure (whether persuasive or informative) is set in the introductory headline. For example, here are two cover titles or headlines from two brochures on graduate programs in journalism. The first is persuasive and the second informative.

    Persuasive:
    Is one graduate program in journalism better than all the others?
    Yes.
    The University of Northern Oregon.

    Informative:
    Graduate studies in journalism
    at the University of Northern Oregon.

    Regardless of your intent, the brochure copy should always be clear on what you expect of your audience. If you are trying to persuade, state what you want the reader to do—buy your product, invest in your stock, vote for your candidate, support your bond issue. Persuasion only works if people know what it is you want them to be persuaded about.

- How will your audience be using your brochure? Is it intended to stimulate requests for information on a topic for which detailed information can be obtained in another form? Are you going to urge readers to send for more information? Is it meant to be saved as a constant reminder of your topic? Many health-oriented brochures, for example, provide information meant to be saved or even posted for reference, such as calorie charts, vitamin dosages, and nutrition information. If your brochure is designed to be read and discarded, don't waste a lot of money on printing. On the other hand, if you want it to be saved, not only should you make the information valuable enough to be saved, but also the look and feel of the brochure should say "don't throw me away." The same is true of any publication. Newspapers, by their inexpensive paper and rub-off ink, say "read me and then throw me away." while a magazine like *National Geographic* says "throw *me* away and you'd be trashing a nice piece of work."

Determine a Format

Format refers to the way you arrange your brochure—its organizational characteristics. As with everything else about brochures, format can go two ways: you can fit format to your writing or you can fit your writing to a predetermined format. For instance, if you are told to develop a Q & A (question and answer) brochure, you'll have to fit both writing and design to this special format. On the other hand, if you are writing a persuasive piece, you might decide to go with a problem-solution format, spending two panels of a six-panel brochure on setting up the problem and three on describing the solution.

Some organizational formats work well in brochures, some don't. Space organization (up to down, right to left, east to west), which can work well in book form or in magazine articles, doesn't seem to fit in a brochure. (See **Chapter 9** for more on organizational formats.) Neither does chronological organization. The reason for this may be the physical nature of the brochure itself. Magazine and book pages are turned, one after the other; and each page contains quite a lot of information. A brochure demands a more concentrated effort, one that is less natural than leafing through pages. Because each panel is limited in space, development has to take place in "chunks." Organizational formats that require continuous, linked development or constant referral to previous information aren't suited to brochures.

Pick a format that is suited to brochure presentation, or design your brochure to suit your format. Creative brochure design is part of the fun of working with this type of publication.

Position Your Brochure

Is your brochure to be used as part of a larger communication package (a press kit, for instance), or is it meant to be a stand-alone piece? If it is part of a larger package, then the information contained in the brochure can be keyed to information elsewhere in the package. If it is a stand-alone piece, it will need to be fairly complete—and probably longer. Knowing how your brochure fits into a larger communications program helps you to position it properly. *Positioning* refers to placing your piece in context as either part of some larger whole or as a standout from other pieces.

The only other consideration to make here concerns writing style. The brochure needs to mimic the style of the package of which it is a component. Obviously, this doesn't mean that it should read like a magazine because it is packaged with a magazine, but it should resemble the companion pieces as closely as possible. If the other pieces are formal, the brochure should be formal; if they are informal, the brochure should be also. The key is consistency.

Decide on Length

Succinctness is an art. Almost all writers are able to write long, but very few can write short without editing down from something originally longer. Your information will probably be edited a number of times to make it as spare and succinct as possible, because short copy is the ideal for brochures.

Your copy must be short because of space limitations, in order to leave enough white space for aesthetic value, for type size considerations (for example, a brochure for senior citizens must utilize a fairly large typeface), or for cost considerations. Whatever the reason, you must learn to write short and edit mercilessly.

The copy in **Exhibit 4.1**—written for the brochure layout shown in **Exhibit 4.2**—is brief by any standards. It is designed to inform in the barest sense. Its audience needs to be aware of the service being offered and urged to call for detailed information.

The copy in **Exhibit 4.3** was written for a brochure—shown in **Exhibit 4.4**— explaining the program of the Public Relations Student Society of America in some detail. Clearly, a brochure written this way would be aimed at those who are already aware of the program and its basic offerings and now want more detail. This copy assumes that the reader has already achieved the "aware" level common to the adoption process (see **Chapter 1**) and is now in the interest stage, while the copy in **Exhibit 4.1** makes awareness its chief objective.

The key to editing brochure copy is to realize exactly how much your reader would need to know about your subject. If you include too much in a piece designed to merely attract attention, you may lose your readers. On the other hand, if you don't provide enough basic information, you may never pique their interest. Although some edited elements may in fact influence the final decision-making process, they may not be important in the awareness stage of the adoption process. Once you have decided on the purpose of your brochure, writing and editing become a much easier job.

Also note the difference in the look of the two brochures. The one with the shorter copy in **Exhibit 4.2** is more open and utilizes a lot more white space. Anyone picking up this brochure would expect from its look to be minimally informed. The longer copy in **Exhibit 4.4** takes up the potential white space and requires a more expert hand at designing to prevent the brochure layout from becoming cluttered and crowded.

Exhibit 4.1—Brochure Copy for a Short Brochure

At the Southern Willamette Private Industry Council, we know that finding the right employee takes time. Time that could be better spent on making your company more profitable.

We work hard at finding the right workers—hard workers—for your business. It's our job and we're good at it.

Here's what we can do for your company:

- Recruit applicants
- Screen applicants
- Test applicants for skills and aptitudes
- Offer customized skills training
- Reinforce employer expectations and good work habits
- Provide a place for employers to conduct interviews
- Provide general employment information

The Private Industry Council has linked approximately 600 Lane County business with some 2,500 workers each year since the Job Training and Partnership Act was legislated in 1983. Employers use our services because we understand the importance of dependable, hard workers. Additionally, our services are prepaid through your tax dollars.

We mean business, so put us to work for you. Call 555-3800 for more information.

The Southern Willamette Private Industry Council. Bringing business and workers together.

Exhibit 4.2—Brochure Layout for a Short Brochure

We mean business, so put us to work for you.

Call 687-3800 for more information

The Southern Willamette Private Industry Council:

BRINGING BUSINESS AND WORKERS TOGETHER

WHAT DOES IT TAKE TO FIND GOOD EMPLOYEES?

Southern Willamette Private Industry Council

The Southern Willamette Private Industry Council is an Equal Opportunity Employer.

Southern Willamette
Private Industry Council

78–B Centennial Loop
Eugene, Oregon 97401
(503) 687-3800

At the Southern Willamette Private Industry Council, we know that finding the right employee takes time. Time that could be better spent on making your company more profitable.

We work hard at finding the right workers—hard workers—for your business. It's our job and we're good at it.

Here's what we can do for your company:

- Recruit applicants
- Screen applicants
- Test applicants for skills and aptitudes
- Offer customized skills training
- Reinforce employer expectations and good work habits.
- Provide a place for employers to conduct interviews.
- Provide general employment information.

The Private Industry Council has linked approximately 600 Lane County business with some 2,500 workers each year since the Job Training and Partnership Act was legislated in 1983. Employers use our services because we understand the importance of dependable, hard workers. Additionally, our services are prepaid through your tax dollars.

Exhibit 4.3—Brochure Copy for a Longer Brochure

A professional association

The Public Relations Student Society of America (PRSSA) is the student-run wing of the Public Relations Society of America (PRSA), the largest professional public relations organization in the nation. There are more than 4,300 students in 150 chapters at colleges and universities all across the United States.

The primary goal of PRSSA is to provide students with learning experiences that support coursework taken in public relations and related areas. Although PRSSA is a student-run organization, PRSA still plays an important and active role in its activities.

Each PRSSA chapter is counseled by a professional advisor and a faculty advisor (both members of PRSA) and is sponsored by a professional chapter. Here at the University of Oregon, PRSSA receives the full support of our parent chapter in Portland as well as a national network of professional and student services.

The student connection

Members of the University of Oregon PRSSA attend a number of events each year including the national conference (where members from all 150 PRSSA chapters meet to exchange ideas and attend seminars and workshops), the annual PRSSA Assembly, local and regional workshops and seminars sponsored by PRSA and PRSSA, and the yearly District Conference here in the Northwest.

We belong to the Northwest District along with PRSSA chapters from Central Washington University, Washington State University, and the University of Idaho. Each year, we gather for a three-day conference where we exchange ideas and attend workshops and seminars given by public relations professionals.

The professional connection

PRSSA members also make invaluable contacts with public relations professionals all over the Northwest through field trips, professional workshops on subjects such as resume writing and portfolio presentation, PRIDE internships (which carry national recognition), and the Professional Partners Program, in which students are matched with public relations professionals in the Portland, Salem, and Eugene areas.

PRIDE stands for Public Relations Internships to Develop Expertise. PRIDE internships are specially designed for members of PRSSA only, and offer PRSSA students an opportunity to develop their knowledge of public relations through close relationships with practicing professionals.

The PRIDE internship requires a contractual agreement between the student and his or her internship supervisor and the student's faculty advisor.

At the end of a successful PRIDE internship, the student's contract is sent to PRSSA national headquarters in New York, which then sends the student a certificate of completion. Although more complex than a standard internship, PRIDE internships offer a more formalized insurance that the student will be working on coordinated projects specifically related to public relations.

The Professional Partners Program matches PRSSA students with PRSA members in an informal, information-sharing partnership.

Students interested in the program fill out a form indicating their area of interest (e.g., special events, corporate PR, agency PR, etc.). The student is then matched with a partner practicing in that area.

Throughout the school year, the student and his or her professional partner meet informally to discuss the field of public relations, the professional's work, the student's particular interests, and public relations in general. The usual method is through lunch meetings in the city in which the professional works, occasional visits by the professional to Eugene, and PRSA monthly luncheons in Portland. In addition, professional partners frequently share a workday in which the student gets to observe his or her partner in action on the job.

Joining PRSSA

Joining PRSSA is easy. All you have to be is interested. You'll receive a membership certificate, a reduced-price subscription to the most widely read professional publication in public relations, *Public Relations Journal*, and a chance to become a member of PRSA at a reduced fee when you graduate.

So, if you think PRSSA has something for you—or even if you just want to know more about us—let us know. Just talk to any member, come to a meeting, or see Dr. Bivins in room 206 Allen Hall.

It could be the most professional move you'll ever make.

Exhibit 4.4—Brochure Layout for a Longer Brochure

PRIDE internships offer a more formalized insurance that the student will be working on coordinated projects specifically related to public relations.

The Professional Partners Program matches *PRSSA students with PRSA* members in an informal, information-sharing partnership.

Students interested in the program fill out a form indicating their area of interest (i.e., special events, corporate PR, agency PR, etc.). The student is then matched with a partner practicing in that area.

Throughout the school year, the student and his or her professional partner meet informally to discuss the field of public relations, the professional's work, the student's particular interests and public relations in general. The usual method is through lunch meetings in the city in which the professional works, occasional visits by the professional to Eugene, and PRSA monthly luncheons in Portland. In addition, professional partners frequently share a workday in which the student gets to observe his or her partner in action on the job.

Joining PRSSA

Joining PRSSA is easy. All you have to be is interested. You'll receive a membership certificate, a reduce-price subscription to the most widely read professional publication in public relations, *Public Relations Journal*, and a chance to become a member of PRSA at a reduced fee when you graduate.

So, if you think PRSSA has something for you—or even if you just want to know more about us—let us know. Just talk to any member, come by a meeting, or see Dr. Bivins in room 206 Allen Hall.

It could be the most professional move you'll ever make.

Public Relations Student Society of America

The Professional Edge

A professional association

The Public Relations Student Society of America (PRSSA) is the student-run wing of the Public Relations Society of America (PRSA), the largest professional public relations organization in the nation. There are more than 4,300 students in 150 chapters at colleges and universities all across the United States.

The primary goal of PRSSA is to provide students with learning experiences that support coursework taken in public relations and related areas. Although PRSSA is a student-run organization, PRSA still plays an important and active role in its activities.

Each PRSSA chapter is counseled by a professional

advisor and a faculty advisor (both members of PRSA) and is sponsored by a professional chapter. Here at the University of Oregon, PRSSA receives the full support of our parent chapter in Portland as well as a national network of professional and student services.

The student connection

Members of the University of Oregon PRSSA attend a number of events each year including the national conference (where members from all 150 PRSSA chapters meet to exchange ideas and attend seminars and workshops), the annual PRSSA Assembly, local and regional workshops and seminars sponsored by PRSA and PRSSA, and the yearly District Conference here in the Northwest.

We belong to the Northwest District along with PRSSA chapters from Central Washington University, Washington State University and the University of Idaho. Each year, we gather for a three-day conference where we exchange ideas and attend workshops and seminars given by public relations professionals.

The professional connection

PRSSA members also make invaluable contacts with public relations professionals all over the Northwest through field trips, professional workshops on subjects such as resume writing and portfolio presentation, PRIDE internships (which carry national recognition) and the Profes-

sional Partners Program, in which students are matched with public relations professionals in the Portland, Salem and Eugene areas.

PRIDE stands for Public Relations Internships to Develop Expertise. PRIDE internships are specially designed for members of PRSSA only, and offer PRSSA students an opportunity to develop their knowledge of public relations through close relationships with practicing professionals.

The PRIDE internship requires a contractural agreement between the student and his or her internship supervisor and the student's faculty advisor.

At the end of a successful PRIDE internship, the student's contract is sent to PRSSA national headquarters in New York, which then sends the student a certificate of completion. Although more complex than a standard in-   ternship,

Fitting It All Together

Whether you write for a specific size or you fit the size to the amount of information you have (especially if your boss simply can't live without that detailed explanation of how beneficial your new widget is to Western technology), your copy will have to fit that unique characteristic of the brochure—the number of folds.

Brochures are designated by how many folds they employ. A two-fold, a sheet with two creases, has six panels—three on one side and three on the other. A three-fold has eight panels, and so on. Each fold adds two or more new panels. Although some very interesting folds have been developed, the usual configuration consists of panels of equal size (see **Exhibit 4.5**).

Each panel may stand alone—present a complete idea or cover a single subject—or may be part of a larger context revealed as the panels unfold. Either way, in the well-designed brochure careful attention is paid to the way the panels unfold to ensure the information is presented

Exhibit 4.5—Typical Brochure Folds

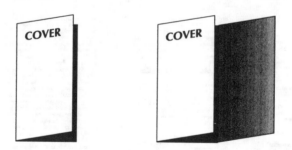

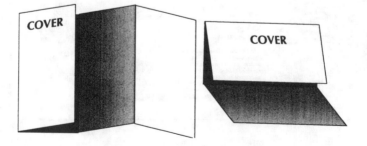

in the proper order. Good brochures do not unfold like road maps, but present a logical pathway through their panels (see **Exhibit 4.6**).

Research indicates that the first thing a reader looks at in a direct mail package is the brochure. The last thing is the cover letter. Exactly how you present the brochure may determine whether it gets read or gets thrown away.

The Order of Presentation

The first thing you must do is establish where the front panel is and where the final panel is. The first panel or front cover need not contain any information, but it should serve as an "eye catcher" that draws the reader inside. It should employ a "hook"—an intriguing question or statement, a beautiful photograph, an eye-catching graphic, or any other device that will get the casual peruser to pick up and read the complete brochure.

Brochures should be constructed much like good print ads. The opening section should explain the purpose of the brochure and refer to the title or headline. This is usually accomplished on the first panel or shortly following it if the first panel is devoted to a visual (see **Exhibit 4.6**).

If you begin your printed matter on the front cover, its headline or title becomes very important. Most informational brochures use a title simply to tell what's inside. After all, most people looking for information don't want to wade through a lot of creative esoterica. A brochure headline should be to the point. "Blind" headlines are of no use in a brochure. For example:

Reaching for the stars?

Is this headline for a product (maybe telescopes)? A service (astrology)?

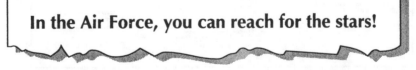

In the Air Force, you can reach for the stars!

Now, both the intent and the sponsor are clear. For the information-seeking reader, a blind headline *might* work; however, if you really want to be sure—and if you want to pick up the browser as well—avoid them.

Exhibit 4.6—Brochure Logic

Panel 2   *Panel 3*   *Panel 4*

WHAT IS PHONE FRAUD?

We've all been asked to purchase something or donate to a cause over the phone.

Most of the people who contact us represent legitimate firms that use the telephone to sell quality goods and services or raise money for worthy causes.

However, there are companies that are involved in telemarketing fraud. According to the Federal Trade Commission, telemarketing fraud is the use of telephone communications to promote goods or services fraudulently. And this can cost you money!

WHAT ARE THEY TRYING TO SELL YOU?

Fraudulent sales callers try to sell us everything from vacations and time-share condominiums to vitamins and magazines subscriptions. They say they represent film clubs, vacation resorts, charities, magazine and book clearing houses, and even churches. Sometimes they want money sent to them directly, or sometimes they just want your credit card number. (This is especially dangerous because they can charge any amount they want with your number.)

WHAT DO THEY SAY TO YOU?

Although fraudulent sales callers may

similarities in their "pitches." These pitches often sound very professional. Sometimes, you are even transferred from person to person to make it sound more like a business setting. Do the following lines sound familiar?

• "You've been specially selected to hear this offer!" (How was the selection process made?)

• "You'll get a wonderful prize if you buy..." (How much is this prize worth?)

• "You have to make up your mind right away..." (They make it seem like this is a now or never opportunity.)

• "It's free, you just have to pay the shipping and handling!" (If they get only $7.00 shipping and handling per person and con 100 people into paying up front, they make $700!)

• "But first, I'll have to have your credit card number to verify..." (To verify what and why?)

WHAT HAPPENS THEN?

If it is a fraudulent sales call, you sometimes actually receive the merchandise—but it is often over priced, of poor quality, or the wonderful prize you won is usually a cheap imitation.

Or, if you've been asked to invest in something, it may turn out to be non-existent.

Or, you find out the worthy cause you donated to only got a tiny part of your actual donation while the caller got the bulk of it.

Or, unauthorized charges start appearing on your credit card bills.

HOW CAN YOU PROTECT YOURSELF?

1. First of all, always find out who is calling and who they represent. Ask how they got your name. Ask who is in charge of the company or organization represented. Get specific names and titles. Ask for the address and telephone number of the firm calling you. Be extremely cautious if the caller won't provide that information.

2. Be cautious if the caller says an investment, purchase or charitable donation must be made immediately. Ask instead that information be sent to you.

3. Be wary of offers for free merchandise or prizes. You may end up paying handling fees greater than the value of the gifts. And, don't ever buy something just to get a free prize.

4. If you're interested in the offer, ask for more information through the mail. Also ask if it's possible to obtain the names and numbers of satisfied customers in your area.

5. If you're not interested in the offer, interrupt the caller and say so. Remember, part of their job is to talk without pause so you can't ask them questions. Don't be afraid to interrupt.

WHAT DO YOU DO IF YOU'RE VICTIMIZED...

Report the facts to :

Financial Fraud Section
Department of Justice
240 Cottage Street S.E.
Salem, Oregon 97210

REMEMBER, YOU HAVE RIGHTS. DON'T BE VICTIMIZED BY TELEPHONE FRAUD!

HOW TO RECOGNIZE PHONE FRAUD AND WHAT
TO DO ABOUT IT, FROM THE STATE OF OREGON
ATTORNEY GENERAL'S
OFFICE. STATE BOOKLET # 32468.

WE THOUGHT YOU'D LIKE TO KNOW ABOUT

PHONE FRAUD

A consumer guide to your rights and obligations when dealing with telephone sales

Panel 5   *Panel 6*   *Panel 1*

The second panel, at least in a two-fold brochure, is the first panel of the inside spread. Its job is to build interest. It is usually copy heavy, and may contain a subhead or crosshead. In fact, panels may be laid out around crossheads. But make sure the reader knows which panel follows which. Never let your copy run from panel to panel by breaking a sentence or a paragraph, or (worst of all) a word in half. Try to treat each panel as a single entity with its own information. This isn't always possible, but it's nice to strive for.

The rest of the inside spread (panels three and four) carries the main load. It may be constructed to present a unified whole with words and graphics bleeding from one panel to the next, or the panels may retain their individuality.

The back panels (panels five and six) serve various purposes. Panel five may be used as a teaser or short blurb introducing the inside spread, or it may be incorporated into the design of panel two (especially useful since this panel is often folded in and seen as you open the front cover). It may also simply continue the information begun on panels two, three, and four. Panel six may be left blank for mailing or contain address information. It doesn't usually contain much else.

Most of us are used to seeing two-folds folded so that the far right panel (inside panel four and outside panel five) is folded in first with the far left panel (outside panel one and inside panel two) folded over it. But this has always presented problems. For instance, what do you put on panel five? It is the first panel you see when you open the cover, yet it is technically on the back of the brochure. You can use it as a teaser, or simply as the informational panel that follows the inside spread. Or, you can experiment with the fold (See **Exhibits 4.7** and **4.8**). So much depends on the presentation of your information, and because they are folded, brochures are among the hardest collateral pieces to present properly. If readers are even slightly confused, you've lost them.

Crossheads

Crossheads should be used liberally in a brochure. They help break up copy and give your brochure a less formidable appearance. Studies have shown that copy formed into short paragraphs, broken by informative crossheads, gives the reader a feeling that he or she can read any section independently without being obligated to read the entire piece. Although in some instances this may be self-defeating, reading one pertinent paragraph is often better than reading none; and, if you run your copy together in one long, unbroken string, you're going to limit

Exhibit 4.7—Traditional Brochure Fold

The standard two-fold folder places the cover on the far right panel of the outside spread. Panel five (inside panel four) folds in first (see below).

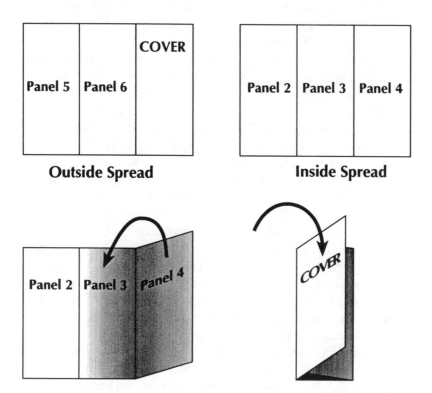

Outside Spread **Inside Spread**

This traditional fold requires two "unfolds" to access the inside spread—the cover and panel five; however, panel five may or may not be intended as part of the inside spread. More often, it follows panels two through four, yet it appears as the first panel seen when the folder is opened.

readership to a hardy few. Your brochure will look better with the increased white space crossheads can add, and white space encourages readership as well.

Exhibit 4.8—Nontraditional Brochure Fold

The standard two-fold folder is redesigned here placing the cover in the center of the outside panel. This allows panel two to fold inside (see below).

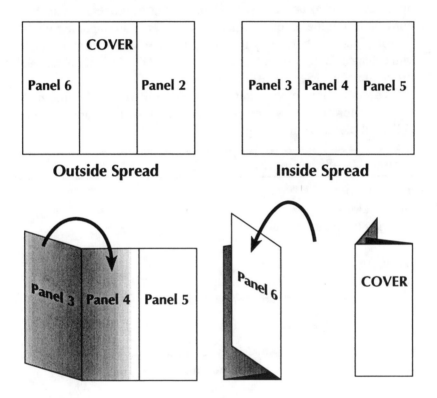

Outside panel two (inside panel three) folds inside becoming the first copy panel seen when the folder is opened. Panel six folds over it to become the back (or mailer). This presents the center outside panel as the cover and sets up two "unfolds" to get to the inside spread; however, there is no doubt that panel two (even though it is folded inside) is the first panel to be read. This fold alleviates the "panel five" problem of the traditional fold.

Copy Format

As you create your brochure, you may have to present the copy to others for approval. It helps to place it into a format that conveys the look of the finished product. Obviously, the best way to show anyone how a finished piece will look is to mock it up; however, copy often must be approved prior to any mockup, so indicating headlines, visuals and copy blocks in the order in which they appear is an important visual aspect of the brochure copy format. Indicating headlines and visuals will enhance continuity between the writer and the designer if they are different people (See **Exhibit 4.9**).

This is as far as most writers go; however, if you work for a small firm or nonprofit agency, you may be solely responsible for producing collateral pieces from writing to layout.

Exhibit 4.9—Brochure Copy Format

"Phone Fraud"
3-fold folder
Attorney General

PANEL 1
HEADLINE: WE THOUGHT YOU'D LIKE TO KNOW ABOUT (graphic
          splits head line here) PHONE FRAUD

VISUAL: Stylized graphic of telephone

SUBHEAD: A consumer guide to your rights and obligations when
          dealing with telephone sales

PANEL 2
SUBHEAD: WHAT IS PHONE FRAUD?

COPY: We've all been asked to purchase something or donate
          to a cause over the phone.

          Most of the people who contact us represent legitimate
          firms that use the telephone to sell quality goods and
          services or raise money for worthy causes.

          However, there are companies that are involved in
          telemarketing fraud. According to the Federal Trade

-more-

Phone Fraud--Page 2

Commission, telemarketing fraud is the use of telephone communications to promote goods or services fraudulently. And this can cost you money!

VISUAL: Cartoon drawing of telephone receiver

SUBHEAD: WHAT ARE THEY TRYING TO SELL YOU?

COPY: Fraudulent sales callers try to sell us everything from vacations and time-share condominiums to vitamins and magazine subscriptions. They say they represent film clubs, vacation resorts, charities, magazine and book clearing houses, and even churches. Sometimes they want money sent to them directly, or sometimes they just want your credit card number. (This is especially dangerous because they can charge any amount they want with your number.)

SUBHEAD: WHAT DO THEY SAY TO YOU?

COPY: Although fraudulent sales callers may have vastly different products or services to sell, there are frequently similarities in their "pitches." These pitches often sound very professional. Sometimes, you are even transferred from person to person to make it sound more like a business setting. Do the following lines sound familiar?

--"You've been specially selected to hear this offer!" (How was the selection process made?)

--"You'll get a wonderful prize if you buy..." (How much is this prize worth?)

--"You have to make up your mind right away..." (They make it seem like this is a now or never opportunity.)

--"It's free, you just have to pay the shipping and handling!" (If they get only $7.00 shipping and handling per person and con 100 people into paying up front, they make $700!)

-more-

Phone Fraud--Page 3

--"But first, I'll have to have your credit card number to verify..." (To verify what and why?)

PANEL 3
SUBHEAD: WHAT HAPPENS THEN?

COPY: If it is a fraudulent sales call, you sometimes actually receive the merchandise--but it is often over priced, of poor quality, or the wonderful prize you won is usually a cheap imitation.

Or, if you've been asked to invest in something, it may turn out to be non-existent.

Or, you find out the worthy cause you donated to only got a tiny part of your actual donation while the caller got the bulk of it.

Or, unauthorized charges start appearing on your credit card bills.

PANEL 4
SUBHEAD: HOW CAN YOU PROTECT YOURSELF?

COPY: 1. First of all, always find out who is calling and who they represent. Ask how they got your name. Ask who is in charge of the company or organization represented. Get specific names and titles. Ask for the address and telephone number of the firm calling you. Be extremely cautious if the caller won't provide that information.

2. Be cautious if the caller says an investment, purchase, or charitable donation must be made immediately. Ask instead that information be sent to you.

3. Be wary of offers for free merchandise or prizes. You may end up paying handling fees greater than the value of the gifts. And, don't ever buy something just to

-more-

Phone Fraud–Page 4

get a free prize.

4. If you're interested in the offer, ask for more information through the mail. Also ask if it's possible to obtain the names and numbers of satisfied customers in your area.

5. If you're not interested in the offer, interrupt the caller and say so. Remember, part of their job is to talk without pause so you can't ask them questions. Don't be afraid to interrupt.

PANEL 5

SUBHEAD: WHAT DO YOU DO IF YOU'RE VICTIMIZED...
Report the facts to :

Financial Fraud Section
Department of Justice
240 Cottage Street S.E.
Salem, Oregon 97210

KICKER: REMEMBER, YOU HAVE RIGHTS. DON'T BE VICTIMIZED BY TELEPHONE FRAUD!

PANEL 6

HEADLINE: HOW TO RECOGNIZE PHONE FRAUD AND WHAT TO DO ABOUT IT, FROM THE STATE OF OREGON ATTORNEY GENERAL'S OFFICE

-30-

Remember, you can write first and then develop a length and size to fit your editorial needs, or you can limit your copy to a preset design and size. Either way, you have to be aware of copyfitting requirements Once you know how much you must write, stick to your guns. If you find that you have written more than will fit your original design concept, you can increase the number of folds and, thus, the number of available panels, or edit your copy.

If your supervisor isn't clamoring for every ounce of information you can provide in 93.5 square inches of space, stick with editing your copy. The best brochures are almost always the short ones.

Flyers

Flyers are a quick way to disseminate information, even to large audiences, cheaply. A flyer is typically a single sheet of paper, usually letter-size, printed on one or both sides. A flyer is most often photocopied, but is sometimes printed if slickness is important.

Flyers, like brochures, can be folded; however, they are most often folded only for mailing. Most often, they are distributed flat, because the most common form of dissemination is still by hand. In fact, the term "flyer" refers to the rapidity with which they can be delivered—historically by kids running through the streets.

Flyers are handed out on street corners, at entrances to events, and practically anywhere large numbers of people gather. Flyers are distributed in employee mail boxes and door-to-door. They are pinned on bulletin boards and office doors. In short, flyers are one of the most useful—and ubiquitous—forms of information dissemination around.

Unlike brochures, good flyers are laid out like good print ads, or sometimes, depending on the amount of information needed, like a good newsletter page. But, like a brochure, the copy is written and the graphics designed to work together to bring the reader's attention directly to the message being imparted.

Tips on Writing for Flyers

When writing for flyers, keep in mind how much information you need to send versus how much space you have to work with. In most cases, you have a considerable amount of space—the same space as a standard brochure with none of the restrictions that panels impose. This leaves plenty of room for creativity.

If you have a lot to say, consider using a newsletter- or magazine-style approach to layout. Divide the page into columns and work within those borders with both words and graphics. Use subheads to break up the copy and plenty of bulleted items for clarity.

Choose your graphics carefully, and for full impact. Only the most striking graphics should appear on flyers, since you usually only have one shot to capture attention. Why? Because you are competing with dozens of other information pieces just like yours for attention.

If you have only a little to say (maybe an announcement of an event), then use full-impact language—as in advertising. Get readers' attention with a big headline and striking graphic. Make them pay attention to your copy, brief though it may be.

The main selling points of a good flyer are its ease of production, the easy way it lends itself to creativity, and its relative inexpensiveness.

So, if you have a quick message to get out in a hurry, try a flyer. Take a look at the examples presented in **Exhibit 4.10 and 4.11** for some idea of the variety of uses a flyer can be put to.

Exhibits 4.10—Letter-size Flyers

Doctoral Studies at Oregon
The University of Oregon Inaugurates Ph.D. Program in Communication & Society

The Program

Our new research degree requires a minimum of 72 quarter hours beyond the master's, embraces diverse methodological approaches, and offers specialization in:

- Social & Cultural Studies
- Law & Policy Studies
- International Communication

The program gives doctoral students opportunities to teach in the School's undergraduate sequences in advertising, communication studies, electronic media production, magazine journalism, news-editorial, and public relations.

The School

Now over 75 years old, the School of Journalism & Communication is nationally recognized as an innovative program. The School's 25 full-time faculty support the seven undergraduate sequences, as well as professional and academic master's programs.

The University of Oregon

Located in Eugene, 120 miles south of Portland, the University is the flagship institution of the state higher education system. With its enrollment of 17,000 students, it is large enough to have the resources of a major research university, yet still small enough to pride itself on close student-teacher contact and the highest quality education.

Admission Requirements

Admission will be granted for fall 1994. Applicants should hold a master's degree and submit transcripts, test scores, recommendations, as well as work samples (professional and/or scholarly) and a personal essay by February 1, 1994. Admission is competitive. Financial aid is available.

For further information and applications contact:

Graduate Studies Office
School of Journalism & Communication
University of Oregon
Eugene, OR 97403-1275
(503)346-2136

Exhibit 4.10 (continued)

Whether you plan to be a part of the media,

or simply an observer,

this workshop is for you.

Media Criticism

This one-credit workshop will explore the Media Criticism movement in the United States, ranging from the early efforts of the conservative Accuracy in Media to the resistance of U.S. media to press councils and to the ombudsman position in daily newspapers.

This is an opportunity to critic and the criticized, interested in participating literacy.

The workshop will be held 6:00–9:00 p.m., and Satu workshop leader will be D in Oregon Hall for CRN 3 workshop will be assessed

We're Steppin' out in style...

with an all-new look to *XyCorp Today*. Your house magazine has a whole new look and we think you'll love it!

So if you haven't seen it, pick up a copy today. The latest issue is available at the information desk or from the public affairs office in suite 612.

Exhibit 4.11—Tabloid-size Flyer

20 communication professionals will be on hand to talk about your chances of getting that first job.

A morning keynote address will be followed by a general session on resumé and cover letter writing. Then, 5 separate panel discussions (Advertising, Newspapers, Magazines, Electronic Media, and Public Relations) will focus on how to prepare for that first job. After a break for lunch, during which you will have an opportunity to talk with professionals one-on-one, the panels will reconvene for an in-depth discussion of interviewing skills, including how to use a portfolio to your best advantage.

Your $4.00 ticket includes morning coffee and donuts, all the conference sessions, and lunch.

Tickets can be purchased in room 211 B Allen Hall (Student Services).

Case Study: Associated Products Corporation

Using the background provided in **Chapter 3**, complete the following assignments.

Assignment 4-1: Brochures

You have been assigned to produce two brochures—one for APC introducing the new IQ software package, and one for NEA/APC introducing the "Byte of the Apple" speaker's bureau. The first brochure will be product oriented and the second will be service oriented. You may continue the motif you have established in your previous package components for the second brochure or develop a new one. The first brochure must not appear to be related to the NEA brochure. The first brochure should be a two-fold; the second, a one-fold. The two-fold brochure should be designed to fit on an 8 1/2" x 11" piece of paper. The one-fold should fit on 8 1/2" x 7" paper. Prepare a completely scripted brochure with headlines, visuals, and copy blocks. Attach a "dummy" brochure layout designating positions of headlines, visuals, and copy blocks.

Assignment 4-2: Brochures

Spec the type for your two brochures. Assume that you will be using 11-point type leaded 2 points. Make sure your copy will fit the specified blocks on your layout. Prepare a layout and a worksheet on copyfitting for each brochure.

Assignment 4-3: Flyer

Design a letter-size flyer for a company picnic at APC. The event will happen two weeks from this coming Sunday, at West Side Park. All employees and their families are invited. Food and drink will be provided by the company and equipment for such games as volleyball, horseshoes, and baseball will be available. West Side Park is located between 17th and 20th Avenues in Westover. Just take I-95 to the Westover exit and turn right on 17th Avenue. The park is about four blocks away. The picnic begins at 12:00 and will run until around 6:00. Try to find or develop an interesting graphic for your flyer. Keep the words to a minimum, but include all the necessary information. Make this as eye-catching as possible. APC wants all its employees to attend.

CHAPTER 5

Newsletters

I really think you should consider a newsletter.

Garry Trudeau

E very day in the United States thousands of newsletters are published and distributed to hundreds of thousands of readers. It is estimated that some 50,000 corporate newsletters alone are published each year in this country. Most newsletters are internal publications in the sense that they reach a highly unified public— employees, shareholders, members, volunteers, voting constituencies, and others with a common interest. In fact, if you ask any self-respecting communications professional for the most effective means of reaching a primarily internal audience, the response will most likely be the newsletter.

Determining the Focus and the Need

Newsletters are as varied as the audiences who read them; however, they do break down into two categories, each based on distribution. Which category a newsletter falls into usually determines its focus. Newsletters that are distributed within a corporation are usually considered **vertical publications** because they are intended for everyone from the mailroom clerk to the CEO. Newsletters that are distributed to a more narrowly defined group with a common interest (such as newsletters on management techniques within a certain industry, or technical publications within an industry) are called **horizontal publications**.

Vertical Publications

There are three main types of vertical publications.

- **Association newsletters** help a scattered membership with a common interest keep in touch. Profit and nonprofit associations and almost every trade association in the United States publish newsletters for their members, often at both national and regional levels.

- **Community group newsletters** are often used by civic organizations to keep in touch with members, announce meetings, and stimulate attendance at events. The local YWCA or Boys Club newsletter might announce their schedules, while a community church group newsletter distributed throughout surrounding neighborhoods might be a tool for increasing membership.

- **Institutional newsletters**, perhaps the most common type of newsletter, are usually distributed among employees. Used by both profit and nonprofit organizations, they are designed to give employees a feeling of belonging. They frequently include a balanced mix of employee-related information and news about the company.

Horizontal Publications

There are also three main types of horizontal publications.

- **Publicity newsletters** often create their own readers. They can be developed for fan clubs, resorts (some resort hotels mail their own newsletters out to previous guests), and politicians. Congressional representatives often use newsletters to keep their constituencies up to date on their activities.

- **Special interest newsletters** developed by special-interest groups tend to grow with their following. *Common Cause*, for instance, began as a newsletter and has grown into a magazine representing the largest lobbying interest group in the United States.

- **Self-interest or "digest" newsletters** are designed to make a profit. The individuals or groups who develop them typically offer advice or present solutions to problems held in common by their target readers. These often come in the form of a sort of "digest" of topics of interest to a certain profession. In the public relations profession, for instance, you'll find *PR Reporter, PR News, Communicate, O'Dwyer's Newsletter, Communication Briefings*, and many more.

Why a Newsletter?

Why indeed? Most newsletters address an internal public, with the exception of those that target single-interest groups—such as professionals and executives—outside a formal organizational structure. The goal of most newsletters, then, is communication with a largely internal public.

Downward and Upward Communication

In the ideal organizational structure, communication flows both vertically (upward and downward) and horizontally. The newsletter is a good example of downward communication. It fulfills part of management's obligation to provide its employees formal channels of communication. Upward communication provides employees a means of communicating *their* opinions to management. Ideally, even downward communication channels such as newsletters permit upward communication through letters to the editor, articles written by employees, surveys, and so forth. Newsletters can also provide horizontal communication, but this type of newsletter is rarely produced *within* an organization; rather it originates from outside.

Newsletter or Something Else?

But, why a newsletter instead of a magazine, booklets, bulletin boards, or (heaven forbid) more meetings? There are several questions you can ask yourself when deciding whether a newsletter is the publication that best suits your purpose.

- What is the purpose of the publication? Is it to entertain? Inform? Solicit?

- What is the nature and scope of the information you wish to present? Longer information is probably better suited to a longer publication such as a magazine; shorter, to brochures or folders. If your information is strictly entertaining or human interest, it may also be better received within a magazine format.

- Who, exactly, are you trying to reach? All employees from the top down? A select few (the marketing department, the credit department, the vice president in charge of looking out windows)?

- How often do you need to publish it to realize the objectives you set in answering the previous questions? Newsletters are best suited to situations requiring a short editorial and design lead time.

Keep in mind also that newsletters are best for small publication runs and information that needs a quick turnover. They handle information that is considered necessary but disposable (much like a newspaper, which in a sense the newsletter mimics). However, this is generally, but not *universally* true. Many fine newsletters are designed to be kept. Health and financial newsletters, for instance, are often hole-punched so that the reader can save them in ring binders. For the most part, though, they are considered disposable.

Setting Objectives and Strategies

Newsletters, like any well-managed publication, will achieve best results if objectives are set and all actions follow logically from them.

Newsletter Content

To determine a newsletter's content, you must first know your audience. Is it totally internal, or a combination of internal and external? Your audience and its interests will dictate, to a large extent, the topic and direction of your articles.

Depending on the type of newsletter you are publishing, the focus will be broad or narrow. For example, when you write for an internal, employee public, you must carefully balance information with entertainment. You must please management by providing information it wants to see in print and you must please the employees by providing information they want to read. Otis Baskin & Craig Aronoff, in their book *Public Relations: The Profession and the Practice*, present a rule of thumb for an appropriate mix in an internal publication (not necessarily a newsletter) aimed primarily at an employee audience.

- 50 percent information about the organization—local, national, and international
- 20 percent employee information—benefits, quality of working life, etc.
- 20 percent relevant noncompany information—competitors, community, etc.
- 10 percent small talk and personals

Given that most newsletters are fairly short, such a complete mix may be impractical; however, a close approximation will probably work. Remember, though, that this mix is only appropriate for vertical publications such as institutional newsletters.

By comparison, most horizontal publications tend to focus on items of interest to a more narrowly defined target public. For example, a newsletter for telecommunications executives may concentrate on news about that industry, omitting human interest items, small talk, or industry gossip. In fact, almost every newsletter targeted to executives contains only short, no-nonsense articles. The reason, of course, is that busy executives simply don't have the time to read the type of article that interests the average employee.

How to Set Objectives

Objectives relate to your publication's editorial statement. Editorial statements shouldn't be pie-in-the-sky rhetoric; they should reflect the honest intent of your publication. If your intent is to present management's story to employees, then say so up front. An editorial statement can be an objective, or it can serve as a touchstone for other objectives.

For example, from the editorial statement in the previous paragraph you could reasonably derive an objective such as "To raise the level of awareness of management policies among all employees by X percent over the next year." Or, "To provide an open line of upward and downward communication for both management and employees." Whatever your objectives, make sure they are measurable. Then, you can point to your success in reaching them over the period of time you specified. You should also have some means by which to measure the success of your objectives. If your objective is simply "To present management's message to employees," how will you measure its success or failure? Don't you want to find out if just presenting the message was enough? How will you tell if anyone even read your message, or, if they did, whether they responded in any way?

Make your objectives realistic and measurable, and once you have set them, follow them. Use them as a yardstick by which to measure every story you run. If a story doesn't help realize one of your objectives, don't run it. If you just can't live without running it, maybe your objectives aren't complete enough.

Writing for Newsletters

Most newsletters are journalistic in style. They usually include both straight news and feature stories and range from informal to formal depending on the organization and its audience. Usually, the smaller the organization, the less formal the newsletter. Large corporations, on the other hand, often have a very formal newsletter with a slick format combining employee-centered news with company news.

The responsibility for writing the newsletter is almost always handled in house, although some agencies do produce newsletters on contract for organizations. In-house personnel tend to be more in tune with company employees and activities. Sometimes the writing is done in house and the production, including design, layout, and printing, is done by an agency.

If you do produce your own newsletter, you are limited only by expense and imagination. A standard newsletter is usually 8 1/2" x 11" or 11" x 17" folded in half. It averages in length from two to four pages and is frequently folded and mailed. Many are designed with an address area on the back for mailing (see **Exhibit 5.1**).

Exhibit 5.1—Newsletter Mailing Options
Clockwise from bottom: standard 11 x 17, four-page folded in thirds and mailed in business envelope; standard 11 x 17, single folded in thirds with Post Office indecia on bottom third (usually folded and stapled); standard 11 x 17 folded in half with indecia on bottom half (usually folded and stapled).

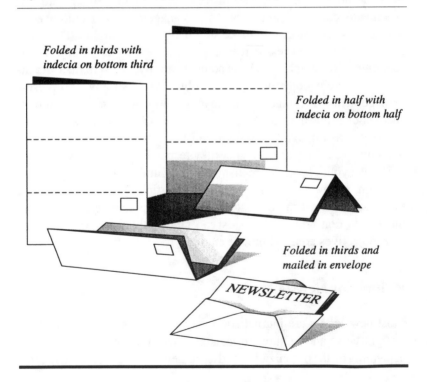

Folded in thirds with indecia on bottom third

Folded in half with indecia on bottom half

Folded in thirds and mailed in envelope

NEWSLETTER

Length of articles varies. Some newsletters contain only one article, while others include several. An average four-page newsletter uses about 2,000 words of copy. Depending on the focus of the newsletter, articles can range in length from "digest" articles of less than 100 words to longer articles of 600 words for newsletters that cover only one or two topics per issue. The trend today is toward shorter articles, especially for the newsletter aimed at the businessperson or corporate executive. Even for the average employee, newsletter articles usually need to be brief. Most newsletters make use of simple graphics or photographs. While most are typeset or, increasingly, desktop published, many are simply typed.

Because newsletters inform and entertain, articles should be written in an entertaining way. Usually, news about the company or strictly informational pieces utilize the standard news story style, except that there is no need to use the inverted pyramid because newsletter stories are seldom edited for space from the bottom up. Employee interest pieces tend to use the feature story style. Feature-type articles for newsletters should be complete, with a beginning and an ending.

Where Do Stories Come From?

There are many ways to come up with acceptable ideas for articles. Sometimes you might receive ideas from employees or management. Sometimes a news release or a short piece done for another publication will spark enough interest to warrant a full-blown newsletter article. Whatever the source of the idea, you must evaluate the topic based on reader interest and reader consequence.

If you're familiar with your audience's tastes, you can quickly determine their interest. To evaluate consequence, ask yourself what they will learn something from the article. Although light reading is fun for some, an organizational publication isn't usually the place to engage in it.

Every newsletter editor will tell you that getting story ideas isn't all that hard. Finding someone to write the stories is. There are several methods for enlisting writers. If you are putting out an in-house publication, try assigning "beats" like a newspaper. If you're lucky enough to have a staff, assign them to different types of stories— perhaps by department or division, or by product or service. If you don't have a staff, rely on certain people in each department or division to submit stories to you. Sometimes the simple promise of seeing their name in print is enough inducement.

You can also send employees a simple request form, spelling out exactly what you are looking for. The information you get back will be sketchy, but you can flesh it out with a few phone calls. (See **Exhibit 5.2**. This is an especially good method of gathering employee-related tidbits that don't deserve an entire story but should still be mentioned. One method for organizing your shorter stories is to group them according to topic. For example, group all stories relating to employee sports, or all stories about employee community involvement, or promotions, and so on.

Of course, if your publication is a narrowly focused horizontal publication, you may end up doing most of the research and writing yourself. Many such newsletters are truly one-person operations. Because desktop publishing allows a single person to act as reporter, editor, typesetter, and printer, this type of publication is enjoying a rebirth.

Whatever system you use to gather stories, as editor you will probably be doing most of the writing as well as the editing.

Researching Stories

If you write most of your own stories, you know that every topic must be researched thoroughly. The first step in a normal research process is to do a "literature search" to determine whether your article has already been written. If it has, but you still want to explore the topic for your specific audience, then try another angle.

Next, gather background information. Try to get specifics. You can't write about something you don't know a lot about personally. It also pays to get first-hand information. Interview people who know something about your topic. Not only will you get up-to-date information, but you may end up with some usable quotes and some new leads. (See **Chapter 1** on interviewing tips.)

Don't forget the library. Many a fine article has been written based on a library visit. Library research is among the most valuable, and one of the cheapest, forms of research. In any event, most articles will be fairly complete and accurate if you do a little background research and conduct an interview or two. Because newsletter articles are usually short, this is about all the information you can use.

Writing the Lead

Now that you have story ideas and have done some research, where do you go next? Always start at the beginning. A good lead is just as

Exhibit 5.2—Employee Information Form

Employee Information Form
For Newsletter Articles

Employee Name: _____

Department: _____

Position: _____

Do you have any information pertaining to promotions, awards, service recognition, etc. that might be of interest to fellow employees? If so, please give details below.

Do you have any story ideas for the employee newsletter?
Please list your suggestions below.

If you are directly involved in any of the above information, would you be willing to be interviewed?

Would you be willing to write any or all of an article relating to any of the ideas mentioned above?

Please return this form to the Corporate Communications Department, #302.

important to a newsletter piece as to a news story. It's still the hook that entices the reader into reading the complete piece.

Although to a great extent newsletters depend on design to attract readers, the well-written article is what draws them back. Like any good story, the newsletter article should have a definite beginning, middle, and end. Of course, if the article is written like a straight news story (inverted pyramid) it will begin with a tight lead and taper off as it progresses. In both cases, the lead is the key.

Your lead must tell the reader what the story is about. It is not necessary to cram everything into the lead; however, you must include enough information that the reader doesn't have to search for your topic. For straight news articles, the lead needs to come right to the point with the facts up front. For a feature, the delayed lead may be used. In this type of lead you create ambience, then place your story within the environment you have created. Other techniques include leading with a quote and placing it in context, or using metaphor, simile, analogy, anecdote, and other interest-getting devices. Although most of us forgot these literary tools the minute we left freshman composition, we shouldn't assume that good writing can get along without them. Look over the following literary uses of metaphor, simile, and analogy and then compare them with the newsletter article leads that follow them.

- A **metaphor** says that one thing *is* another:

  Cauliflower is nothing but a cabbage with a college education. (Mark Twain)

  Tree you are,
  Moss you are,
  You are violets with wind above them. (Ezra Pound)

- A **simile** says that one thing is *like* another:

  Though I must go, endure not yet
  A breach, but an expansion,
  Like gold to airy thinness beat. (John Donne)

  In time of peril, like the needle to the lodestone, obedience, irrespective of rank, generally flies to him who is best fitted to command. (Herman Melville)

- **Analogies** make hard-to-understand ideas easier to grasp by placing them in reader context; or, in the following example, by making a point of view more understandable through humor:

  Soap and education are not as sudden as a massacre, but they are more deadly in the long run. (Mark Twain)

The following leads show even the most mundane subject is of interest to someone and deserves the most interesting treatment possible. Pay particular attention to the number of scene-setting or descriptive words used in these leads.

Leading with a quote:
"Steelhead trout are an elitist fish; they're scarce, big, beautiful and they're good fighters," says Bob Hooton, Fish and Wildlife biologist responsible for steelhead on Vancouver Island. (*Salmonid*, newsletter of the Canadian Dept. of Fisheries and Oceans)

Leading with an anecdote:

If past experience is an indication, the telephones at our Client Services Center in Laurel, Maryland, will rarely stop ringing on December 16. That day the Center begins accepting calls for appointments to review diaries from the Fall radio survey. (*Beyond the Ratings*, national newsletter of Arbitron)

April 1st marks the beginning of a new era in banking—and a new dawn of satellite communications. On that day a clerk in Citicorp's Long Island, N.Y. office will make history by picking up the phone and dialing a Citicorp office in California. (*Telecommunications Week*, national newsletter published by Business Research Publications, Inc.)

Leading with an analogy:

You've heard the adage "two heads are better than one." What about 40? The Division's plants, more than 40 of them, are "putting their heads together" in the form of a Division-wide information sharing project recently released. (*Action Connection*, employee newsletter of Weyerhaeuser Packaging Division)

Setting the scene:
It's 5:30 on a Monday afternoon and you've just finished one of *those* days. Not only did the never-ending pile of work on your desk cease to go away, but you just received two additional "A" priority assignments. On top of that, the phones wouldn't stop ringing and the air conditioning wouldn't start working, even though the temperature hit 95. (*Spectra*, employee newsletter of the SAIF Corporation)

It's pretty quiet at Merwin Dam in southwest Washington. Two generators are running. The water level is down a little so folks along the reservoir can repair some docks while the weather stays nice.
For the 21 people working at the dam, it's business as usual. But, there is a subtle change. There's no longer a threat hanging over their heads that Pacific might not own or operate the dam. The court case that could have forced Pacific to give it up was finally resolved at the end of February. (*Pacific Power Bulletin*, employee newsletter of Pacific Power)

Leading with a metaphor/simile:
Recession fears faded like Presidential Candidates this
spring. Markets were jolted by the February employment
release which showed an increase in employment of over
500,000.... The mood has gone full circle as there is re-
newed focus on the strength of the economy with its 5.4
percent unemployment rate, and the whiff of higher inflation in the air. (*Northwest Business Barometer,* a quarterly
economic review for customers from U.S. Bank)

News Style

Remember the inverted pyramid we used when writing press releases
in **Chapter 3**? It's just as valid for news stories written for newsletters.
The inverted pyramid makes sense for short straight news stories.
Consider the straight news story in **Exhibit 5.3**, which appeared in a
student newsletter. Notice how the story opens with a straight news
lead, much like a press release, and covers the basic who, what, when,
where, and how of the story.

Although the most common straight news lead is the *summary lead,*
other types are also used. In the *delayed lead,* the point of the story is
delayed slightly while an interesting angle is developed, or a character
is set up through a quote, or a scene is set through description. For
example:

> School children all over the country will soon be learning
> the three *R*'s on a *C* thanks to a $1 million grant from
> Associated Products Corporation (APC). APC has recently
> donated the money to set up a fund for the purchase of
> educational computers that, when combined with APC's
> newest software, will teach reading, 'riting, and 'rithmetic in
> a whole new way—on computers.

This reads less like straight news than the lead of the story in **Exhibit
5.3**. A delayed lead is rarely used in straight news. Delayed leads most
often appear in feature-type stories because they are excellent ways to
set a scene, introduce a character, or simply attract and hold attention.

Feature Style

Feature style is usually less objective and provides less hard information
than straight news style. Features generally take a point of view or
discuss issues, people, and places. The style is more relaxed, more
descriptive, and often more creative than straight news style. Look at
the opening paragraphs of the feature story in **Exhibit 5.4**. This story

Exhibit 5.3—Straight News Story

Expressions Newsletter
AMHCA story
Page 1 of 1

Counselors' Association 'hires' PRSSA

The American Mental Health Counselors Association
(AMHCA), a representative association for community counselors,
has hired PRSSA to develop and implement a series of
communication projects. The projects began last spring when a
committee of five PRSSA members developed a PR plan for AMHCA.
The comprehensive plan is targeted at present and potential
members. The two main objectives of the plan are to strengthen
AMHCA as a membership organization and to create awareness of
AMHCA among its target audiences.

After receiving approval for the plan from AMHCA board
members, PRSSA was asked to develop more specific projects. This
fall, a committee of eight PRSSA members worked on two projects.
The first was to develop a logo and slogan for AMHCA to be used on
all informational materials. The logo, now finished, symbolically
represents the safety and shelter of a hearth, utilizing a stylized
Hebrew symbol for home and well being. The second project
involved redesigning an existing AMHCA brochure. The committee
developed a whole new layout and cover design.

The committee will also continue to develop projects winter
and spring terms. The main project will be a series of brochures for
AMHCA. The brochures will range from information on membership
to information on mental health counseling. Other upcoming
projects include writing a series of public service announcements to
be broadcast nationally for Mental Health Week in March.

"Overall, the project has been a great experience for all of
us involved," said committee chairperson Wendy Wintrode.

-30-

is on the same topic as the previous straight news example, but the approach is extremely different.

The facts are still here, but the focus in on creative information presentation. The lead is a question (a typical delayed lead strategy). Answering that question becomes part of the story itself. Quotes are used liberally. They not only validate and lend credibility to the subject discussed, they add human interest.

Human interest is a key characteristic of much feature writing. It can be simple inclusion of the human "voice" in a story, or it can be an entire *profile*, featuring a single person. Although the term profile usually refers to a feature story done on a person or on one aspect or issue relating to a person, individual companies or products may be profiled as well.

Exhibit 5.4—Feature-style Article

Expressions Newsletter
AMHCA story
Page 1 of 1

<u>Clearing up the confusion over mental health</u>

What's the difference between a therapist, psychologist, psycho-therapist, psychiatrist, and counselor? If you don't know, you're among the millions of people who are confused about the multi-tiered mental health counseling field.

In an effort to clear up some of the confusion, the American Mental Health Counselors Association (AMHCA) has "hired" a university student group to produce a public information campaign for them.

The Public Relations Student Society of America (PRSSA) at the University of Oregon has been retained by the Association to develop a program of information that will better define the various roles contained under the umbrella term "mental health counselor." Jane Weiskoff, regional director of AMHCA, says that the confusion seems to stem from a misconception over what constitutes a "counselor." "In the mental health profession, there is a perceived

-more-

Mental Health -- 2

hierarchy," she says. "Psychiatrists are seen as being at the apex of the field with psychologists, therapists, and other counselors falling into place under them. We'd like to clarify and possibly alter that perception."

Part of the plan, which has already been produced and approved, is to establish and maintain contact with current AMHCA members through a series of brochures and an updated and redesigned association newsletter. These informational pieces will carry the message that mental health counselors come in a variety of forms with a variety of educational and training backgrounds, and that each of these levels is suited to certain types of counseling. The goal is to establish credibility for certain of the counseling functions not fully recognized at this time by the general public and the mental health profession....

[for illustration purposes, part of the story has been deleted here.]

... If committee chairperson Wendy Wintrode has her way, the term "mental health counseling" will soon have a completely different, and definitely more expanded, definition. "We want everyone to know that professionalism doesn't begin and end with a small clique at the top—it is the guiding force behind the entire field of mental health counseling."

-30-

The following is from a profile on a corporate legal department and its new head. Notice how the scene is set in the lead before the subject is introduced.

> Sitting behind a cluttered desk, boxes scattered around the office—some still unopened—is the new head of Associated Products Corporation's Law Department, Ed Bennett. Ed is a neat man, both in appearance and in speech. As he speaks about the "new" Law Department, he grins occasionally as though to say, "Why take the time to interview someone as unimportant as a lawyer?" That grin is deceiving because, to Ed and the other attorneys who work for Associated Products Corporation, law is serious business.

To add human interest is merely to add the human element to a story. Information without this element is only information. With it, information becomes more interesting, more personal, more attuned to readers' experiences. As a further example, consider the following lead.

> Somewhere north of Fairbanks, long after the highway disappears into the low growth and stubby trees, Seth Browner is stalking an elusive prey—his health. Seth is one of 20 hikers involved in the inaugural "hiking for health" program. Seth hopes the program will give him an opportunity to see the outdoors up close for the first time in his life, and provide him with something he badly needs right now. Six months ago, Seth's doctor told him if he didn't exercise he would die.

And, if you're trying to reach people with your message—I mean really reach them—injecting human interest is often the best way to do it.

Writing the Story

Once the lead is conceived and written, the story must elaborate on it. If possible, make points one by one, explaining each as you go. Get the who, what, when, where, and how down in the most interesting way possible—but get to the point early.

The body of the article must support your main point, preferably already made in the lead, and elaborate on it. Anticipate questions your reader might have, and answer them satisfactorily. Remember to utilize logical transitional devices when moving from one point to another. Subheads, although they are helpful to the reader, don't alleviate the need for thoughtful transitions.

Back up your statements with facts and support your generalizations with specifics. Although newsletter articles seldom use footnotes, they are not completely inappropriate. Usually, however, citation can be taken care of in the body of the text. If, however, you are quoting someone, be sure to use attribution. Don't just give the person's name. A person's title or job may lend your quote authority if that person is considered knowledgeable or an expert on your subject.

In a feature, cover the news angle in a more people-oriented way. Paint word pictures to help readers hear, smell, and feel the story. If your story has a possible human-interest angle, use it. It helps your readers relate to the message through other human beings. Above all, don't be afraid to experiment with different approaches to the same topic. Try a straight news approach, then a human-interest angle or maybe a dramatic dialogue. In every case, try to make your story specific to your audience. Remember, they are major players in your scripts, in reality or vicariously (see **Example 5.5**).

Exhibit 5.5—The Newsletter Story

Boxis story
Page 1 of 2

Fully Loaded: Playing Tag with the Competition

Can the lowly load tag become a competitive advantage? Several plants are learning the answer is yes, if it's a load tag produced on BOXIS. BOXIS, the Packaging Division's Box Information System, has been around a while, and most plants are currently using computer generated load tags. But Portland folks, among others, are getting a feel for just how useful BOXIS load tags can be—for themselves and their customers. "Most load tags are handwritten, often difficult to read," notes Don McLaurin, BOXIS manager in Tacoma. "BOXIS produces a computer generated tag that's easy to read, even in dark warehouses."

But the beauty of the BOXIS load tag is more than skin deep. It also carries bar code information, the foundation of automated operations that improve productivity and customer service. For instance, while an order is still being produced, load tags help the finishing department run more smoothly. According to Portland's Chuck Goodrich, production supervisor, the load tag's bar coding has helped Portland increase strapper throughput 15 to 20%. "As a unit comes down the line, a laser scanner reads the bar code information on the load tag. The information is used by a computer to set the strapping pattern, automatically strap the unit, and send it down the correct spur line," Chuck explains. Automated strapping is an easy way to make sure the load is strapped to the customer's specs. It also can improve finishing department productivity, decrease bottlenecks at the strapper, and free employees to dress the load and correct problems before they happen.

-more-

Boxis – 2

"It has really made a big difference," adds Chuck. "Before, the line would get so backed up, we'd have to put three people on the strapper. Now, we're able to run it smoothly most of the time with just one person." Another advantage of the bar code system is that it provides instant access to order status. "By simply scanning the bar code on a completed unit, we can tell a customer exactly how many units of the order have been completed that moment," explains Don. But load tag customer service doesn't stop there. Packaging Division customers are learning how our load tags can help them with computerized inventory and other needs.

Tom Booth, production planner at Salinas, says the flexibility of the load tag and help from information systems expert Del Green allowed them to quickly and easily modify the load tag when a key agricultural customer, Bud of California, asked them to add a special numeric inventory code.

"Hey, this is a competitive business," Tom says, "and any time you can provide an additional service – particularly when it doesn't cost much – that's a real advantage. The customer was very, very pleased." Brendan Doherty, Charlotte sales rep, says a customized load tag was one factor solidifying Charlotte's position in a trial with Kimberly Clark. "We developed a special corner tag that included a calendar. They were impressed. We're still on a trial basis, but it looks very good. The load tag is an advantage that sets us apart just that much more.

That's not the end of the story; BOXIS users are still learning just what the system can do. But one thing's certain: once they see Weyerhaeuser load tags, customers are beginning to request similar load tags from all their packaging suppliers. A major Rochester customer, Central New York Bottle, liked the tag so much they asked competitors to produce a similar one. "This customer buys $5 million of corrugated a year," says senior sales rep John McCormick. "We are currently a minority supplier. But this could easily gain us $200,000 in new business because our competitors are scratching their heads wondering how they will do it."

"They don't have the system."

Formatting Your Content

Depending on the nature of your publication, contents can vary widely. Here are some of the most common editorial inclusions.

- **Articles**
- **Table of contents**: Usually run on the first page.
- **Masthead**: Gives publication information (editor, publisher, etc.) and usually run on the second or back page.
- **Announcements**: Usually run as boxed information, but sometimes as regular columns for job placement, promotions, etc.
- **Letters:** If the publication is designed for two-way communication, a letters column is a common addition.
- **Editorial**: Can be in the form of a "President's Column," a signed editorial from management or the publication's editor.
- **News notes**: A quick (and brief) look at what's happening—often a boxed item or sometimes run in very narrow columns as *marginalia*.
- **Mailer**: This is the spot reserved for mailing labels, postage-paid information and return address; however, it is often used as a place to put masthead information.
- **Calendar**: Upcoming events of interest to readers.

Although there are variations on these elements, most newsletters include at least some of these items.

How Much Is Enough?

How many articles to run depends on the focus and length of your publication, but fortunately, newsletters are extremely flexible. If you run a four-page newsletter but you always have more information than room, you can expand to six or eight pages. A one-page insert (loose, or run on a larger sheet with a brochure-type fold) will give you enough room for two or three more stories—more if your articles are short (see **Exhibit 5.6**).

There is no set figure for how much is enough. The key questions are: how much can you spend, how much information do you have to impart, how much will your audience read, and how large a publication do you personally want to edit?

Making Your Articles Fit

Most newsletters lead off with the most topical or interesting story on the front page—as a newspaper does. Your choice of lead article will be based on management dictates or your assessment of reader interest.

Before you begin to lay out your newsletter, you should list all your potential articles, their lengths, and approximate placement by importance/interest in the newsletter. This way, if space gets tight, you can edit from the bottom up. A secondary choice is to carry over articles that aren't "time bound"—that is, articles that could just as well wait for the next issue. And, finally, you can edit each story until *all* of them fit in the space you have. This assumes that some information in each article is superfluous which, under ideal editorial circumstances, shouldn't happen. But, as any experienced editor can tell you, there is always something you can cut.

Standing columns—articles such as editorials or employee recognition that recur from issue to issue—should already have a reserved space in your layout. It is in your best interest to allot a certain amount of space to these recurring articles and stick to it. That way, your other articles will have the space they need and deserve.

If you run out of space and can afford it, consider adding two pages (a single page run on both sides) either as an insert or an extra fold. If you only have enough copy to add literally one page (a single sheet printed only on one side) don't do it. Nothing is as unattractive as a publication page printed only on one side.

Editorial Considerations for Display Copy

Display copy, from an editorial viewpoint, includes headlines, subheads, captions, and pull quotes. Each of these elements has to be written for best effect. Ideally, each should contribute to the article to which it refers by adding to, elaborating or amplifying on, or drawing attention to information already presented in the article.

Writing Headlines

Headlines are important to any publication, but especially so for newsletters. Headlines should grab the readers' attention and make them want to read the article. They should be informative and brief. Here are some guidelines that should help you in constructing good headlines.

- Keep them short. Space is always a problem in newsletters. Be aware of column widths and how much space that sentence-long headline you are proposing will take up. Every column inch you

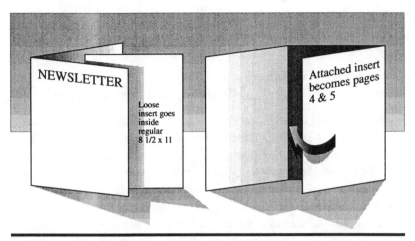

Exhibit 5.6—Newsletter Inserts

A one-page addition (printed both sides) can be inserted as a loose page into a standard four-page newsletter; however, many of these loose pages fall out or become lost during distribution or reading. If you opt for an attached page as part of a two-fold format, the last page should fold inward.

devote to your headline will have to be subtracted somewhere else. Headlines don't have to be complete sentences, nor do they have to be punctuated unless they are.

- Avoid vague words or phrases. Your headline should contribute to the article, not detract from it. Cute or vague headlines that play on words should be left for entertainment publications like *Variety* (famous for its convoluted headlines). Don't use standing heads for recurring articles such as "President's Message" or "Employee Recognition." It is better to mention something of the article's content in the headline, such as "Packaging Division wins company-wide contest."

- Use short words. Along word in a headline often has to be hyphenated or left on a line by itself. You can always come up with an alternative that is shorter.

Writing Subheads and Crossheads

Subheads are explanatory heads, usually set in a smaller type (or italics), that appear under the headline. For example:

ACME buyout impending
Statewide Telecom makes takeover bid

In most cases, a headline is sufficient; however, there are times when a rather lengthy subhead is necessary, especially if the headline is brief or cryptic.

'A drama of national failure'
A best-selling author talks about reporting on AIDS

Subheads should be used sparingly, if at all, and only for clarity's sake.

Crossheads are the smaller, transitional heads within an article. You shouldn't need them in a typical newsletter article. About the only time they might be useful is in a longer article—perhaps a newsletter devoted to a single subject. Crossheads should be very short and should simply indicate a change in subject or direction. Most writers use crossheads in place of elaborate transitional devices. Space is always a consideration, and using a crosshead instead of a longer transitional device may save you several column inches.

However, if you do use crossheads, make sure that more than one is warranted. Like subpoints in an outline, crossheads don't come solo. Either delete a single crosshead, or include another one.

Writing Captions

Captions, or cutlines, are the informational blurbs that appear below or next to photographs or other illustrations. They are usually set in a smaller point size. Like headlines, they should contribute to the overall information of an article, not detract from it.

Keep captions brief. Make sure they relate directly to the photograph. (The best captions also add information that may not be included in the article itself.)

If your caption is necessarily long, make sure it is clear. If you are naming a number of people in a photo, for example, establish a recognizable order (*clockwise from the top, right to left, from the top, from the left*, etc.)

Captions, like headlines, should not be vague or cute. You simply don't have enough space to waste developing that groaner of a pun.

Writing Pull Quotes

Pull quotes are relatively new to newsletters. Traditionally a magazine device, they draw a reader's attention to a point within an article. They almost always appear close to the place in the article from which the quote is taken.

Pull quotes don't have to be actual quotes, but they should at least be an edited version of the article copy. Pull quotes usually suggest themselves. If you have a number of good quotes from an interviewee, you can always find a good one to use as a pull quote. Or, if you simply want to stress an important point in an article, use it as a pull quote.

Pull quotes are useful both as editorial and as design elements. Editorially, a pull quote draws attention to your article by highlighting an interesting quote. As a design element, a pull quote can create white space or fill up unused space left over from a short article. If, for instance, you have several inches left over on your page, simply add a pull quote to the middle of the article in the length you need to take up the extra space (see **Exhibit 5.7**). A good pull quote can be as long or as short as you want and still make sense. It can span several columns, be constrained to a single column, head the page, appear in the center of a copy-heavy page, or help balance some other graphic element on the page.

Remember, good pull quotes reflect the best your article has to offer. A mundane pull quote is wasted space.

Exhibit 5.7—Pull Quotes as a Design Element
As a design element, a pull quote can be used to take up space on a page. The normal restrictions for trapped white space don't apply here as the increased white space can be used as a point of emphasis. Notice that the extra white space falls below the pull quote.

Lorem ipsum dolor sit amet, consectetuer adipiscing elit, sed diam nonummy nibh euismod tincidunt ut laoreet dolore magna aliquam erat volutpat. Ut wisi enim ad minim veniam, quis nostrud exerci tation ullamcorper suscipit lobortis nisl ut aliquip ex

'From the opening baton to the last, lingering note, this season will be a winner.'

Lorem ipsum dolor sit amet, consectetuer adipiscing elit, sed diam nonummy nibh euismod tincidunt ut laoreet dolore magna aliquam erat volutpat. Ut wisi enim ad minim veniam, quis nostrud exerci tation ullamcorper suscipit lobortis nisl ut aliquip ex ea commodo consequat. Duis autem vel eum iriure dolor in

Lorem ipsum dolor sit amet, consectetuer adipiscing elit, sed diam nonummy nibh euismod tincidunt ut laoreet dolore magna aliquam erat volutpat. Ut wisi enim ad minim veniam, quis nostrud exerci tation ullamcorper suscipit lobortis nisl ut aliquip ex

'From the opening baton to the last, lingering note, this season will be a winner.'

Lorem ipsum dolor sit amet, consectetuer adipiscing elit, sed diam nonummy nibh euismod tincidunt ut laoreet dolore magna aliquam erat volutpat. Ut wisi enim ad minim veniam, quis nostrud exerci tation ullamcorper suscipit lobortis nisl ut aliquip ex

Lorem ipsum dolor sit amet, consectetuer adipiscing elit, sed diam nonummy nibh euismod tincidunt ut laoreet dolore magna aliquam erat volutpat. Ut wisi enim ad minim veniam, quis nostrud exerci tation ullamcorper suscipit lobortis nisl ut aliquip ex

'From the opening baton to the last, lingering note, this season will be a winner.'

Lorem ipsum dolor sit amet, consectetuer adipiscing elit, sed diam nonummy nibh euismod tincidunt ut laoreet dolore magna aliquam erat volutpat. Ut wisi

Design Considerations

No discussion of newsletters would be complete without some mention of design. Most people who engage in newsletter writing and editing today also lay out their own newsletters as well. And with the advent of desktop publishing, that job has become increasingly easy.

We've already seen how most newsletters are simply 11" x 17" pages folded in half, giving us four "panels" or pages to work with. However, once we include the design elements that will make our newsletter attractive enough to be picked up by readers, there's not all that much room left for words. Exactly how much room will depend on your design capabilities.

What most designers love the most about newsletters is the wide variety of available formats. Just picking one can be a challenge. A newsletter can take on any number of disguises, ranging from the standard 11" x 17" format folded down to a four-page 8½" x 11" size, to a lengthy magazine-like format folded and stapled, to a tabloid newspaper, to a tabloid-sized magazine-type format known as a *magapaper*. Audience needs and cost are the most important deciding factors in picking a format for your newsletter.

The thing to remember is that no matter what format you ultimately decide on, you will be stuck with it for quite some time. If you are going to have enough information to fill a twelve-page magazine format four times a year—good, use a magazine format. If not, try something smaller. If you need to insert your newsletter in a monthly billing envelope, try something even smaller. If size is what attracts your audience, and you usually don't have to mail your newsletter, try a magapaper or a tabloid (even these can be mailed—they just cost a lot more).

Whatever you decide on, remember that your design elements must fit your format. Large formats call for larger artwork. Small formats call for shorter articles. White space is an extravagance in a bill stuffer, but not in a tabloid. Folding and mailing differs immensely among the various sizes. Suit your format to your needs. Once you *have* decided on a basic format, the job of design begins in earnest, and requires a good deal of practice.

Take a look at **Exhibit 5.8** for some of the essential elements of a newletter front page, for example. While there isn't time or space to cover newsletter design in detail here, let's explore a few basics, such as formats and type faces. Once your interest is piqued, however, you'll want to take a look at some books dealing with newsletters in more detail.

Associated Products Corporation Newsletter • Vol. 2, No. 4

New APC software will revolutionize education.'

INSIDE

'*We're strong on education at APC, and this software shows it in a big way.*'

Teachers and students across the country may soon get some relief from overcrowded classrooms thanks to a revolutionary new software line developed by APC. The software, called *InfoQuick* or *IQ*, will help students learn through the use of interactive computer programs according to APC President James L. Sutton.

on cites statistics showaverage teacher in a grade school class of 30 students spends only ten minutes a day with each student. He believes that *IQ*'s interactive format will help provide that needed personal attention. According to a recent study, the interactive format of a computer program also helps students information more quickly.

IQ is an "entirely new concept in educational software," says Sutton, the originator of the

idea. Through different interactive computer programs, students learn not only about computers, but also from computers, and they have fun at the same time. *IQ* is designed to ask questions and provide students with answers, advice and guidance. "The *IQ* system of learning is easy and fun, and teachers will welcome a computer program that takes some of the load off their shoulders," Sutton says.

But, Sutton points out that *IQ* is not just a series of computer games. APC has devoted five

---

Exhibit 5.8—A Newsletter Front Page

Some of the more important design elements of a typical newsletter front page are: 1) The banner or name of your newsletter. Make sure it neither overpowers your front page nor is overpowered by other elements on the page. 2) The headline. Typically, there should be only one major head on the front page. Make it large enough to draw attention, but not so large as to overpower your banner. 3) Photos and illustrations. Don't scrimp on size. Draw attention to your stories with large photos and illustrations. Just make sure they are of a quality worthy of the attention. 4) Body copy. Flush left, ragged right if columns are wide (2 or 3 columns), justified if narrow (4 or more columns). 5) Table of contents. Don't assume it has to be boxed. Try an open format for a change. 6) Rules. Use them to delineate your columns or to set items apart.

Grids

Grids, basically, refer to the number of columns you will be using. The most common formats are 3- 4-column layouts. Both are quite flexible, 3-column being more appropriate for smaller formats and 4-column for larger. Remember, the more columns you have, the narrower they will have to be and the smaller you type will need to be to accomodate the column width.

If you're just beginning, try a basic 3-column grid for all your pages. The column width is enough to give you a readable type and to use graphics in legible sizes. The basic rule of laying out a newsletter is to use the columns as your grid and lay all your elements out (in our 3-column grid) in one-, two-, and three-column widths. See **Exhibit 5.9**.

Exhibit 5.9—Three-column layout

As you can see, all the elements of this front-page spread conform to the 3-column grid. Not only do the headlines and text fit within one colum, but the photos are designed to fit either one or two columns. Try not to use fractions of columns as your layout will look jumbled.

Type

There really is a bewildering array of choices facing you; however, if you learn a few basics now, that array can be narrowed down to just a few choices for you and your newsletter.

The first thing to know is how to classify type. Let's start with the most general, and useful, classification for publication purposes. First of all, type is measured in points (in type, this is a vertical measurement). There are 72 points in an inch. Imagine trying to designate 11-point type in inches and you know why printers and typesetters have traditionally used a different scale. Small type, up to 14 points, is called *body type*. Type that is 14 points and above is called *display type* (normally headlines). Most typefaces come in both body and display sizes; however, there are subtle differences between the sizes. The best way to spec type is to look at a complete alphabet in all the sizes and weights you are going to be using and check out the differences for yourself. Next, type can be broken down into five other, fairly broad categories; but, for our purposes, we'll look at just three: serif, sans serif, and italic.

1. *Serif.* Most serif faces are distinguished by a variation in thick and thin strokes, and by serifs—the lines that cross the end strokes of the letters. (See **Exhibit 5.10**.)Serif type can be further broken down into *romans* and *slab* or *square serif* faces. Romans have the traditional thick and thin strokes while slab serif faces have relatively uniform strokes and serifs. Serif faces are usually considered easier to read, especially in body type sizes.

2. *Sans serif.* These are faces without serifs (*sans*, from the French, meaning *without*). (See **Exhibit 5.11**.)They are usually, but not always, distinguished by uniformity of strokes. They usually impart a more modern look to a publication, especially if used as display type. Setting body type in sans serif is unwise because

---

Exhibit 5.10—Serif Type

Times

Serifs are the small lines that cross the end strokes of the letters in serif type. Roman serifs have the traditional thick and thin strokes.

Lubalin

Square or slab serifs have fairly uniform thicknesses of both the letter strokes and their serifs.

---

the uniformity of the strokes tends to darken your page and makes for difficult reading. There are some exceptions. Optima, for example, has some variation in stroke and reads fairly well in smaller sizes. Stone Sans, a new face designed by Sumner Stone of Adobe Systems, makes excellent use of thin and thick strokes.

Exhibit 5.11—Sans Serif Type

Helvetica

In this example of sans serif type (Helvetica), notice the uniformity of stroke width. This is characteristic of most, but not all, sans serif type.

Optima

Optima is one of several sans serif typefaces with some interesting variation in strike width. This variation (along with a hint of serifs) tends to make the face more readable.

3. *Italics.* Some typographers don't consider italics a separate category of type since most typefaces today come with an italic version. However, true Roman italic versions of many typefaces are completely different from their upright versions. (See **Exhibit 5.12.**) Since the advent of desktop publishing, editors have had the option of italicizing a typeface with a simple keystroke. This method typically only slants the existing face; it does not always create a true italic version of that face. Only by selecting a face that has been designed specifically as an italic do we get true italics. Because they are slanted, italics tend to impart an informality and speed to your message. But, also because of the slant, they are more difficult to read and should be used for accent only. Also, italic refers only to a version of a serif face.

Exhibit 5.12—Italic Type

Type Type

There is quite a bit of difference between a true italic face (Goudy italic) left, and a slanted version of the upright face, right. Type designers would just as soon you didn't distort their original typeface designs.

Type Type

Sans serif typefaces don't have italic versions per se. Instead, they have obliques. Like italics, obliques are specifically designed to be set at a slant. They are not simply slanted versions of the upright face.

A slanted version of a sans serif face is called *oblique*. Like italics, true obliques are designed as separate *fonts* (a complete alphabet, number series and set of punctuation points and miscellaneous marks) and are not simply the original face at a slant.

How to Choose Type

If you are putting your newsletter together on a typewriter, try to stick to one typeface. Although there are interchangeable elements for some typewriters, they can't replicate the look of typeset copy and headlines. If you are typesetting your newsletter, then you will have to select typefaces. Following are some of the most common questions regarding that selection.

1. **Can I use just one typeface**? The safest route to take is to stick with one typeface. Using a single face lends your newsletter unity and consistency. Pick one that comes in as many variations as possible style, weight, size, and width.

   Most typefaces come in *regular* and/or *light* versions. These are sometimes called *book* or *text*. They also come in *upright* (roman) and *italic* or *oblique*. In addition, they may have *demi-bold,* and *bold* versions in both upright and italic or oblique (or these versions may be called *heavy* or *black*; or heavy and black versions may be in addition to bold). And the semi-bold and bold versions may come as extended and/or condensed (referring to the width of the letters).

   The greater the variety available, the more flexibility you have in a single typeface. For example, you could use the regular version for body type, the bold version for headlines, and the regular italic version for captions, pull quotes, and subheads (in different point sizes).

2. **Can I use more than one typeface**? Novices with access to a computer and a type library of twenty faces tend to use all twenty just because they have them. Try to limit yourself to no more than two different typefaces in a publication, and make sure they don't conflict with each other. This is the most difficult part of using more than one face. Here are a few guidelines to remember.

   • If your body type is serif, try a sans serif for headlines. Two different serif faces will probably conflict with one another.

- If you are using a light body type (as opposed to its regular version), use a regular or semi-bold headline type. You don't want your headline weight to overpower your text weight.

- Above all, don't pick your type just by looking at a type chart. Have a page set, complete with body copy and headlines, to see for yourself whether your two faces are going to harmonize or not.

3. **Where do I go to select type?** If you are working on a computer, you probably have anywhere from two to a hundred choices, depending on the sophistication of your desktop publishing system. Stick with what you have. It's easier and saves a lot of frustration in the long run. If all you have is Times Roman, use it. If you have Times Roman and Helvetica, use Times for the body copy and Helvetica for the headlines. Under no circumstances use Helvetica for the body copy. It is not very readable set in blocks of small type. If you have access to a larger type library on computer, explore your options by experimenting with several combinations, printing out a page with each one.

Don't forget to try several different point sizes for body copy. There can be a great deal of variation in readability between 12-point Times and 12-point Palatino, as well as between 12-point Palatino and 10-point Palatino, for example.

Be aware that your type will also look different when printed on different printers. Decide which printer you're going to use to print your final camera-ready copy and check its print quality against your type choice. Typefaces with thin serifs may not print as well on a dot-matrix printer as on a laser printer, or as well on a laser printer as on an imagesetter. Bold or heavy faces (especially if condensed) will tend to clog and fill on dot-matrix and laser printers, but will print cleanly on an imagesetter. If you don't have access to computer type, ask your printer or typesetter for samples of type set in copy blocks and as display type. Most printers can provide you with more than just a type chart.

Alignment

Alignment refers to the way your copy is arranged in relation to column margins. The two most typical alignments are *flush left* (sometimes called *ragged right*) and *justified*. (See **Exhibit 5.13**.) Flush left copy is getting to be quite common for newsletters. It imparts a less formal look, involves less hyphenation, and takes up more space.

Justified copy looks more formal, is more hyphenated, and takes up less space. However, when using justified copy, keep in mind that the width of your columns severely affects *word spread*. The narrower your columns, the more your words will separate from one another in order to maintain justification. Computers allow for minute adjustments to word and letter spacing to help correct this spread, but the best way to avoid it is to keep your columns at the average or maximum width for your type size.

There are other alignment possibilities, such as *flush right* and *centered*. Flush right copy should be avoided because it is difficult to read. It is, however, sometimes useful for very brief text blocks such as pull quotes that appear in outside left margins. Centered body text should always be avoided. Centered headlines are not in fashion these days, although centered pull quotes are still found quite a bit.

Exhibit 5.13—Text Alignment

Notice that the justified text (left) takes up less space than the flush left text (center). The flush right text (right) is nearly impossible to track (move from end of one line to the beginning of the next).

What's the difference between a therapist, psychologist, psycho-therapist, psychiatrist, and counselor? If you don't know, you're among the millions of people who are confused about the multi-tiered mental health counseling field.	What's the difference between a therapist, psychologist, psycho-therapist, psychiatrist, and counselor? If you don't know, you're among the millions of people who are confused about the multi-tiered mental health counseling field.	What's the difference between a therapist, psychologist, psycho-therapist, psychiatrist, and counselor? If you don't know, you're among the millions of people who are confused about the multi-tiered mental health counseling field.
In an effort to clear up some of the confusion, the American Mental Health Counselors Association (AMHCA) has "hired" a university student group to produce a public information campaign for them.	In an effort to clear up some of the confusion, the American Mental Health Counselors Association (AMHCA) has "hired" a university student group to produce a public information campaign for them.	In an effort to clear up some of the confusion, the American Mental Health Counselors Association (AMHCA) has "hired" a university student group to produce a public information campaign for them.
The Public Relations Student Society of America (PRSSA) at the University of Oregon has been retained by the Association to develop a program of information that	The Public Relations Student Society of America (PRSSA) at the University of Oregon has been retained by	The Public Relations Student Society of America (PRSSA) at the University of Oregon has been retained by

The best idea is to pick either flush left or justified for your body copy and not to deviate. Stick with flush left for headlines. And use either flush left or justified for pull quotes and captions.

Style Sheets

In order to maintain consistency in your newsletter from issue to issue, you will need to develop a *style sheet*. A style sheet is a listing of all of the type specifications you use in your newsletter. It should be as complete as possible, and every member of your staff should have a copy. Style sheets are especially important if you are sick or on vacation and someone else has to produce an issue or two of your newsletter. It will tell them at a glance what it probably took you hours to determine when you first started. **Exhibit 5.14** shows a typical style sheet.

Exhibit 5.14—Style Sheet

Style Sheet: <u>On Line</u>
Newsletter of the Public Relations Student Society of America,
University of Oregon Chapter

<u>Page size</u>—11 by 17 inches, one-page, printed front and back, vertical tabloid layout. Margins 3/4 inch on all sides. Folded in thirds for mailing. Self-mailer on bottom third of back page. 60 lb. white, semi-matt finish.

<u>Grid</u>—Five columns for normal text layout. Four or five columns for boxed or feature items. One pica between columns with a hairline rule.

<u>Body text</u>—10-point Times, auto leaded, flush left, first indents 1/4 inch.

<u>Captions</u>—9-point Times italic, flush left, run width of photo, 1/2 pica beneath photo.

<u>Lead article headline</u>—24-point Optima bold, set solid, reversed on 40% screen. Run full width of page (five columns).

<u>Two and three-column heads</u>—18-point Optima bold, leaded 19, flush left running width of article. Reversed on 40% screen.

<u>Pull quotes</u>—14-point Optima italic, centered, one to three-column width as needed. Two-point line one pica above and one-point line below as needed to fill space.

<u>Masthead copy</u>—9-point Optima, flush left, one-column width..

<u>Ink color</u>—Black ink run on pre-printed blanks with banner in PMS 4515.

As you can see from this simple style sheet, you'll have to make numerous design considerations as editor of your own newsletter. The fun is in the experimenting. For example, take a look at **Exhibit 5.15**. These are just three of the nearly unlimited ways in which you can lay out a newsletter front page to tell the same story. Don't give up until you have it the way you want it.

Exhibit 5.15—Front Page Layouts

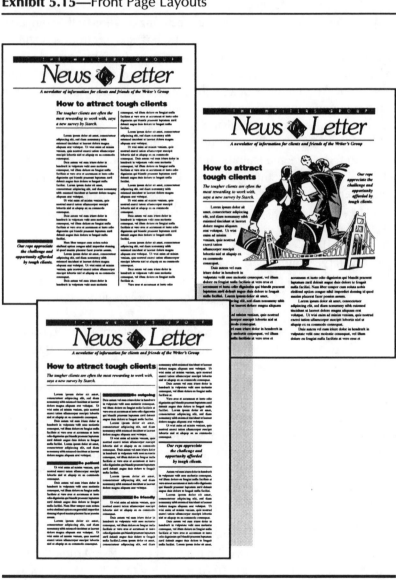

Case Study: Associated Products Corporation

Use the following additional information for the newsletter assignments. Be sure to review the original background information in
Chapter 3 as well.

APC Electronics Division

The Electronics Division of Associated Products Corporation, located
in White Plains, N.Y., is a major manufacturing division of the company.
APC was originally called Traxton Electronics, and electronics is still its
primary concern. Although the headquarters of the company is located
in Syracuse, N.Y., the Electronics Division was moved to White Plains
in 1979 to take advantage of a relatively new plant site purchased from
another manufacturing firm the year before.

The new Electronics Division is located on a ten-acre lot outside
White Plains but within the city limits and provides the city with
substantial tax revenue from both property and local income taxes. In
addition, the division employs 800 workers, 350 from White Plains. The
remainder have transferred from other divisions or from headquarters
or are new hires, who specialize in electronics, from various parts of the
state and country.

The facility is composed of four buildings and two large parking
lots. The largest building is given over to the assembly lines where the
electronic products are manufactured. The other buildings house the
offices, research labs, meeting rooms, a large auditorium, and the
facility's cafeteria.

The InfoQuick software, a product of the Electronics Division, is
created in two basic stages. First, the physical diskette is manufactured
in two parts—the magnetic inner disk and the synthetic paper outer
covering. The magnetic disks are then electronically bulk coded with
the software information from a master program. Of course, the transfer
is made electronically instead of physically. The disks are then covered
with the outer sleeve and sealed, all by machine. The only workers
involved in the process are those who run the primary machines;
however, a number of assembly line people are involved in the final
packaging in which the software is inserted into boxes and wrapped in
cellophane for shipping.

Robert McArthur, Electronics Division Manager

Senior vice president and division manager Robert McArthur has been
with APC for over ten years. Before coming to APC, McArthur was

assistant vice president for manufacturing at Philcronics, another electronics firm purchased by APC in 1974. He has a close working relationship with APC president James L. Sutton, and sits on the executive board of the company. Although he had no hand in either the idea or the development of InfoQuick, McArthur is playing a major role in the manufacturing process. As division manager, he is responsible for the mass production of the software, including raw materials purchase, quality control, and meeting production deadlines. Some quotes:

> "I agree with Jim [Sutton] when he says that this idea is revolutionary. I've raised two kids myself [McArthur's wife died in 1970] and I know firsthand how difficult it is to keep them interested in learning."

> "The Electronics Division is *the* division at APC (don't tell Harve Johnsen over in the Paper Products Division I said that) and we pump a lot of money into R&D [research and development] to support that claim. Without R&D, we wouldn't have IQ on the market today. It takes a lot of thinking and sweating to come up with that kind of product."

> "If it didn't have a market, we wouldn't make it. Let's face it—if we can't make any money, then we go out of business. I mean, I appreciate what IQ is going to do for kids all over the country, but it's also going to make us a bundle."

> "The people who work here in the White Plains plant are a great bunch of folks—all 800 or so of them. Every single worker knows his job and does it. We don't get a lot of flack from the line people. They know that in today's economy, they're lucky to have jobs. I don't mean to sound high and mighty, but that's the bottom line. It doesn't mean that we try to get away with anything, we don't. They get top money and honest treatment."

> "We're thinking of instituting a profit-sharing plan sometime this year. The employees already know about it and they're real pleased. It gives them incentive to work hard, put in a full day, and come up with cost-saving ideas. They know that they'll profit too."

Ellen Burke, Assembly Line, Electronics Division

Ellen Burke is an assembly line worker for the Electronics Division. She's been with APC for four years, is married, and has one child, three years old. Some quotes:

"Some people don't like assembly line work, but I don't mind it. I try to understand what it is I'm doing. I don't just go through the motions eight hours a day."

"This InfoQuick stuff is a great idea. I understand that President Sutton came up with it. Good for him. My daughter will be going to school in a few years, and I sure want her to get to use it."

"The profit-sharing plan we've been hearing about is a great idea. I could use a little profit. Not that I don't get paid good money. I do. But, when I get part of the profits, then the company kind of belongs to me too—and everybody else around here."

Lorna Allen, Programmer III, Electronics Division

Lorna Allen is a computer programmer hired by APC five years ago when work on the IQ line began. She had just received her masters in computer science from Cornell and was job hunting. Along with eight other programmers, Allen was responsible for coming up with the technical requirements necessary to put the educational ideas into computer language. Some quotes:

"I was extremely lucky to have been hired by APC right out of graduate school. Now, I'll be able to stay on here in the Electronics Division as long as IQ is carried as a product line—which we all hope will be a long time."

"When we first began, we only had the barest of ideas how we'd proceed. What evolved was an excellent working relationship between the programmers and the educators we hired as consultants."

"We've really done something to be proud of here—not only as computer programmers, but as inventors. I mean, I feel kind of like Ben Franklin or Thomas Edison—a pioneer in my field."

Assignment 5-1: Newsletter

As part of your job as public relations writer for APC, you must contribute articles for the employee newsletter, *APC Action*. You have been assigned the task of writing an article of 500 words to be this month's feature article on the new IQ software line and APC's involvement with NEA. Because there is a lot of information, you will have to keep to the point—500 words is only about two typed pages.

This is an employee newsletter. You should try to make the article newsy but interesting. Look for an angle that you think might attract the employees—something they may all have in common. Because this is a feature story, use feature article construction.

Assignment 5-2: Newsletter

Most school districts subscribe to a national newsline featuring news of interest to educators. Individual districts often put out their own newsletters based on newsline information, sometimes using stories from the newsline *in toto*. Write a brief news story (about 250 words) on the NEA speaker's bureau for the newsline. Use standard news story format (inverted pyramid).

Assignment 5-3: Newsletter

You've been given the assignment of writing a newsletter feature for the corporate monthly newsletter about the Electronics Division at White Plains plant and its involvement with the IQ line. This can be an all-purpose article because it's as much about the plant and the division as it is about the software. The article is to be about 600 words.

## CHAPTER 6

Magazines & Trade Publications

The magazine in the end will be the most influential
of all departments of letters.

Edgar Allen Poe

W hen we speak of magazines most of us think of our favorite
consumer publication (*Time, Newsweek, National Geographic,* the *Atlantic*, etc.); however, for our purposes, we
are speaking primarily, but not exclusively, of the **house publication**.
Recent research has shown that house publications are the *least* looked
to form of organizational communication. Guess what's first? Face-to-
face communication. That's not surprising, but it doesn't mean that the
house magazine is dead. What it does mean is that it should *contribute*
to open communication rather than be relied upon as the sole source. In
addition, it plays another role. Unlike most print media an organization
might have access to, the house publication is a totally controlled
medium—that is, the organization producing it has sole editorial
control. The company can go on record through its house organ, state
its position on a controversial issue, or simply tell its story its way. In
other words, the house organ is still a good public relations tool.

The typical house organ is meant for an internal public—usually
employees, shareholders, and retirees. Sometimes, though, it is offered
to the external public. A publication like *Exxon USA* stresses a broader
emphasis, with articles often dealing with the industry as a whole and
subjects of interest to those outside the company. Because the house
organ is, at bottom, still a public relations piece, its thrust remains
company oriented. Even a seemingly unrelated story will, in some way,
eventually relate to the organization.

The house publication is usually in either magazine or newspaper format (or sometimes a hybrid called a "magapaper"). Both communicate with their various publics efficiently. Unless the company is large enough to produce a slick in-house publication, the house organ will be sent out to an agency for design and printing. Sometimes the agency will even provide writers to work up the stories; however, the best articles still come from writers inside the company who know and work with the people they write about.

Content and Format

Like their smaller cousin, the newsletter, house magazines usually present the following editorial mix:

- 50 percent information about the organization—local, national, and international
- 20 percent employee information—benefits, quality of working life, raises, etc.
- 20 percent relevant noncompany information—competitors, the community, etc.
- 10 percent small talk and personals

How you organize these elements is important. You should lead your reader through your magazine in a logical order, and one that is pleasing and interesting.

There is no single organizational format for house magazines. What is important is that you find a place for all relevant information, a place inclusive enough to house similar information from issue to issue.

Before you even start (or if you're overhauling an existing publication) you need to set some objectives. To make sure your reasons for publishing a house magazine are realistic, ask yourself some questions.

- Are my goals and objectives consistent with the goals and objectives of the organization itself? What am I really trying to get out of this? The temptation is very real, especially for creative people, to produce a magazine for simple ego gratification. Don't succumb to it. Have good, solid reasons for publishing.

- Can I attain these objectives through another, more effective method? Can I achieve good downward communication through an existing newsletter or more frequent meetings?

- Can I attain these objectives in a more cost-effective way? House magazines are expensive to produce. As usual, your budget restrictions will have the final say.

Once you have answered these questions, and you have satisfied yourself that your prospective audience will benefit from your publication, you can decide on its proper organizational format.

Most house magazines contain very much the same type of editorial information as newsletters. The following items are listed in the approximate order in which they might appear (allowing for overlap in the case of articles).

- **Table of contents**: Usually run on the front page.
- **Masthead**: Gives publication information (editor, publisher, etc.) and usually run on the table of contents or second page.
- **Editorial**: Can be in the form of a "President's Column," a signed editorial from management or the publication's editor.
- **Letters:** If the publication is designed for two-way communication, a letters column is a common addition.
- **News Notes**: A quick (and brief) look at what's happening around the organization. You can get a lot of these in two or three pages. This is a good place for employee information as well.
- **Articles:** News and feature articles make up the bulk of the magazine and should have a consistent order of their own. For instance, the cover story should always appear in the same approximate location each issue.
- **Announcements**: Usually boxed, but sometimes run as regular columns for job placement, promotions, etc. This is another good place for employee interest pieces.
- **Calendar**: Upcoming events of interest to readers.

Remember, there is no hard and fast rule for formatting your magazine, but stick to whatever method you choose. Your readers look for consistency. If the format changes every two issues, you'll quickly lose them.

Writing Articles

House publication articles range from straight news to complete fiction, and include everything in between. Most, though, are either straight news or feature. Since straight news has been covered adequately in earlier chapters, we will concentrate on feature writing here.

A feature can be construed as almost anything that isn't straight news. In fact, *feature* has several meanings. As used in the term "feature story," it simply means the main story or cover story in the publication. In its broader sense it means an article that features something as its central point or theme. This something may not necessarily be the message of the story or its publicity angle. It is most often the story itself. For example, you've been asked to do a story on a new product—say, a plastic lining that can be used as a bed for soil or sod to keep it from eroding or slipping. Instead of doing a straight news story on the product itself, you opt to do a feature story on a user of the new product. Maybe you find a golf course that's using the new underliner to rebuild its greens and the focus of the story becomes the golf course. The publicity angle or the message about the new product becomes almost secondary. Featuring the golf course adds an extra dimension to your product story and sets it in context. In fact, the most useful element of a feature story approach is that it presents a context. Not every straight news story can do that.

A vast array of writing styles can justifiably be called "magazine writing." Articles or ideas for articles that don't seem to fit one particular magazine format, or even one section of a magazine, may well fit into another. For example, let's say you interview an employee on a job-related topic such as benefits. In the course of your conversation you discover that he builds model ships for a hobby and, in fact, has won several competitions. You actually gather enough information for a how-to article on building model ships as well as enough for a feature on the employee. Neither of these ideas may fit into the story you originally set out to do; however, they may fit into another section on employees or one on hobbies. The lesson, of course, is never discard information just because it doesn't fit into your present assignment. Even if the tone or style of the article or information doesn't seem to fit one category, it may well fit another.

The Profile

Although several standard types of feature articles are appropriate for magazines, the most common is the *profile*. The profile is most typically a feature story written specifically about a person, a product or service, or an organization or some part of it. It literally profiles the subject, listing facts, highlighting points of interest, and—most importantly—tying them to the organization. Regardless of the subject of your article, you are writing for a specific organization and the article must have some bearing on it—direct or indirect.

The personality profile. Personality profiles are popular because people like to read about other people, whether these people are just like them (so they can easily relate) or very different (so they can aspire or admire). Of course, a personality profile should do more than just satisfy human curiosity, it should inform the reader of something important about the organization itself by putting it in the context of a biographical sketch. For example, this lead was written for a brief profile on an award-winning engineer:

> When Francis Langly receives the Goodyear Medal this spring, it will represent the symbolic crowning of a lifetime of dedication to the field of chemistry. Awarded by the Rubber Division of the American Chemical Society, the Goodyear Medal is the premier award for work in the field of specialty elastomers—an area that Langly helped pioneer. When Langly makes his medalist's address to the gathering in Indianapolis in May, his comments will be a reflection of almost 50 years of innovation and development which began in 1938 when he joined Rogers Experimental Plastics Company as a research chemist.

What does this say about the organization? It implies, for one thing, that the company is obviously a good one to have such a well-respected person work for it for so long. A profile like this calls attention to the merits of the organization by calling attention to someone who has something to do with it—or, in some cases, to someone who benefits from its services or products. Consider the following lead:

> Guy Exton is a superb artist. His oils have hung in galleries all over the country. But, for nearly five years, he couldn't paint anything. In order to paint, you typically need fingers and a hand, and Guy lost his right hand in an auto acci-dent in 1983. But now, thanks to a revolutionary new elastomer product developed by Rogers Experimental Plastics Company, Guy is painting again. He can grip even the smallest of his paint brushes and control the tiniest nuance through the use of a special prosthetic device designed by Medical Help, Inc. of Franklin, New York. The device, which uses REP's "Elastoflex" membrane as a flexible covering, provides minute control of digits through an electro-mechanical power pack embedded in the wrist.

One of the most common types of personality profiles is the Q & A (question and answer format). This style typically begins with a brief biographical sketch of the person being interviewed, hints at the reason for the interview, and sets the scene by describing the surroundings in which the interview took place. For the remainder of the piece, speakers are tagged Q or A. Sometimes, the interviewer is designated with the magazine's name (for example, *The Corporate Connection* might be shortened to *CC*). Likewise, the interviewee might be designated by his or her last name.

The descriptive narrative tells the story of the individual being profiled from a second-person point of view. Naturally, quotes from the subject may be included, but sometimes a successful profile is simply a biographical sketch, and won't necessarily need them. The profile in **Exhibit 6.1** is a mixture. Although there are some brief quotes, most of the profile is simple biography.

Exhibit 6.1—Personality Profile

A Lifetime of Service

When Francis Langly receives the Goodyear Medal this spring, it will represent the symbolic crowning of a lifetime of dedication to the field of chemistry. Awarded by the Rubber Division of the American Chemical Society, the Goodyear medal is the premier award for work in the field of specialty elastomers—an area that Langly helped pioneer. When Langly makes his medalist's address to the gathering in Indianapolis in May, his comments will be a reflection of almost 50 years of innovation and development which began in 1938 when he joined Rogers Experimental Plastics Company as a research chemist.

Born in Brooklyn, New York, in 1915, Langly received his BA in chemistry and his PhD in organic chemistry from Cornell in 1939. His first position at REPC was in the Chemical Department at the Experimental Station near Ravenswood, Vermont. At the outset of World War II, he was working on the synthetic rubber program addressing the problem of an adhesive for nylon tire cord for B-29 bomber tires. These studies eventually culminated in the development of the vinyl pyridine adhesives so widely used today.

-more-

Langly's background in organic chemistry led to his transfer to the Organic Chemicals Department at the Johnson Laboratory in Stillwater, Oklahoma, where he discovered the first light-fast yellow dyes for cotton; and during the next 10 years, he led the task force that developed dyes for the new synthetic fibers that were fast becoming a mainstay of American fashion.

From his work in dyes, Langly moved on to work in fluorine chemical research. The small research team he headed is credited with the discovery of a family of new elastomers. The team at that time had what Langly calls, "a very special business in fluorine chemicals," but no solid applications yet for these quickly developing products. Langly and his group knew that they had something distinctly different and new in the field of elastomers. To an inventor, of course, the invention comes first. It didn't seem to trouble him that there was little or no market at that time for these new products. "There was no surprise in development," Langly says. "We understood the properties of the products we were developing and were sure that markets would eventually open up."

Chief among these early fluorelastomers was "Axon," a polymer that could resist extremely high temperatures, toxic chemicals, and a broad range of fluids. Other products, however, were gathering attention in industry and defense and the company was eager to market these already-accepted materials. In fact, the "Axon" project was sidetracked in the early 1950s when it was thought that the Langly research team could be better utilized in work on an already existing product. In a way, this turned out to be a profitable diversion. Although the proposed research turned out to be a dead end, a small pressure reactor system that had been designed to build EP rubbers was converted to make fluoropolymer and used as a pilot plant to produce "Axon."

According to Langly, "you rarely have a chance to fill a vacuum with something entirely new." And "Axon" was entirely new. The Air Force had been searching for some time for a product that could withstand very low and very high temperatures and was impervious to oil for use as engine seals on jet aircraft. "Axon" fit the bill perfectly. The Air Force quickly adopted it for use in jets, and the product went commercial for the first time in 1959.

When interest in space led the United States into the space race in the late 1950s, "Axon" gained another and larger market for use in

-more-

rocket engine seals. Because of its ability to seal against "hard" vacuum, "Axon" was one of the first rubbers that could be used in space.

As the markets for "Axon" continued to expand—to automotives, industry, and oil exploration uses— Langly progressed through a series of promotions. When the Elastomer Chemicals Department was formed in the mid-1960s, he was transferred to corporate headquarters in Freeport as Assistant Director of Research and Development.

Until his retirement in 1979, Langly continued to develop his interest in the field of elastomers. To date, he has 35 patents issued in his name and some 15 publications. In the 25 years since the birth of "Axon," Langly has seen the product grow to its present status as the premium fluoroelastomer in the world with a new plant recently opened in Belgium providing the product for a hungry European market.

But, Langly numbers the discovery and development of "Axon" as only one in a long line of accomplishments attained during his half-century of work in the field of chemistry. Since his retirement, he has remained active in the field, working in art conservation, developing new techniques for the preservation of rare oil paintings. In a year and a half of work with the City Museum in New York, he set up a sciences department for the conservation of paintings. He is currently scientific advisor for the Partham Museum in Baltimore. He continues to consult, working closely with industry. He serves as expert testimony at court trials involving chemicals. And, he has given a speech before the United Nations on rubber.

Yet, Langly remains low key about his accomplishments and his current interests. "I'm just trying to keep the fires going," he says. Despite this modesty, it is apparent to others that when Francis Langly receives the Goodyear Medal this year it will represent, not a capstone, but simply another milestone in a lifetime of service.

-30-

The product or service profile. Profiling a product or service means describing it in a way that is unusual in order to draw attention to the product and the organization. This is often done in subtle ways. For example, the personality profile on the artist Guy Exton is really a way of mentioning a product. Clearly this doesn't detract from the human-interest angle, but it does accomplish a second purpose (probably the primary purpose), which is publicity. The same techniques you use in other article types can be used in profiling products.

The organizational profile. In the organizational profile, an entire organization or some part of it is profiled. The organizational profile and the personality profile are accomplished much the same way, except that you need to interview a number of key people in the unit you are profiling in order to obtain a complete picture of that unit. The following profile looks at a department within a large corporation (**Exhibit 6.2**). **Exhibit 6.3** shows how the article might look laid out for a corporate magazine.

Exhibit 6.2—Organizational/Departmental Profile

The Legal Department at APC

Sitting behind a cluttered desk, boxes scattered around the office—some still unopened—is the new head of Associated Products Corporation's Law Department, Ed Bennett. Ed is a neat man, both in appearance and in speech. As he speaks about the "new" Law Department, he grins occasionally as though to say, "Why take the time to interview someone as unimportant as a lawyer?" That grin is deceiving because, to Ed and the other attorneys who work for Associated Products Corporation (APC), law is serious business.

Questions of law are rarely debated around APC. According to Ed, when something is not legal, it simply is not legal. No vote is taken by anyone; no decision needs to be arrived at. For this reason, "house counsel" (those attorneys who work for and in companies rather than for individuals) are often thought to be against all suggestions—paid to say no to projects or suggestions. This isn't so, says Ed. "It just so happens that a number of things that people wish to do must meet certain requirements. In most cases," he says, "it's not a question of 'you can't do it' but rather a matter of 'you have to do it this way.'"

According to Ed, this often puts the bearer of this news in an awkward position—much like the messenger who brings the Chinese Emperor bad tidings and has his head cut off for his efforts. It is a lot

-more-

better in Ed's mind to make the adjustments to a particular project now than to wait until they can no longer be made and find out that the entire project is unworkable.

In APC's Law Department, each attorney handles a specific area dealing with particular projects. Like many of the other departments in APC, Law is experiencing a period of transition. Consequently, specific areas of assignment are only tentative. Still, the four-person legal staff now employed by APC is specialized to the extent that each member has an area of expertise in which he or she works a majority of the time.

Denise Silva, newly arrived at APC from work with the State, is involved primarily with local and state government matters. Gary Williams is involved primarily in contractual matters, often between APC and other large companies. Keith McGowan has been handling research and certain other issues, frequently dealing with the Federal government.

Ed, just recently elected Vice President and General Attorney, describes his role as that of a player-coach. Aside from his specific responsibilities, he must also present the legal overview of the company's actions, and accept the consequences of his advice. "Along with responsibility comes accountability," he says.

Ed, who has been with APC for nearly two years, was assistant center judge advocate at Walter Reed Army Medical Center prior to coming to APC. He received his Juris Doctor from the University of Pennsylvania Law School and graduated from the College of William and Mary. Before coming to work for APC, Ed was a judge advocate officer at the Headquarters, U.S. Army Fort Dix, New Jersey from 1972 to 1975.

Together with the three other attorneys, Ed helps comprise a relatively small department. Despite its size, it may well be one of the most important functions within the company. "The myriad of legal and regulatory requirements, particularly in a business like this, creates a jungle," Ed says. "It is impossible to get to the other shore of this particular river by rowing in a straight line. There are cross currents and tides with the wind blowing from a hundred different directions."

The metaphor may be mixed, but the point is clear. According to Ed, the various State and Federal regulations governing our operations are by no means consistent. Neither, frequently, are the goals of the company as expressed by the input of each of the departments.

-more-

Consequently, it is also the responsibility of the Law Department to make uniform, or parallel, the various desires of the company.

"The end is always the same though," says Ed. "It is not to turn out neat legal briefs which, though often well researched and executed, are not useful if a manager can neither understand nor conform to them. It is to strike a balance between our own professional conscience and the utilitarian nature of the work."

"Of course," says Ed, "we'd like to spend six months on each item, carefully researching it, but by then we have lost the element of timeliness, which is often equally important."

The attorneys who make up the Law Department are, in the highest sense, professional. In fact, they have a professional responsibility quite separate from the company. Every attorney is a member of a bar association, and thus has imposed upon him or her the Code of Professional Responsibility unique to the profession. "We are not exempted," says Ed, "simply because we are 'house counsel,' from the dictates of that Code." Thus, their advice has to be correct, or as correct as it can be under prevailing circumstances. All of APC's attorneys are members of at least one bar and some are members of up to four.

The role of the APC attorney is similar to that of the "outside" attorney in that they are here to represent the company in legal matters. But APC's Law Department does more than that. It not only represents the company when it gets into difficulty, but expends a great deal of time and effort in keeping the company out of difficulty. To that end, the house counsel of APC must maintain sufficient contact with the company, its people, and its activities in order that it may render timely advice and thus prevent difficulties.

In a way, the modern attorney is still much like the medieval predecessor, who, hired to represent his client on the field of combat, used every honorable device in his power to win. Perhaps the armor and shield have been replaced by the vested suit and briefcase, but the same keen edge that decided many a trial-by-combat is still very much apparent.

-30-

Exhibit 6.3—Corporate Magazine Layout

Here is an example of how the article in Exhibit 6.2 might look laid out for a typical corporate magazine.

Writing the Story

Magazine articles, unlike straight news stories, must have a definite beginning, middle, and end. Developing these elements takes patience, practice, and organization.

The Lead

Always start at the beginning. A good lead is just as important to a magazine piece as it is to a news story. You must hook your reader into reading further and you must keep his or her interest through to the end.

In your lead, you must tell the reader what the article is about. You don't have to cram everything into the lead; however, you should include enough information so that the reader doesn't have to search for the topic. Consider the following leads.

A lead for a horse-racing trade:
> For some time now, the sound of heavy machinery has been echoing through the rolling green countryside and heavily forested groves of Eastern Maryland. But that sound will soon be replaced by the sound of galloping horses as they take to the newly banked turns and straightaway at what is being billed as "the most innovative thoroughbred training and sports medicine facility in North America."

One for the hospital industry:
> The scene is a standard hospital room designed with fire safety in mind: a very low fuel load, floors of asbestos tile, walls of gypsum board on steel studs, and a ceiling of fiberglass panels. The hospital is built in accordance with the National Fire Protection Agency Life Safety Code and has received the Joint Commission on Accreditation of Healthcare Organizations maximum 2-year approval.
>
> Late in the evening, a patient accidentally ignites the contents of his trash can which, in turn, ignite the bed clothes and, eventually, the mattress. The ensuing fire is a disaster, and despite the correct operation of all fire systems, multiple fatalities occur and the entire hospital wing is a total loss. Why? There are no fire standards on the upholstered furniture in this hospital and the mattresses meet a federal code designed to retard fires from smoldering cigarettes, not open flames.

A lead for a new product aimed at highway engineers:
> You're traveling along at high speed—the familiar "clackety-clack" of the rails beneath your feet. But wait a minute. You're not on a train, you're in an automobile, and that familiar sound beneath your feet is the result of deteriorating pavement joints that have been repaired with the usual "hot pour" method.

And an article for golf course superintendents:
Valleyview Country Club had a problem—the twelfth hole
was sinking again. For almost 40 years, the facilities people
at Valleyview had been rebuilding the green. In fact, it had
been rebuilt three times over that period of time, but each
time with the same results—in a matter of a few years, the
green would begin to sag again. This time, it was almost
bowl-shaped and was acting as a funnel for rainwater that
was draining from its outer edges into its concave center.

Although you may not have guessed it, all of these leads come from
articles announcing new products or new applications for established
products. Remember, even the most mundane subject can benefit from
a creative treatment. Your readers will only read your story if they like
your lead.

The Body of the Article

The body of your article should contain all the information your reader
needs to understand what you are trying to say. Obviously, it's in your
best interest to present your ideas clearly. Working from an outline is
the best way to ensure that you have covered all your key points in a
logical order. (Several methods for organizing an outline are presented
in **Chapter 14.**)

The body of the article must support your main point (hopefully
already made in the lead) and elaborate on it. You should anticipate
questions your reader might have, and answer them satisfactorily.
Remember to utilize logical transitional devices when moving from one
point to another. Subheads, although helpful to the reader, don't alleviate
the need for thoughtful transitions. Back up your statements with facts and
support all generalizations with specifics. Although magazine articles
seldom use footnotes, they are not completely inappropriate. Usually,
however, citation can be taken care of in the body of the text.

Articles for house publications tend to be shorter than those for
consumer magazine articles or even trade journals. The average length
of most house publications in magazine format is around twelve pages.
Article length runs about 1,000 words or less for features (about four
typed pages). Considering that magazine column width is about 14
picas for a three-column spread, and that articles are usually accompanied by photographs or artwork and headlines, subheads, and blurbs—
a 750-word article may cover several pages.

In **Exhibit 6.4** notice the organizational concept and transitional
devices that move the article from point to point, and the contributions
of the lead and ending.

Exhibit 6.4—Organizing the Article

APC's Answer Man

(1) You might have noticed, if you've been in the new headquarters building at Associated Products Corporation long, a rather harried figure dashing madly up and down the halls. That man with the worried expression is Dave Martin. Dave, in a sense, is the ombudsman for APC's new building. He's the man who fields all the complaints, large and small, that have to do with everything from desk positioning to major malfunctions.

> *The lead paragraph incorporates many of the basic elements of a news-type lead, including who, what, where, and how. It also delays the discovery of the topic until the second sentence by setting the scene first.*

(2) Dave's official title reads: Manager, Headquarters Facilities and Services. This constitutes a promotion for Dave, who was Manager, Technical Services. It also constitutes quite a lot of "heartburn."

> *The second paragraph is the "bridge" from the lead to the body of the story. It begins with a factual statement and ends with another teaser.*

> *Paragraphs 3 through 6 follow a sort of chronological order based on the construction of the new building, and provide background information.*

(3) The job was almost a matter of evolution for Dave, who became associated with the project through working with Bob Allen, Project Manager for the new building. Dave continually found himself involved with planning of space allocation, because this was a natural carry over from his former job. He cites the speed at which the building was completed as one of the major factors for his almost sudden immersion in the project.

-more-

(**4**) An undertaking of this magnitude usually takes years to complete. The space layout itself, which usually takes six to eight months, only took six to eight weeks. Dave and the planners worked night and day setting up seating arrangements for each department. These arrangements had gone through each department weeks before but had to be thoroughly scrutinized by the architects and planners before implementation.

(**5**) Dave realizes, of course, that not everyone is going to be completely happy with his or her particular arrangement, but no major changes can be made until after the first of the year. There are several reasons for this. "The move itself will take up to 60 days to complete," says Dave, "during which time furniture will constantly be arriving." According to Dave, each piece has been designated for a particular spot in the new building, and last-minute changes would only serve to confuse further what will doubtless be a confusing move as it is.

(**6**) Telephones have already been assigned to particular individuals and can't be moved, and the special ambient lighting fixtures built into the desks provide light for a specific grouping of furniture. Moving a desk would mean disrupting the lighting scheme for a particular area, which would affect more than just one person. All of these factors lead Dave to stress acceptance of the new floor plan, at least for the time being. According to Dave, psychological adjustment to new surroundings normally takes about 30 days. Complaints handled prior to that time are likely to be adjustment oriented. Those are the complaints he would like to avoid initially.

> *Paragraphs 7 and 8 come back to the subject (focusing on the human angle) and expand on position and point of view.*

(**7**) Dave's new position will have him on the fourth floor as part of the Industrial Relations Department, where he will be in charge of the expanded reproduction facilities as well as Office Services, which handles supplies, PBX operation, mail service, and messenger service.

-more-

(8) Dave is going to be monitoring almost every aspect of the new building. He will handle the janitorial contract, the plant contract (yes, Virginia, there will be greenery inside too), and snow removal. As Dave says, "If the building has a problem during the day, I'll hear about it first." Dave's only concern right now is that he will receive too many complaint calls such as "I don't want to sit next to Joe," or, "I can't see the window from here." With all of the major problems involved in a move of this magnitude (by the way, he's also in charge of getting everybody into the building) Dave is hoping that the personal problems can wait until the major trauma of the move is over.

> *The closing paragraph refers to the opening paragraph as a technique for gaining closure.*

(9) So, if you see this man with the harried expression in his eyes rushing around the halls of APC's new headquarters building, have a heart. Remember that Dave, like a modern-day Atlas, bears the weight of six floors on his shoulders. Just say "hi," give him a smile, and learn to live with your new desk for a while.

-30-

The Ending

The most powerful and most remembered parts of your article will be the beginning and the end. Good endings are as difficult to write as good beginnings. However, there are only a few ways to wrap up an article and bring your readers to closure (a sense that they are satisfactorily finished): summarize your main points (summary ending), refer back to the beginning in some way (referral ending), or call for action (response ending), although this last is rarely used in magazine article writing. Consider the following leads with their respective endings.

Posing a question in the lead/summary ending

Lead:
Name the oldest civilization in North America. If your anthropological information is such that you pinpointed the Aleut peoples of Alaska, you are both well-informed and correct.

Ending:

"Intellect and knowledge, technical skills, helpfulness, and concern for the truth are still the hallmarks of Aleut culture," observes the Connecticut anthropologist, Laughlin. Such virtues are valuable assets, ever more useful as the 21st century approaches, and the bedrock on which the best that is Aleut may find permanence and continuity.—Richard C. Davids for *Exxon USA*

Setting the scene in the lead/referral ending

Lead:

For one emotion-filled moment on July 28, when the Olympic torch is lit atop the Los Angeles Memorial Coliseum, this sprawling California city will be transformed into an arena of challenges and champions. But that magic event, shared with two billion television viewers around the world, will mark more than the beginning of the XXIII Summer Olympic Games.

Ending:

For GTE employees worldwide, perhaps some of that special thrill can be shared by just watching the Games on television, and knowing that whenever gymnastics, fencing, water polo, volleyball, yachting, or tennis are televised, those images and sounds will have passed through the hands of 425 fellow employees—GTE's Team at the Olympics.—Bill Ferree for *GTE Together*

An anecdotal lead/summary and referral ending

Lead:

In 1737, Benjamin Franklin wrote in the Pennsylvania Gazette of an auroral display so red and vivid that some people thought it was a fire and ran to help put it out.

Ending:

Although the effects of auroral activity on the lower levels of the earth's atmosphere are more apparent, the effects on the upper atmosphere are not, and we are only now beginning to understand them. With more understanding, we may eventually view the aurora with a more scientific eye, but until that day comes, it still remains the greatest light show on earth.—Tom Bivins for *National Bank of Alaska Interbranch*

Writing Headlines

Writing headlines for magazines is much like writing headlines for newsletters, but there are some exceptions. First, some definitional differences. A *headline*, strictly speaking, is for news stories, while a *title* is for features. For example, a news story on a new product might read like this:

New software will 'revolutionize education' says APC president

Now, contrast that headline with the following title:

Talking to the past— Learning about the future

The headline tells something about the story, so that even the casual reader can glean some information from reading it alone. The title, on the other hand, entices the reader or piques his or her interest. Therefore, a basic rule of thumb for writing headlines and titles is: use headlines for news articles and titles for feature articles. And, as with all writing, try to be clear. If your headline or title confuses the readers, they won't read on.

Editing Your Article

Magazine articles probably get, and deserve, the most editing of the various types of writing discussed in this book. Length has something to do with it, but more than that, it's the freewheeling attitude of some article writers (especially novices) that contributes the most to this need. Since many writers of basic company publications end up dealing with pretty dry topics, an assignment to do an article for the house magazine might be seen as an invitation to creativity. This usually leads, in turn, to a looser style, wordiness, and lack of organization. Whatever the reason, even the best-written article can benefit from intelligent editing.

A quick word here about the term "intelligent editing." This implies that you are being edited by (or are yourself, if you're doing the editing) someone who knows about writing—both grammar and style. Unfortunately, as many of us who have worked on in-house publications for years know, editors are often chosen because of their position within the organizational hierarchy (or the obligatory approval chain) and not for their literary talents. One of the best (if perhaps a little cynical) rules of thumb for dealing with "inexpert" editing is to ignore about 80 percent of it. You quickly get to recognize what is useful to you and what is not. Basically, editing that deals with content balance and accuracy is usable. Most strictly "editorial" comment is not. A vice president's penchant for ellipses or a manager's predilection for using *which* instead of *that* are strictly stylistic preferences (and often ungrammatical). In many cases, even if you do ignore these obligatory edits, these same "editors" won't remember what they said when the final piece comes out. A rule of thumb for most experienced writers is to try to avoid being edited by non-editors. If you can't, at least see how much you can safely ignore.

As for editing yourself, there are several methods for cutting a story that is too long, even if you don't think you can possibly do without a single word.

- Look at your beginning and end to see if they can be shortened. Often we write more than we need by way of introduction or closing when the real meat is in the body of the article.

- If you used a lot of quotes, cut the ones that are even remotely "fluff." Keep only those that contribute directly to the understanding of your story.

- Are there any general descriptions that, given later details, may be redundant? Cut them.

- Are there any details that are unnecessary given earlier general descriptions? Cut them. (Be careful not to cut both the general description *and* the details.)

- Are there any people who can be left out? For instance, will one expert and his or her comments be enough or do you really need that second opinion?

- Finally, look for wordiness—instances in which you used more words than you needed. This type of editing hurts the most, because you might have struggled over that wording for an hour.

Your goal is to get the article into the size you need without losing its best parts or compromising your writing style. **Exhibit 6.5** shows how some of these guidelines can be applied. **Exhibit 6.6** shows the layout of the edited article.

Exhibit 6.5—Editing an Article
Take a close look at this article and notice to what degree the edited sections add to the article. If they add indispensable information, they shouldn't be edited out.

DGA Wins UL Certificate

The sign on the door reads "Grade 'A' UL Central Station." To the people at Dallas General Alarm (DGA) and to the hundreds of businesses and homes they protect, this means the availability of some of the best alarm and intrusion detection systems in the country. In fact, almost every improvement made at DGA over the past few years has had as its goal the attainment of UL certification.

In 1924, Underwriters Laboratories, Inc. began offering a means of identifying burglar alarm systems that met acceptable minimum standards. The installing company can apply for investigation of their services and, if found qualified, may be issued UL certification.

To the customer, this certification can mean a large reduction (sometimes up to 70 percent) in insurance premiums, depending on the exact grade and extent of the UL-approved service used.

> *The next four paragraphs, although adding additional information, can be cut without loss to the overall information impact of the story because they deal with details we can get along without. Given enough space, however, we would opt to leave the story intact.*

However, Dallas General Alarm doesn't sell only UL service. "We sell and lease our systems on the merit of the system and the particular need of the customer," says Dave Michaels, Director of Quality Control for DGA. "Of course, those who do have the UL Grade 'A' system installed can usually pay the extra cost entailed with the savings they make on insurance alone."

What makes this Grade "A" system so effective that insurance companies charging sometimes thousands of dollars a year for coverage are willing to cut 40, 60, or even 70 percent off their premiums?

-more-

"The UL people are really tight on their standards," says Michaels. "They conduct a number of 'surprise' inspections of DGA on a regular basis. If we fall down in any of their requirements, we get our certification cancelled."

DGA has its own tight security system consisting of television monitors on all doors and verbal contact with people entering the offices. The central control room is always manned and locked. A thick glass window allows the operators on duty to check personally all people entering the premises. Other UL requirements are extra fire proofing for the building itself and a buried cable containing the thousands of telephone lines used to monitor the alarm systems that are run from the building. The cable is unmarked, preventing an adventurous burglar from cutting it and thus disabling the hundreds of systems served by DGA.

The over-a-thousand customers who either lease or buy alarm or detection systems from DGA range from some of the biggest businesses in Dallas to private residences. In addition, all of the schools in the Dallas area are monitored from the DGA central station against break-in and vandalism.

The monitoring devices located at the DGA central control vary from a simple paper tape printout to voice communication with the premises being protected. For instance, the card-key system used by Atlantic Richfield Company allows access to certain areas through the use of a magnetic card inserted into a slot in the door. Access is forbidden to those lacking the proper clearance, and the number and time of the attempted access are printed out at the DGA central station.

> *Whatever you do, don't edit out the purpose for writing the article in the first place. In this case, it's mention of a product in the next two paragraphs.*

By far the most impressive system is the *Hyper Guard Sound System*, which allows the central station operators actually to listen into a building or home once the system is activated. If the building is entered, the sound sensitive system is activated, causing an alarm to go off at the DGA central station. By the use of

-more-

microphones installed on the premises, the DGA operators can then determine the presence of an intruder. The owners, of course, sign in and out verbally when they open and close. Most of these customers also carry the special "holdup" feature of this system that allows them to trigger, unnoticed, an alarm in the event of a robbery.

"We tried out a lot of other sound-activated systems," says Michaels, "but the Hyper Guard made by Associated Products Corporation is the best I've ever seen." Michaels says that the Hyper Guard system is probably 20 times more sensitive than most other brands DGA has tried. "And, in our business, sensitivity is a key component of a successful detection."

Once an alarm is received from any of the hundreds of points serviced by DGA, it is only a matter of seconds before security guards, police, ambulance, or fire department are notified and on their way. DGA maintains direct, no-dial lines to all of these agencies.

DGA currently contracts with Smith-Loomis, which dispatches two or three security guards to each of DGA's calls. "Our average response time is under 4 1/2 minutes," says Dave Michaels. "Of course, we often have to wait for the owner to show up to let us in." Michaels says that if DGA keeps a key to the premises, another 10 percent often can be taken off on insurance premiums because it allows a faster response time and a higher apprehension rate. "Recently, we got two apprehensions in three alarms at a local pharmacy," he says. "We roll on every suspicious alarm. UL only allows one opening and one closing time per business unless prearranged," says Michaels. "This way, we know exactly when there should be nobody on the premises."

DGA offers a number of different systems. Some respond to motion, and some to sound. There are systems with silent alarms and systems with on-sight alarms fit to frighten the toughest intruder. DGA also handles smoke and heat detection systems. But, the key to a UL Grade "A" certified system, says Michaels, is the central control. "That's the added factor in a Grade 'A' system," he says. "We know immediately when something has occurred, and we respond."

-more-

The next two paragraphs are a good example of an extra character who can be deleted without substantial loss to the story. Although this kind of testimony adds credibility to any story, in this case, the story is about DGA, and their spokesperson actually provides the first-person credibility needed for the purpose—which is to get one of the products mentioned.

Frank Collins, president of Southwestern Gemstones, Inc., has had his Grade "A" system since September. "I was robbed last year of over $400,000 worth of merchandise," he says, "and I was uninsured. That won't happen again." Collins is impressed with his system.

From his office in the Calais Building, Collins can watch everyone who enters his showroom via television monitor. A telephone allows visitors to identify themselves from outside the front door before entry. The showroom has an impressive array of precious gems and gold and a great many antique art objects, frequently hand-made turquoise and silver pieces. "I got the complete works," Collins says, "audio sensors, motion sensors, TV monitor, everything," resulting in a good-sized cut in his necessarily high insurance premiums.

For the many high-risk businesses served by Dallas General Alarm, the UL Grade "A" system seems to be the answer.

"We don't expect more than a couple of hundred customers for the UL system over the next few years," says Dave Michaels, "but that's all right. Our customers know their needs and they know that they can't get a better system for the price." Collins smiles. "For the three or four dollars a day this system costs, they couldn't even afford a guard dog."

-30-

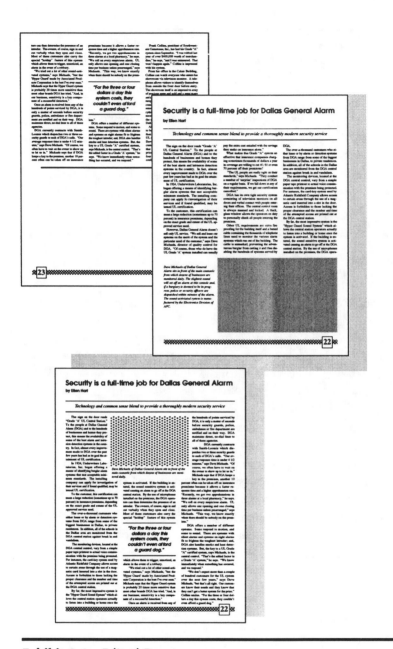

Exhibit 6.6—Edited Pages

As you can see from these layouts, the unedited version of the DGA story from
Exhibit 6.5 *takes up approximately one and a half pages including pull quote,
photo and caption. The edited version takes up only a single page, including a
reduced photo, edited caption, and the full-sized pull quote.*

Trade Journals

Trade journals are a valuable source of information for those who work within a specific industry. They provide news and stories dealing with the concerns and products of that industry. Trade journals accept product press releases readily and are an excellent target for placement. They usually have a section devoted specifically to new products and will normally place your release, edited of course, in this section.

For those desiring more attention, trade journals also accept articles written on products, concepts, and services of interest to their specific audiences (i.e., the industries they serve). These are normally submitted in the manner of any freelance magazine article. First, you query the journal by letter explaining that you have an article idea, what it is, and why you think it might fit the journal's format and be of interest to its readership. If you receive a positive response, send the article, carefully following the journal's editorial style. Trade journals, like consumer magazines, often have a sheet of "author's guidelines" explaining their style, average length, manuscript requirements, and so on. Follow these guidelines explicitly if you want to get published or get your client the publicity you were hired to provide.

The variety of trade journal articles is immense. They can range from feature-type articles using human interest, through straight news stories on products and services, to light fluff articles on travel and entertainment. In order to determine what style best fits your idea and their magazine, obtain a copy of the publication and read it thoroughly. Never submit an article to a magazine you haven't read.

Get a copy of one of the numerous "publicity checkers" that list all of the publications by industry. For my money, Standard Rate and Data Service (SRDS) provides the most comprehensive look at trade publications of any on the market. Almost every industry has a trade journal, sometimes a number of them. For instance, there are trade journals for golf course groundskeepers, race track owners, thoroughbred breeders, paper manufacturers, supermarket owners, table waiters, bartenders, railroad workers, airline workers, and almost every other trade imaginable. One or more of these will fit your needs.

Case Study: Associated Products Corporation

Use the background provided in **Chapters 3** and **5** to complete these assignments.

Assignment 6-1: Corporate Magazine Article

You have been charged with developing a magazine article for APC's house publication, *APC Plus*, a magazine that goes out to all of APC's subsidiaries and is read by about 1,000 employees. Like the newsletter article you wrote in **Assignment 5-1**, it should be on the new IQ software line and APC's involvement with the NEA. You can use the same theme or angle, or come up with another one. You should use a feature style, but don't omit the newsworthy product-development information. Your article should be about 750 or 800 words in length. You should come up with a headline, but subheads, photo recommendations, and other fillers are optional.

The most difficult part of this type of writing is organizing the information. Organization is usually dictated by the lead. Look carefully at your information, decide on an angle, and write several trial leads to see if they indicate a direction for your story. Once you have decided on a lead, produce an outline of exactly where you want to go with your story and what you want to include. Try a topic sentence outline in which you write the complete topic sentence for each section.

Assignment 6-2: Trade Magazine Article

Take the information you have gathered on James L. Sutton and write it into a profile. Sutton obviously is the angle, but, again, IQ is the publicity "bottom line."

Your profile is to be submitted to *Computer World* magazine's "People in Computing" section. *Computer World* is a consumer trade publication with a circulation of 150,000.

Along with the profile, you will include a picture of Sutton working at a computer terminal with the new software; a picture of a classroom of students using computers; and a publicity photo of one of the new software packages.

Assume you have spoken on the telephone with the editor of *Computer World*, Fran LeFavre, and she showed some interest in the story idea. Attach a letter mentioning your conversation along with the article. The address is:

Computer World
One, Presidents' Circle
Chicago, IL 60640

You have also received from *Computer World* a brief sheet of "Author's Guidelines." These guidelines are as follows:

1. Most of the articles submitted to *Computer World* are meant for a lay audience, one which, though familiar with computing concepts, is not technically oriented. Therefore, your information should be free of all but the most basic jargon.

2. Articles should be no more than 2,000 words for cover story material and features. Articles for the "Business Briefs," "People in Computing," and "Inside Computing" sections should be no longer than 800 words.

3. All articles should be typed on plain white bond paper in plain type. Lines should be double-spaced and all formulae and symbols should be clearly designated.

4. References should be limited to those that can be easily mentioned within the text. Please do not footnote.

5. Attachments (photos, transparencies, charts, schematics, etc.) should be included as appendices following the article with clear designations within the article as to placement.

Make sure that your article follows these guidelines closely.

CHAPTER 7

Annual Reports

Never ask of money spent
Where the spender thinks it went.
Nobody was ever meant
To remember or invent
What he did with every cent.

Robert Frost

nnual reports are probably the least read of all house publications. Recent research indicates that about half the shareholders who receive them spend less than 10 minutes looking at
them. And 15 percent of all stock analysts don't read them at all. So why
is corporate America spending $5 billion a year producing annual
reports?

Part of the reason is that the federal government requires it. The
Securities Exchange Act of 1936 requires publicly traded companies to
provide their investors with a yearly financial statement. This law also
requires that an annual report be delivered to stockholders no later than
15 days before the annual meeting. Quarterly reports also have to be
filed.

Beginning in 1980, the Securities and Exchange Commission
(SEC) mandated that additional information be added, including financial data covering the past five years and an expanded discussion and
analysis of the company's financial condition. It's not surprising, then,
that annual reports increase in size and complexity each year—so much
so, in fact, that a few years ago General Motors asked the SEC to allow
them and other companies to develop and file an abbreviated, "summary" annual report.

In 1987, the SEC ruled that companies could indeed publish such
a report as long as they included all of the elements required by law as
either appendices to the abbreviated report or in another formal document, such as the already required Form 10-K. Critics worry that this

new flexibility allows companies to selectively cut bad news from their most visible communication vehicle. They argue that most stockholders will read *only* the annual report, believing it complete. Although some companies have experimented with the "summary" annual report, at this writing, most companies still produce the lengthy report already familiar to stockholders.

Annual Report Audiences

When you produce an annual report, you're writing for a primarily internal audience, one with a vested interest in the well-being of your organization. That's why many annual reports gloss over the bad news, even though research shows that most stockholders would feel a lot better about a company if it were open and honest with them.

However, stockholders aren't the only audience for annual reports. These organizational summaries are excellent information sources for media people, especially financial reporters. They also provide valuable background for financial analysts, potential stockholders, nonshareholding employees and customers, and opinion leaders such as legislators and community leaders.

Before you write an annual report, you must first decide which of these audiences you are writing for. Don't ever assume that you are talking only to shareholders; rank the other potential audiences in order of their importance to you and be sure to address them, too.

Annual Report Contents

No two annual reports are alike; however, the SEC does require certain elements be present including:

- Certified financial statements for the previous two years
- An explanation of any difference between these financial statements and statements filed in another form with the SEC
- A summary management analysis of operations for the past five years
- Identification of the company directors' principal occupations
- Stock market and dividend information for the past two years
- Notice of Form 10-K availability

- A brief description of both business and line-of-business in the "audited footnote."
- Any material differences from established accounting principles reflected in the financial statements
- Supplementary inflation accounting

The form this information takes is what makes annual reports different from each other. To accommodate the SEC guidelines, annual reports have developed certain standard mechanisms for housing the required information.

- A description of the company including its name, address (headquarters, subsidiaries, and plant sites), its overall business, and a summary of its operations, usually in both narrative and numerical form.

- A letter to stockholders including an account of the past year's achievements, an overview of the industry environment and pertinent markets, and a discussion of future business and investment strategies.

- A financial review as set forth by SEC regulations listed above.

- An explanation and analysis of the financial review that outlines the factors influencing the financial picture over the past year.

- A narrative report covering anything from a discussion of subsidiaries to details on corporate philanthropy. Many companies use the annual report as a forum in which to discuss social issues or beat their own public relations drum, as it is one of the best publicity tools available.

Writing for Annual Reports

There are generally two ways to produce an annual report: you can write it in house, or you can farm it out to an agency. Frankly, agencies—including those that specialize in annual reports—produce the bulk of these publications. However, with the advent of desktop publishing, more organizations are considering in-house writing and production.

No matter who writes it, the bulk of an annual report is taken up with tables, charts, and flashy photographs. In fact, critics charge, annual reports often try too hard (and too blatantly) to sweeten a bitter financial pill with a lot of pretty sugar coating. Many annual reports do stand guilty of this, but countless others perform a valuable informational service to shareholders and members. In fact, because they *are* good message vehicles, a great many nonprofit organizations are now producing annual reports even though they don't really have to. The modern annual report has become a major tool in any organization's public relations arsenal.

Writers produce only a small portion of the annual report, but it is the portion most read by shareholders—the president's letter and the narrative report.

The President's Letter

There are some really awful president's letters in annual reports. The reason most cited is the SEC guidelines telling them what they have to talk about. Fortunately, these guidelines don't tell writers *how* to talk about what they *have* to talk about. There is no reason these letters have to be crashingly dull, wordy, and confusing. What impresses the everyday shareholder is honesty, a straightforward writing style, and no fluff.

Both of the following examples opt for the "numbers up front" approach on the mistaken belief that readers want it that way.

> [Company name] expanded its financial base in 19__ and substantially increased the number of property interests in its investment portfolio. A $47 million common stock offering, completed in June, plus a $40 million public offering of mortgage notes and common stock purchase warrants in December 19__ were among the financial resources that permitted [company name] to increase the number of its property interests to 191 by adding 99 real estate investments during the year.

> •

> The year 19__ was a successful one for [company name]. Net income was up substantially, over 27 percent greater than 19__'s results, to a record $305.6 million, as the economy moved into a strong recovery. On a per share basis, our earnings were $9.50, an increase of 13 percent, reflecting both the issuance of additional common stock during this past year, as well as the preferred stock issued during 19__.

The next example at least begins with an interesting image of a "corporate renaissance."

> We are in the midst of a corporate renaissance, and 19__ was a strong reflection of the growth, diversification, and enthusiasm that typifies [company name].

We had a record performance in 19__ in many areas. For the first time, net income exceeded $1 billion, at $1.2 billion. Sales reached an all-time high of $13.4 billion—up more than $2 billion from the 19__ level. The list of records also included earnings per share at $6.47; and operating income, which at $2.3 billion was up 69 percent from the previous record.

And what about bad news? This letter buries it under a barrage of industry buzzwords such as "maximizing profitability."

[Company name] continued its strategy of maximizing profitability in basic markets and businesses in 19__. All these areas of the Corporation had a truly excellent year. Unfortunately, the property and casualty reinsurance lines of the Insurance Group, which are not a part of our basic long-term strategy, incurred continuing heavy losses, significantly lowering our overall profitability. Reflecting this impact, [company name]'s consolidated net income of $106.3 million was about flat with 19__, although earnings per share increased marginally to $4.02 from $3.96 reflecting a slightly reduced number of common shares outstanding.

Finally, here's a letter that approaches a mixed year with an interesting, number-free narrative approach.

External forces produce both opportunities and challenges— and 19__ had its share of both for [company name] and its businesses.
During the year, some of the external forces facing our four business segments served to expand revenues and growth. Others had a dampening effect, calling for effective counter-measures.
The mix of forces at work included... [bulleted list follows]

We worked to take advantage of those external forces that offered opportunities, and to overcome the challenges posed by others.

If you can write the letter yourself, and simply route it for the president's approval, you'll get better results than you would if the president drafted it. When you do it yourself, keep in mind a few points. Because most of the rest of the report is numbers, it's best to keep numbers in the letter to a minimum. Keep your letter short, and keep its language friendly and simple. This way, you'll be able to cover the SEC bases without boring your readers.

The Narrative Report

The body of the annual report is your only chance to write anything without numbers—or, at least, with a minimum of numbers. Here is where you get to describe the company, its operations, its people (a favorite focus of many reports), and its future in detail. The only problem is one of space. Remember, you can't leave out anything required by the SEC. And you don't want to leave out anything that really makes your company look good.

One of the best ways to decide on content is to have the people in charge of the various divisions or subsidiaries submit brief lists of the year's highlights from their "down in the trenches" perspective. Make your needs known in plenty of time to get responses from your contacts. And leave the final compiling and writing to one person so that the entire report has a single style.

A quick word about that style. Depending on a company's image, the style of an annual report can vary greatly. Some are formal to the point of being stiff. Others are too informal and leave shareholders with a feeling that the company is being loosely run. The best and most appropriate style is somewhere in the middle.

As with the president's letter, you don't have to begin your narrative report with numbers. In fact, it benefits greatly from a little introduction. There is no reason why annual reports have to be boring reading. The following introductions to the narrative report sections of two different annual reports are fairly good examples of what can be done to lend a modicum of interest to an otherwise often dull subject.

> To come up with a winner in global competition, you have to provide the highest quality... the greatest number of choices... and the most innovative solutions to a customer's needs, regardless of location.
>
> In meeting that challenge, [company name] uses a system of "global networking" to choreograph its worldwide response by product, function, and geographic area. Networking teams enable [company name] to draw upon its resources around the world and to respond quickly no matter where customers may be headquartered.

> •

> There are many ways to define shareholder value ... and many ways that companies strive to create it. But at [company name], the strategy has been three-pronged:
>
> • Utilizing existing resources within the company to diversify into four separate businesses.

- Acting on opportunities to build and strengthen these existing businesses.
- Keeping abreast of trends that hold promise for the future.

Use numbers to *augment* your narrative—don't let numbers be the entire focus. Although annual reports are intended to spell out a company's financial environment, they communicate more often with average people than with financial analysts. Financial analysts won't rely on an annual report as their sole information source. Many shareholders will, so it has to be written in a style they will understand.

Striking just the right tone, in both writing and design, is the most important ingredient in producing an annual report. In fact, so much depends on design that many annual reports emphasize form at the expense of its function.

Design for design's sake is still common. Be careful not to let your "look" overpower your written information. Ideally, form and function should work together to achieve a real sense of the company that readers care enough to own part of.

CHAPTER 8

Writing for Television, Radio & Audio-visual Media

The play's the thing...

Hamlet

B roadcasting is pervasive. Since the advent of radio, people have become more and more dependent on the broadcast media for their information and entertainment. Today, more than ever before, the public views the world through the window of the television. The average American family spends more than six hours a day watching television, and, according to recent research, they find it the most credible news source by a wide margin. Radio reaches more people each day than any other medium, with more than 500 million radios in American homes and cars.

For the public relations practitioner, utilization of these two powerful and influential media is often restricted. While approximately 90 percent of the non-advertising content of print media is informational, 90 percent of the non-advertising content of broadcast media is entertainment. There is simply very little time available for news-related items. Radio usually airs news, but often in an abbreviated format. Each of the 30-minute network television news shows has only 22 minutes of actual news, which would fill about one-quarter of the front page of a daily newspaper.

There are some obvious advantages to using the broadcast media, however. They reach millions of people each day. Moreover, television and radio involve their audiences more than print does, and can be highly memorable. People tend to react more personally to broadcast than they do to other media. Think of the influence television celebrities have on the youth of today. Consider the power of newscasters such as Peter Jennings or Dan Rather in influencing opinion.

Reaching Broadcast Audiences

Getting public relations material aired on network radio and television is difficult; however, local broadcast media offer some avenues for the experienced practitioner.

There are five basic methods for the public relations writer to reach broadcast audiences: News releases (see **Chapter 3**), video news releases (VNRs), radio and television tapes and actualities, interviews and talk shows, and public service announcements or corporate advertising.

Video News Releases

Video news releases are a fairly new phenomenon. Originally, they were simply prepackaged publicity features meant to be aired on local, regional, or national television. Now they have become staples of many local news shows searching for time-filling informational pieces.

The entertainment industry was among the first to recognize the potential in producing their own videos for publicity purposes. For example, the publicity department for a new motion picture would produce a tape including collages of footage from the film in varying lengths, special "behind the scenes" looks at production, and interviews with key stars. Each of these segments would have both an "A" and "B" sound track. The "A" sound track would contain both music and voiceover. The "B" sound track would contain music only. The varying lengths would allow a station to air a segment suited to its particular time requirements. The choice of sound tracks would allow the station to drop in its own announcers' voices to give the piece a local feel.

It is in local television that VNRs are most successful. Filling an hour with local news is sometimes difficult for programmers, and program managers are constantly seeking out "fillers" to plug 30-, 60-, or 90-second holes in newscasts. In fact, a recent A.C. Nielson poll showed more than 75 percent of all TV stations regularly used VNRs.

Organizations and their PR agencies and departments have been quick to capitalize on this opportunity. The key is to produce fillers in various lengths that have certain news value yet are not time bound. This way, stories can be produced, packaged, and mailed to stations around the country with no fear that the news will be old before it is received. Medialink, a New York-based company, developed the nation's first dedicated video newswire and has become a leading distributor of VNRs, with Medialink wires in over 600 television newsrooms around the country. This type of distribution network allows organizations to get even the most time-sensitive news on the air soon enough to be effective. For example, a company can stage an important news conference, tape interviews and visuals from the event, combine this with pre-produced or stock footage of the company, and send it out via satellite all over the country in a matter of hours.

There are some problems with this infant publicity vehicle, however. A major criticism in the news industry is that much of what is packaged as video "news" releases is really advertising in disguise. This may be true, in part—VNRs are an excellent means of plugging a product by wrapping it in a soft news format. The same thing, of course, has been done for years in product-oriented articles for trade publications; however, the difference is that VNRs are being sent to mainstream media outlets who trade in hard news, not product publicity. The old advertising adage, "buyer beware," should hold here. Alert journalists should always be aware of the publicity angle inherent in any sort of release—print, video, or otherwise. On the PR side, practitioners won't gain any media support by deliberately disguising product plugs as hard or soft news. The best approach is to tag clearly any VNR as to its sponsor and content and let the media do the gatekeeping.

How you write for a VNR depends on the format of the release. Taped press conferences and the like should follow a straight news format, as do straight news print releases. Features should follow feature style. Most of the techniques discussed below also apply to writing for VNRs. Simply be aware of the format and target media, and conform to their accepted styles. Remember, as with all other media, the broadcast media will accept only that which fits their needs and format.

Radio and Television Tapes and Actualities

Radio and television rely heavily on taped actualities in covering the news. An actuality is simply a firsthand account, on tape, of a news event. Actualities lend credibility to any newscast. They may feature newspeople describing the event, interviews with those involved in the event, or they may simply provide ambience or background for a voiceover. Rarely will the public relations writer be in the position to provide a finished actuality to a radio or television news program. Most of the time, he or she will act as the intermediary or spokesperson for the organization. Or, the PR practitioner may arrange a taped interview with another company spokesperson, typically outside of the public relations department. In some cases, the medium may be interested enough to send out a reporter or news team to cover an event firsthand. In that case, the public relations practitioner usually acts as liaison, arranging the schedule and making sure that everything is in order for the taping.

Interviews and Talk Shows

It may be that a radio or television station has a local talk show or similar vehicle for which information about your organization is suitable. The public relations practitioner, here again, usually acts as liaison, arranging the interview for a spokesperson, getting preparatory materials together, and making sure the spokesperson gets to the interview or talk show on time. As the media specialist, you may also be called on to coach the spokesperson or even write his or her responses.

Public Service Announcements and Corporate Advertising

There is a difference in the way the broadcast media treat PR materials prepared by profit-making organizations and those provided by non-profit organizations. Realizing that profit-making organizations don't usually need free air time, the Federal Communications Commission (FCC) requires them to purchase time, even for messages presented in the public interest. Free public service time, on the other hand, is available only to legitimate non-profit organizations.

Corporate advertising. Corporate or institutional advertising takes three basic forms depending on the purpose of the message.

1. **Public interest** usually provides information in the public interest such as health care, safety, and environmental interests. In order to have these placed free, they have to meet stringent guidelines.

2. **Public image** tries to sell the organization as caring about its employees, the environment, the community, and its customers. Unlike the public service ad, the public image ad will always focus on the company and how it relates to the subject.

3. **Advocacy advertising** presents a definite point of view. This may range from political to social, and positions, by inference, the company as an involved citizen of the community or the nation.

The object of corporate or institutional advertising is not usually to sell a product, but rather to promote an idea or image. All forms of corporate advertising are, in fact, image advertising because, in each the organization is projecting an image of itself as concerned, caring and involved. Image advertising has become as important to most organizations as product advertising, and most major advertising agencies now handle as much image advertising as sales promotion.

Public service announcements. Like corporate public interest advertising, the public service announcement or PSA is aimed at providing an important message to its target audience. However, unlike corporate advertising, even that done in the public interest, the PSA is reserved strictly for nonprofit organizations—those that qualify as nonprofit under federal tax laws.

Remember, however, that public service announcements and image advertising, while different under the law, are identical in format and style. They are both an attempt to sell something, whether it's a product, an idea, or an image. What follows is applicable to both.

Writing for Television

Broadcast messages, whether paid-for advertising or PSAs, are called *spots*. Producing a complete television spot is usually beyond the expertise of the public relations writer and is best left to professional film and video production houses. Many practitioners, however, prefer to write their own scripts, so a knowledge of the proper form is essential. A good script tells the director, talent, or anyone reading it exactly what the spot is about, its message, and the image it should convey. In a well-written script, virtually nothing is left to the imagination. A good working knowledge of film and video techniques is necessary if you are to be able to visualize your finished product and transmit that vision to someone else. Before beginning a script, therefore, you need to become familiar with some basics of television production and the language of script writing.

Basic Concepts

Television spots are produced either on film or videotape. Because both formats involve similar aesthetics, a discussion of one will serve to cover both. Television spots, and all commercials and programs for that matter, are composed of a series of scenes or shots joined together by transitions. A scene usually indicates a single locale, so that a 30-second commercial might be composed of a single scene that is in turn composed of several camera shots. Or, a 30-minute program might be composed of many scenes composed of many camera shots. These scenes and shots are joined by transitional devices usually created by switching from one camera to another (a form of on-the-spot editing), or in the case of a single-camera production that is edited later, by switching from one kind of shot to another. The script tells the director, camera operators, and talent what sort of composition is required in each shot.

Camera shot directions are scripted in a form of shorthand. The most common designations are described below. For our purposes, we will assume that the shots are of a person.

CU or **closeup**—A shot that takes in the neck and head but doesn't extend below the neck.

ECU or **extreme closeup**—A much tighter version of the CU, usually involving a selected portion of the object, such as the eyes.

MS or **medium shot**—A shot that takes in the person from about the waist up.

Bust shot—A shot of a person from the bust up.

LS or **long shot**—A shot of the entire person with little or no room at the top or bottom of the screen.

ELS or **extreme long shot**—A shot with the person in the distance.

There are variations on these basic shots, such as **MCU** or **medium closeup, MLS** or **medium long shot, 2-shot** or a shot of two people, **3-shot** a shot of three people, etc. When designating shots in scripts, you need to be in the ballpark—you don't have to have it down to the millimeter. Whatever you write in your script may ultimately be changed by the artistic collaboration between the director and the camera operators.

Camera shots are accomplished in one of two ways: by movement of the optical apparatus (or lens), or by movement of the camera itself. The most common designations for lens movement are *zoom in* and *zoom out*. Physical movements are as follows:

Dolly in/out—Move the camera in a straight line toward or away from the object.

Truck right/left—Move the camera right or left, parallel to the object.

Pan right/left—Move the camera head to the right or left.

Tilt up/down—Move the camera head up or down.

Each of these movements creates a different optical effect, and each will impart a different impression to the viewer. Dollies and trucks, for instance, impart a sense of viewer movement rather than movement of the object being filmed or taped. The camera becomes the viewer. This type of shot is frequently called **point of view** or **POV**. Pans and tilts appear as normal eye movement, much as if the viewer were moving his or her eyes from side to side or up and down. Remember that the camera is actually the eyes of the viewer limited by the size of the screen.

Transitions are the sole domain of the director and editor. In the case of a studio production, such as a live talk show, the director and technical director work together—the director giving transitional directions, and the technical director following those directions by electronically switching between the cameras. Transitions in field productions and single-camera productions are taken care of in postproduction editing through a cooperative effort between the director and the editor. The following are the most used transitions:

Cut—An instantaneous switch from one shot to another.

Dissolve—A gradual replacement of one image with another.

Wipe—A special effect in which one image is "wiped" from the screen and replaced by another. This was used extensively in silent movie days and in adventure films of the 1930s and 1940s.

Fade—A gradual change, usually to or from black designating either the beginning or end of a scene.

Other shorthand notations are specific to audio directions. The most common are:

SFX or **sound effects**.

SOF or **sound on film**—The sound source is the audio track from a film.

SOT or **sound on tape**—The sound source is the audio track from a videotape or audio tape.

SIL or **silent film**.

Music up—Signifying that the volume of the music bed is raised.

Music under—Signifying that the volume of the music bed is lowered, usually to allow for narration.

Music up and out—Usually designating the end of a production.

VO or **voice over/voice only**—Indicating that the speaker is not on camera.

OC or **on camera**—Indicating that the speaker or narrator can be seen. This is usually used when the speaker has been VO prior to being OC. In other words, it indicates that he or she is now on camera.

Writing for the Eye

When you write for television, you write for the eye as well as the ear, which means that you have to visualize what you want your audience to see and then put that vision on paper. Your image must be crystallized into words that will tell others how to recreate it on tape or film.

In order to end up with the best possible script, you must begin with an idea. Try to think in visuals. Take a basic concept and try to visualize the best method for presenting it to others. Should you use a studio or film outdoors? Will you use ambient sound or a music background? Will you have a number of transitions or a single scene throughout? Answering these questions and others will help you conceptualize the television spot.

Television Scripts

Script Treatment

Once you have a basic idea of what you would like to say, the next step is to write a *script treatment*. A treatment is a narrative account of a television spot. It is not written in a script format but may include ideas for shots and transitions. The key is to keep it informal at this point. There will be plenty of time to clean it up in later drafts. **Exhibit 8.1** is a treatment for a promotional ad for a documentary to be shown on television.

Working Scripts and Shooting Scripts

The next step is to sharpen your images in a working script. The working script should include all of the information necessary for a

---

Exhibit 8.1—Television Script Treatment

"IDITAROD"
30 second promo
Treatment

Opening shot of dog team against setting sun across long stretch of tundra. Cut to flashes of finish line hysteria, dogs running, racers' faces frozen or exhausted, stretches of open ground, trees, checkpoints, etc., perhaps terminating at starting gun. Images continue under narration.

Voice over: WHAT MAKES SOME PEOPLE SPEND LITERALLY AN ENTIRE YEAR TRAINING BOTH THEMSELVES AND THEIR DOGS, OFTEN WITH HEARTBREAKING RESULTS? WHAT DRAWS A PERSON TO DOG SLED RACING? IS IT A MYSTIQUE UNIQUE ONLY TO ALASKA, OR IS IT SOMETHING COMMON TO ALL PEOPLE AT ALL TIMES?

Cut to closeup of winner of last year's Iditarod race ... exhaustion ... joy ... satisfaction. Zoom in to freeze-frame of face.

Voice over: JOIN US FOR A TWELVE-HUNDRED MILE RACE ACROSS ALASKA WHEN NATIONAL GEOGRAPHIC PRESENTS "IDITAROD: THE RACE ON THE EDGE OF THE WORLD."

NGS logo... super day and time.

# # # # #

---

complete understanding of your idea. In it, you should begin to flesh out camera shots, transitions, audio—including music and sound effects—and approximate times. The working script is still a draft, but in it you should begin to solidify your ideas. The shooting script is constructed from the working script. The director will use it to produce your spot for television. In it you must include all of the proposed camera shots, transitions, narrative, audio of all types, and acting directions.

Here are some guidelines that will help you as you move through both working and shooting scripts.

1. Open with an attention-getting device: an interesting piece of audio, an unusual camera shot, or a celebrity. The first few seconds are crucial. If your viewers are not hooked by then, you've lost them.

2. Open with an establishing shot if possible—something that says where you are and intimates where you are going. If you open in a classroom, for instance, chances are you are going to stay there. If you jump too much, you confuse viewers.

3. If you open with a long shot, you should then cut to a closer shot, and soon after, introduce the subject of the spot. This is especially applicable if you are featuring a product or a celebrity spokesperson.

4. Vary shot composition from MS to CU throughout, and somewhere past the midpoint of the spot return to a MS, then to a final CU and a super (superimposition) of logo or address. (A *super* involves placing one image over another.)

5. Don't call for a new shot unless it adds something to the spot. Make your shots seem like part of an integrated whole. Be single-minded and try to tell only one important story per spot.

Although a director will feel free to adapt your script to his or her particular style and to the requirements of the production, you should leave as little as possible to the imagination.

Exhibit 8.2 is a page from a working script. Notice the difference between it and the shooting script version in **Exhibit 8.3**.

Accompanying Scripts

The accompanying script is the version sent with the taped spot to the stations that will run it. It is written on the assumption that the shooting script has been produced as it was originally described. The accompanying script is stripped of all but its most essential directions. It is intended to provide the reader a general idea of what the taped spot is about and is to be used only as a reference for broadcasters who accept the spot for use.

Exhibit 8.2—Television Working Script

PRODUCTION: A.P.P.L.E. 9/17 Revised   Page 1 of 33

PRODUCER: University of Alaska Media Services

VIDEO	AUDIO
Scene opens with aerial view of grassy area on which are displayed 5 boxes of different sizes and colors. Cut to ground level view as camera pans over boxes. They are labeled "nonrenewable resources," "hazards," "ownership," and "land use." Shot should end on nonrenewable resources box with a tight shot. Pull back to catch entrance of mime. This should be an edit so that the other boxes are no longer in the shot.	ALASKA'S LAND IS PRETTY COMPLEX AND UNDERSTANDING IT CAN BE COMPLICATED. THERE ARE A FEW BASIC THINGS, HOWEVER, THAT YOU SHOULD KNOW SO THAT WHEN THE TIME COMES FOR YOU TO MAKE DECISIONS ABOUT LAND, YOU CAN MAKE GOOD ONES. YOU SHOULD KNOW ABOUT RESOURCES, RENEWABLE AND NON-RENEWABLE. YOU SHOULD KNOW WHO OWNS THE LAND NOW AND WHO MIGHT OWN IT IN THE FUTURE AND HOW THEY USE IT. AND YOU NEED TO KNOW ABOUT THE LAND'S OWN NATURAL HAZARDS SO THAT YOU CAN USE IT WITH CAUTION IF YOU HAVE TO. YES, USING THE LAND CAN BE COMPLEX, BUT IT CAN ALSO BE VERY INTERESTING.

Exhibit 8.3—Television Shooting Script

PRODUCTION: A.P.P.L.E.   9/17 Revised   Page 1 of 33

PRODUCER: University of Alaska Media Services

VIDEO	AUDIO
ELS moutain range, AERIAL	(ambient sounds of birds)
Camera PANS range, descends through wooded area, zeroing in on the edge of a grassy clearing.	(sound of wind)
DISSOLVE to LS grassy clearing	NARRATOR: ALASKA'S LAND IS PRETTY COMPLEX AND
Colorful objects can be made out scattered within the clearing.	UNDERSTANDING IT CAN BE COMPLICATED. THERE ARE A FEW BASIC THINGS,
DISSOLVE to MLS grassy clearing	HOWEVER,THAT YOU SHOULD KNOW SO THAT WHEN THE TIME
At ground level, camera slowly PANS across objects and stops on box labeled "non-renewable resources."	COMES FOR YOU TO MAKE DECISIONS ABOUT LAND, YOU CAN MAKE GOOD ONES.
	YOU SHOULD KNOW ABOUT
DISSOLVE to MS mime	RESOURCES, RENEWABLE AND NON-RENEWABLE.
Camera PANS as mime enters scene and approaches box.	

It is customary to send out taped spots in packages that include a cover letter explaining what the package is, a form requesting the receiver to designate when and how often the spot is used, and an accompanying script for each spot. Sometimes a storyboard is also sent with an abbreviated frame-by-frame summary of the major points, both audio and video, of the spot. The accompanying script in **Exhibit 8.4** was sent with the finished promo seen as a treatment in **Exhibit 8.1**.

Exhibit 8.4—Accompanying Script

PRODUCTION: Iditarod DATE: 9/17/94   Page 1 of 1

PRODUCER: Northstar Associates

VIDEO	AUDIO
Open on LS dog sled racing into setting sun.	(National Geographic music up)
Series of quick CUTS of finish line excitement, checkpoints, racing, and scenery.	
Narration begins as series of shots of winning team flash by.	NARRATOR: WHAT MAKES SOME PEOPLE SPEND LITERALLY AN ENTIRE YEAR TRAINING BOTH THEMSELVES AND THEIR DOGS, OFTEN WITH HEART-BREAKING RESULTS? WHAT DRAWS A PERSON TO DOG SLED RACING? IS IT A MYSTIQUE UNIQUE ONLY TO ALASKA, OR IS IT SOMETHING COMMON TO ALL PEOPLE AT ALL TIMES?
Quick series of CUs and MSs of racer.	
PAN of faces in crowd at finish line.	
CUT to CU of winner's face showing joy and exhaustion.	JOIN US FOR A TWELVE-HUNDRED MILE RACE ACROSS ALASKA WHEN NATIONAL GEOGRAPHIC PRESENTS "IDITAROD: THE RACE ON THE EDGE OF THE WORLD."
FREEZE FRAME of face MATTED on magazine cover.	(music up and out)
SFX logo.	# # # # #
SUPER station air date.	

Choosing a Style

The two styles most common to television spots are *talking heads* and *slice-of-life*. In a *talking heads* spot, the primary image appearing on the television screen is the human head—talking. This style is often chosen for reasons of cost—talking heads spots are relatively cheap to produce—but it can be very effective. **Exhibit 8.5** is an example.

Talking heads spots have criticized for being boring or unexciting, but this does not need to be the case. The key is to make what is said forceful and memorable while, at the same time, introducing enough camera movement and varied shot composition to make the video image visually interesting. By incorporating the simplest of camera movements into your scripts, you can hold the attention of the audience long enough to impart your verbal message. With this in mind, read through **Exhibit 8.5** and notice how closely the subtle camera movements are tied to the verbal message.

As its name implies, the *slice-of-life* television spot sets up a dramatic situation complete with a beginning, middle, and end. In the slice-of-life spot, the focus is on the story, not the characters. The message is imparted through an interesting sequence of events incorporating but not relying on interesting characters. Slice-of-life spots usually use a wide variety of camera movements and post-production techniques, such as dissolves and special effects. Although this type of spot is often shot with one camera, the effect is one of multiple cameras due to the post-production process. Slice-of-life spots may be more difficult to produce than talking heads spots, but they are just as easy to script. (See **Exhibit 8.6**.)

Timing Your Script

How do you know when you have written a script that will end up running only 60 seconds on the television screen? Timing a script isn't easy and requires a certain amount of "gut feeling." The best way to time a script is to read through what you have written as if it were already produced. Always exaggerate your delivery. You usually talk faster than you think you do. Pause for the music, sound effects, and talent reactions. You also need to simulate movements as if they were occurring on screen. If your script calls for the talent to walk up a classroom aisle, for instance, walk the equivalent distance while you read the narrative. This type of "live action" walk-through will give you a ballpark idea of how long your script will be when finally shot.

Exhibit 8.5—"Talking Heads" Script

The American Tuberculosis Foundation
1212 Street of the Americas
New York, NY 00912

"Your Good Health"
30-Second TV Spot   Page 1 of 1

VIDEO	AUDIO
Open on CU of young woman's face against a neutral background. She is smoking.	NARRATOR:(VO) YOU KNOW THE DANGERS OF CIGARETTE SMOKING.
Woman looks unconcerned. She takes another puff as narrator talks.	SMOKING CAUSES HEART DISEASE, EMPHYSEMA, AND CANCER. BUT DON'T STOP SMOKING JUST BECAUSE YOU MIGHT DIE FROM IT.
Pull back to MS to reveal child of about 4 yrs. looking up at her.	STOP SMOKING BECAUSE SOMEONE YOU LOVE MIGHT DIE FROM IT. WHEN YOU SMOKE AT HOME, YOUR CHILDREN BREATH THE SAME CANCER-CAUSING SMOKE YOU DO... AND THEY
Child covers his mouth and coughs.	DON'T HAVE ANY CHOICE. THEY CAN'T DECIDE TO QUIT SMOKING. BUT YOU CAN. IF YOU WANT TO STOP SMOKING, WRITE US. WE'LL SEND YOU A
Slow zoom to CU woman, still holding cigarette. Looks concerned.	FREE PROGRAM THAT WILL HELP YOU STOP IN 30 DAYS.
	REMEMBER, SOMEONE YOU LOVE CARES ABOUT YOUR GOOD HEALTH.
Fade to black, super address.	# # # # #

Exhibit 8.6—Slice-of-life Script (continued on following 2 pages)

Institute for Higher Education
Box 1873, Washington, D.C. 19806

"Payoff"
60-Second TV Spot   Page 1 of 3

VIDEO	AUDIO
Open on MLS large crowd shot, city street, people walking. We see a young man in front of crowd as it stops at crosswalk.	(Music up: "You've Earned Your Chance")
Continue MLS as light changes and crowd crosses.	"THE CITY'S HOT, THE DAY'S BEEN LONG, BUT YOU'VE BEEN OUT THERE HANGING ON.
ARC LEFT and AROUND as young man crosses street and FOLLOW shot behind him as he reaches other side.	THE FACES START TO LOOK THE SAME, YOU WONDER IF THEY KNOW YOUR NAME.
CUT TO MLS as young man stops in front of building, checks address on slip of paper in his hand, and enters.	THERE'S ONE MORE SHOT BEFORE YOU'RE THROUGH. YOU KNOW YOU'RE TIME IS COMING DUE.
CUT TO MS young man as he rushes to squeeze into elevator.	IT'S YOUR TURN NOW, YOUR DUES ARE PAID. YOU'VE EARNED YOUR CHANCE,
CUT TO MCU young man looking uncomfortable in crowded elevator. He looks to right and left as others ignore him.	YOU'VE MADE THE GRADE." (Lyrics end, music under)
CUT TO MS of elevator doors opening as young man exits, looks both ways and turns screen left.	-more-
CUT TO MS of young man pausing before door, checking number, and entering.	

"Payoff"

60-Second TV Spot   Page 2 of 3

VIDEO	AUDIO
CUT TO MLS young man entering front office. Secretary is seated at desk and glances up as he enters room.	
CUT TO CU secretary's face	<u>SECRETARY</u>: MAY I HELP YOU?
CUT TO CU young man's face CUT TO 2-SHOT secretary and young man.	<u>MAN</u>: YES. I'M HERE FOR AN APPOINTMENT WITH MR. ALDRICH.
	<u>SECRETARY</u>: YOU MUST BE MR. ROBINSON. MR. ALDRICH IS EXPECTING YOU. I'LL LET HIM KNOW YOU'RE HERE. WHY DON'T YOU HAVE A SEAT. I'M SURE HE'LL BE RIGHT WITH YOU.
Follow MS young man as he seats himself. He picks up a magazine and begins to read.	<u>ANNOUNCER</u>: YOU'VE PREPARED FOR THIS MOMENT FOR FOUR YEARS. NOW IT'S PAYOFF TIME. YOU'RE CONFIDENT AND POLISHED. YOU'VE GOT A COLLEGE EDUCATION AND THE
CUT TO MCU young man as he glances at office door.	TRAINING YOU NEED TO GO WHERE YOU WANT TO GO, AND DO WHAT YOU WANT TO DO IN LIFE. YOU HAD THE INSIGHT AND THE DRIVE TO BETTER YOURSELF THROUGH HIGHER EDUCATION,
CUT TO CU young man's face exuding confidence.	AND NOW IS THE MOMENT YOU'VE WAITED FOR.
	-more-

"Payoff"
60-Second TV Spot

VIDEO	AUDIO
CUT TO MLS as office door opens and interviewer steps out to shake young man's hand.	
CUT TO CU interviewer's face.	INTERVIEWER: MR. ROBINSON? I'VE BEEN LOOKING FORWARD TO MEETING YOU. I'VE GOT TO TELL YOU--YOU'RE JUST THE KIND OF PERSON WE'RE LOOKING FOR. WE'VE GOT A LOT TO TALK ABOUT.
CUT TO CU young man's face, smiling.	ANNOUNCER: MAKE YOUR DREAMS A REALITY. GO TO COLLEGE. EDUCATION PAYS OFF. FOR MORE INFORMATION, WRITE:
CUT TO MEDIUM 2-SHOT as two men chat.	
LOSE focus and SUPER address.	INSTITUTE FOR HIGHER EDUCATION BOX 1873 WASHINGTON, D.C. 19806
FOCUS on MEDIUM 2-SHOT as two men enter office and close door behind them.	(Music and lyrics up) "YES, YOU'VE EARNED YOUR CHANCE, NOW GIVE IT ALL YOU'VE GOT."
	# # # # #

Remember, the director will ultimately make the adjustments necessary to fit your script into the required time slot; but it's always in your best interest (as far as your reputation as a writer is concerned) to be as close as possible.

Cutting Your Script

Cutting a script means understanding the message you want to impart, and then making sure that it is still intact after editing. Remember, a 30-second spot is half the length of a 60-second spot. That may sound obvious, but 30 seconds lost out of a 60-second spot can result in the deletion of a lot of valuable set-up and development time. That 10 seconds you took to pan slowly around the classroom scene now has to go. What do you do instead? Here are some guidelines for cutting your script.

1. Always begin with the longer script. It is easier to cut down than to write more.

2. Look first at the opening and closing sections to see if you can eliminate long musical or visual transitions or fades.

3. Next, check for long dissolves or other lengthy transitions within the body of the script to see if these can be replaced with shorter transitional techniques, such as cuts, or eliminated altogether.

4. See if you can eliminate minor characters. Cutting a character with only one or two lines will save you a lot of time.

5. See if you can eliminate any narrative assigned to your major spokesperson. Leave only the key message, slogan, any necessary contact information—and enough narrative transition to allow for coherent development.

6. Finally, try out the cut-down version on someone who hasn't seen the longer version to make sure it flows and makes sense.

Read **Exhibit 8.7**, the 30-second version of the "slice-of-life" spot in **Exhibit 8.6**. Notice what was left out and what remains. Is the message still clear? Did the "story" lose anything in the cutting?

Exhibit 8.7—Edited Script

Institute for Higher Education
Box 1873, Washington, D.C. 19806

"Payoff"
30-Second TV Spot   Page 1 of 2

VIDEO	AUDIO
Open on LS young man entering front office. Secretary is seated at desk and glances up as he enters room..	
CUT TO CU secretary's face.	SECRETARY: MAY I HELP YOU?
CUT TO CU young man's face.	MAN: YES. I'M HERE FOR AN APPOINTMENT WITH MR. ALDRICH.
CUT TO 2-SHOT secretary and young man.	SECRETARY: YOU MUST BE MR. ROBINSON. MR. ALDRICH IS EXPECTING YOU. I'LL LET HIM KNOW YOU'RE HERE. WHY DON'T YOU HAVE A SEAT. I'M SURE HE'LL BE RIGHT WITH YOU.
Follow MS young man as he seats himself He picks up a magazine and begins to read.	ANNOUNCER: YOU'VE PREPARED FOR THIS MOMENT FOR FOUR YEARS. NOW IT'S PAYOFF TIME. YOU'RE CONFIDENT AND POLISHED. YOU'VE GOT A COLLEGE
CUT TO MCU young man as he glances at office door.	EDUCATION AND THE TRAINING YOU NEED TO GO WHERE YOU
CUT TO CU young man's face exuding confidence.	WANT TO GO, AND DO WHAT YOU WANT TO DO IN LIFE.
	-more-

"Payoff"
30-Second TV Spot

VIDEO	AUDIO
CUT TO MLS as office door opens and interviewer steps out to shake young man's hand.	ANNOUNCER (CONT.): YOU HAD THE INSIGHT AND THE DRIVE TO BETTER YOURSELF THROUGH HIGHER EDUCATION, AND NOW IS THE MOMENT YOU'VE WAITED FOR.
CUT TO CU interviewer's face	INTERVIEWER: MR. ROBINSON? I'VE BEEN LOOKING FORWARD TO MEETING YOU. I'VE GOT TO TELL YOU—YOU'RE JUST THE KIND OF PERSON WE'RE LOOKING FOR. COME IN. WE'VE GOT A LOT TO TALK ABOUT.
CUT TO 2-SHOT as both enter office and shut door behind them.	ANNOUNCER: MAKE YOUR DREAMS A REALITY. GO TO COLLEGE. EDUCATION PAYS OFF. FOR MORE INFORMATION, WRITE:
SUPER address on door.	INSTITUTE FOR HIGHER EDUCATION BOX 1873 WASHINGTON, D.C. 19806
	-30-

Effective TV PSA Production

As you begin to plan your PSAs, here are some production tips that may enhance your chances of getting on the air.

- Keep your PSAs simple. Covering one or *maybe* two points in 30 seconds is the best you should shoot for. Any more will simply dilute your message. It's usually best to stick to one point and repeat it in several different ways.

- This also means fewer scenes. Although a soft drink commercial may have the money and energy to jump through 30 scenes in 30 seconds, such a frenetic pace doesn't suit most PSAs. Don't take the chance of confusing your audience.

- Work from the general to the specific. A problem-solution format is usually best. Tell or show your audience the problem and then how it can be solved; however, don't dwell on the problem, it'll turn off your audience.

- Demonstrations work well in the visual media. Show how your service works or what you want people to do.

- Always start with something interesting. Remember, you only have a few seconds to hook your audience. After that, they'll simply tune you out.

- Use testimonials when appropriate. People who are directly involved in your work, especially those being helped by it, can be very effective spokespersons. Don't avoid ordinary people. If they know what they're talking about, they can be much more effective than a celebrity who doesn't.

- In fact, avoid celebrities unless they are or can be made to appear to be really involved in your cause. Using celebrities simply because of their celebrity status can be self-defeating. Your audience may remember them but not your message.

- On the other hand, if you are lucky enough to attract someone who is well-known and who believes in what you are doing, you can create a memorable spot.

- Unless you *have* attracted a practiced professional, avoid stand-ups if possible. A stand-up is basically one person delivering your message. So, unless you have a superb speaker—one who can really engage an audience with just a voice and a direct gaze—

stay away from this approach. Also, make sure that whoever you pick can deliver your message sincerely, from a sound understanding of what you do and represent. Your audience will know if the message rings false.

- If you've got something interesting to show, however, use voice-over. It's ultimately better to show something other than just a face. In many cases, celebrities are easily identifiable by their voices or can identify themselves at the end of the spot. In fact, some celebrities would rather do just a voice-over because it saves them time and they don't have to go through all the preparation it takes to be seen on television.

- If you decide to show your phone number or address on the screen, keep it up long enough for viewers to write it down— usually at least eight seconds. Remember all those handy gadget commercials, "but wait, there's more!"? They read their phone numbers so many times you can recite them by heart. That's what you have to do.

- On the other hand, if it's not really important to have people call or write you—for instance, you goal is to motivate people—you may not need a number at all. Decide what the purpose of your spot is, and leave out anything that doesn't contribute directly to that purpose, even if it's your phone number.

- In the same vein, if you do superimpose information on the screen, make sure what is being seen by your viewers is also being talked about. If it's a written message or an address, your audio should be reading it at the same time.

- Viewers won't listen if they are watching something that doesn't match what's being said. For example, a few years ago, a famous national news anchor produced a piece on a presidential candidate that showed him stumping the country, smiling and delivering his message of hope and good cheer. However, her voice-over lambasted the candidate for avoiding the issues and merely wrapping himself in the flag. She received a phone call the next day from the candidate's press secretary thanking her for the excellent coverage. "But, didn't you get it?" she said. "I spent nearly three minutes berating your candidate for avoiding the issues." "Do you think anyone was listening to you?" he replied. "All they were seeing were the great images of my candidate you put up for them to watch." In other words, if what you're saying doesn't match what you're showing, most people will go with what you're showing.

- If you must use music, use good music, either written and performed specifically for your spot or paid for from a commercial source. Be sure to match the feel of your music to your message.

Writing for Radio

The radio spot, like the television spot, must be absolutely clear in order to be understood—both by the listener and by the broadcaster who will be airing it. Remember, radio scripts are written for the ear. You must be clear and simple, reducing ideas to their essence. Radio may be the most flexible of media because it can rely on the imagination of the listener to fill in visuals. In radio, it is possible to create virtually any scenario that can be imagined by the audience.

With the appropriate sound effects, you can have elephants perform on stage, or lions in your living room; you can position yourself in the middle of the Amazon jungle or on the highest mountain peak. Radio spots are also much cheaper to produce than television spots and can be changed on much shorter notice. Lengths of radio spots vary. While television spots are typically either 60 or 30 seconds in length, radio spots are anywhere from 10 seconds to 60 seconds and any length in between. The standard lengths for radio spots are:

10 seconds or about 25 words

20 seconds or about 45 words

30 seconds or about 65 words

45 seconds or about 100 words

60 seconds or about 125 words

Live Radio Announcements

The simplest type of radio spot is the spot announcement involving no sound effects or music bed and meant to be read by station personnel. This type is usually sent in a package of two, three, or four spots and can be general in nature, geared to a specific program, or tied to some specific time of the year or holiday.

Like television scripts, radio scripts must be uniformly formatted. Never send a spot on a 3" x 5" card. Although most stations will transfer the information from a spot announcement to a card for ease of handling, you should always send your spots on standard bond paper. Some other rules include:

1. Head up your spot with the name of the originating agency and its address and telephone number. Include a contact.

2. Title your spot and give the length at the beginning, not the end.

3. Because spot announcements are never more than one page in length, you may be able to get more than one per page. The standard is usually five or six 10-second spots per page; two 30-second spots per page; and one 60-second spot per page. As with press releases, end all spots with # # # # # .

4. Type all radio spots upper case, double-spaced for ease of reading. Talent directions, if there are any, should be upper and lower case in parentheses.

Since spots are typically written as a series, it is necessary to develop a theme that will carry over from spot to spot. This is best accomplished by the use of key ideas and phrases, repeated in each spot. The concepts and ideas should be such that they can be developed more fully as the spots increase in length and time.

The spots in **Exhibit 8.8** employ some standard methods for creating a cohesive series. Whenever you produce a series of spots, they should reflect a continuity of theme and message. Ask yourself these questions about the spots:

1. What is the underlying theme or concept throughout the spots?

2. How is this theme carried out from spot to spot?

3. What are the key ideas and phrases that are repeated in all the spots?

Notice that the longer spots elaborate on the theme in some way. The shorter spots, especially the 10-second spots, are the basic message—often only the phrase or idea that will be repeated in the longer spots. The longer spots, particularly the 60-second spot, can take time for development and enumeration of points barely mentioned in the shorter versions.

Exhibit 8.8—Live Radio Spots (continued on following 2 pages)

The American Tuberculosis Foundation
1212 Street of the Americas
New York, NY 00912

<u>"YOUR GOOD HEALTH" :10 SEC. LIVE RADIO SPOTS</u>

THE AMERICAN TUBERCULOSIS FOUNDATION AND THIS STATION
CARE ABOUT YOUR GOOD HEALTH. DON'T SMOKE... SOMEONE
WHO LOVES YOU WANTS YOU TO QUIT.
# # # # #

(station call letters) AND THE AMERICAN TUBERCULOSIS
FOUNDATION CARE ABOUT YOUR GOOD HEALTH. IF YOU SMOKE,
TRY TO STOP. IF YOU'RE THINKING OF STARTING, THINK TWICE.
# # # # #

SMOKING NOT ONLY HARMS YOUR LUNGS, IT HARMS THE LUNGS
OF THOSE AROUND YOU. SOMEONE YOU LOVE WANTS YOU TO
QUIT. THE AMERICAN TUBERCULOSIS FOUNDATION CARES ABOUT
YOUR GOOD HEALTH.
# # # # #

IF YOU'RE THINKING OF STARTING TO SMOKE... THINK TWICE.
SMOKING HARMS YOU AND THOSE YOU LOVE. THE AMERICAN
TUBERCULOSIS FOUNDATION AND THIS STATION CARE ABOUT
YOUR GOOD HEALTH.
# # # # #

GOOD HEALTH MEANS TAKING CARE OF YOURSELF. DON'T START
SMOKING. AND IF YOU ALREADY SMOKE... TRY TO STOP.
SOMEONE YOU LOVE CARES ABOUT YOUR GOOD HEALTH. A
MESSAGE FROM (station call letters) AND THE AMERICAN
TUBERCULOSIS FOUNDATION.
# # # # #

The American Tuberculosis Foundation
1212 Street of the Americas
New York, NY 00912

"YOUR GOOD HEALTH" :30 SEC. LIVE RADIO SPOTS

DO YOU SMOKE? IF YOU DO, DO YOU REMEMBER WHEN YOU
STARTED? MAYBE YOU WERE A TEENAGER AND YOUR FRIENDS
THOUGHT IT MADE THEM LOOK "ADULT." WHATEVER THE REASON,
SMOKING ISN'T GROWN UP ANY MORE... IT'S JUST PLAIN STUPID.
THE AMERICAN TUBERCULOSIS FOUNDATION AND THIS STATION
WANT YOU TO KNOW THAT SOMEONE YOU LOVE CARES ABOUT
YOUR GOOD HEALTH. WE WANT YOU TO HAVE THE CHANCE TO
ACT LIKE A GROWN UP. IF YOU'D LIKE TO STOP SMOKING,WRITE US.
OUR ADDRESS IS:

THE AMERICAN TUBERCULOSIS FOUNDATION
BOX 1892
NEW YORK, NEW YORK 00911

# # # # #

WHEN YOU SMOKE, YOU'RE NOT JUST HURTING YOURSELF, YOU'RE
HURTING THOSE AROUND YOU... AND MAYBE EVEN SOMEONE YOU
LOVE. THE AMERICAN TUBERCULOSIS FOUNDATION WANTS YOU
TO KNOW THAT YOU CAN QUIT. WE'VE DEVELOPED A PROGRAM
THAT WILL HELP YOU STOP SMOKING IN 30 DAYS, AND WE'LL SEND
YOU THAT PROGRAM FREE. ALL YOU HAVE TO DO IS WRITE US AT:

THE AMERICAN TUBERCULOSIS FOUNDATION
BOX 1892
NEW YORK, NEW YORK 00911

WE CARE ABOUT YOUR GOOD HEALTH.

# # # # #

The American Tuberculosis Foundation
1212 Street of the Americas
New York, NY 00912

<u>"YOUR GOOD HEALTH" :60 SEC. LIVE RADIO SPOT</u>

SMOKING CAUSES HEART DISEASE, EMPHYSEMA, AND CANCER.
BUT DON'T STOP SMOKING JUST BECAUSE YOU MIGHT DIE FROM IT.
STOP SMOKING BECAUSE SOMEONE YOU LOVE MIGHT DIE FROM IT.
THAT'S RIGHT... SECOND-HAND SMOKE IS A PROVEN CONTRIBUTOR
TO HEALTH PROBLEMS IN NON-SMOKERS. WHEN YOU SMOKE AT
HOME, YOUR CHILDREN BREATHE THE SAME CANCER-CAUSING
SMOKE YOU DO... AND THEY DON'T HAVE ANY CHOICE. THEY
CAN'T DECIDE TO QUIT SMOKING. BUT YOU CAN. IF YOU WANT TO
STOP SMOKING, WRITE US. WE'LL SEND YOU A FREE PROGRAM
THAT WILL HELP YOU STOP IN 30 DAYS. WRITE:

THE AMERICAN TUBERCULOSIS FOUNDATION
BOX 1892
NEW YORK, NEW YORK 00911

(repeat address)

REMEMBER, SOMEONE YOU LOVE CARES ABOUT YOUR GOOD
HEALTH.

# # # # #

"As-Recorded" Spots

Unlike the television spot, radio spots come not only in different lengths
but in different formats. Television spots are rarely written to be read
by a television announcer as a drop-in as are radio spots. The radio spot,
on the other hand, can be prerecorded, utilizing many of the same
techniques as television—sound effects, music beds, multiple talent,

sound fades and dissolves, and changes in scenes. Of course, these effects are more difficult to pull off when you are restricted to audio only, but the challenge is in the trying.

As-recorded spots are produced by the originating agency and are ready to be played by the stations receiving them. They are usually sent in the format used by the particular stations or on reel-to-reel tape, which will probably be transferred to the proper station format. As with television spots, an accompanying script is sent along with the standard cover letter and response card.

As-recorded radio spots differ in format from television scripts but contain much of the same information. However, if you are basing your radio spots on already produced or written television spots, you will need to transfer the video cues to audio cues. For instance, if you are using a celebrity spokesperson who is easily recognizable on your video spots, she will have to identify herself on radio. Scene setting, which can be easily enough accomplished on video, will have to be taken care of verbally or through sound effects for radio. Consider the example in **Exhibit 8.9**.

Exhibit 8.9—As-Recorded Radio Spot

Northwest Library Association
1342 Placer Ave.
Seattle, WA 98901

"Werewolf" 30 Sec. PSA—As Recorded

(sfx: sounds of wind, howling, and footsteps running)

WOMAN: DID YOU HEAR THAT? IT SOUNDED LIKE A WEREWOLF!
MAN: DON'T WORRY. WE'RE SAFE.

(sfx: loud sound of bushes rattling and sudden snarling)

WOMAN: (very frightened) IT IS A WEREWOLF! WHAT ARE WE
           GOING TO DO?

-more-

MAN: (reassuringly) I TOLD YOU NOT TO WORRY. I HAD
     PLENTY OF GARLIC ON MY PIZZA TONIGHT,
     REMEMBER?

WOMAN: (sarcastically) I CERTAINLY DO.

WEREWOLF: (in terror) GARLIC! (screams)

(sfx: sounds of rapidly retreating footsteps and howling fading into distance)

WOMAN: (relieved) HOW ON EARTH DID YOU KNOW THAT
     GARLIC WOULD FRIGHTEN A WEREWOLF AWAY?

MAN: I READ IT IN A BOOK AT THE PUBLIC LIBRARY.

WOMAN: (sarcastically again) AND DID THIS BOOK EXPLAIN THE
     EFFECTS OF GARLIC ON YOUR DATE?

MAN: WHOOPS...

ANNCR: YOU'D BE SURPRISED WHAT YOU CAN LEARN AT YOUR
     PUBLIC LIBRARY. GIVE READING A TRY... IT MAKES
     GOOD SENSE.

MAN: (voices fading as couple walks away) OH, COME ON
     CAROL, IT SAVED OUR LIVES DIDN'T IT... I'LL CHEW
     SOME GUM... I'LL BRUSH MY TEETH...

        # # # # #

How to Get Your PSAs on the Air

Ask each media outlet for its guidelines for PSAs. If an outlet doesn't have them in writing, ask for a verbal explanation. The best way to ensure your spots get on the air is to follow their guidelines to the letter. Some of the things you should look for in these guidelines are:

- Deadlines—The media are deadline oriented. If you don't work within their deadlines, they won't run your PSA. Find out what their deadlines are, and plan as far ahead as you can.

- Length of spots—Most stations typically run shorter spots, usually 30 seconds. Find out what lengths they will run, and produce in that length.

- Submit rough versions of your scripts or ideas to the stations if time permits. Ask for their advice to make sure you needs meet theirs.

- Find out whether any of the stations will produce your spots for you. Some will, if you provide the script and it suits their needs. Look especially for co-sponsorship opportunities through which the station can publicize its involvement with you.

  Be careful, though. Other, competing stations may not want to run spots produced by a rival station, especially if you use that station's "personalities." However, if a station merely produces your spots for you, find out if you can then run those on other stations.

- Find out when each station is most likely to run PSAs. Although it might be best for you to get your message out during the Christmas season, the stations will probably be inundated with similar requests. You'll find that most stations have more available air time following major holidays.

Other Audio-visual Media

Slide Presentations

Writing for other types of audio-visual productions is a natural extension of radio and television writing. Scripts employing slides as visual accompaniment are formatted similarly to television scripts, with visuals on the left and narration on the right. There are several types of presentations utilizing slides and sound. Among the most common are:

1. Live narration (usually in the form of a scripted speech) accompanied by slides. This is the form of many presentations ranging from educational to sales promotion. The slides can be changed by hand, or by remote control.

2. Taped audio with slide accompaniment. The simplest method is to change slides manually as you play a tape. More elaborate systems allow for audio tones to signal slide changes automatically. The advantage of taped audio is that virtually any sound technique that can be used in radio can be used for slide/tape presentations, including music, sound effects, multiple voices, etc. Some systems don't even require a screen but can be viewed on a built-in television-like screen.

   For organizations with limited budgets, the slide-tape combination is an excellent way to produce an inexpensive television spot. Some stations may even produce your presentation on videotape for you if submit your slides and audio script. Of course, you can also produce the audio tape yourself and send it with your slides to the stations.

3. Slides and audio dubbed to videotape. This allows the presentation to be viewed on a VCR and simplifies the logistics of lugging around slides, projectors, screens, and audio tapes. If slides are committed to videotape, you might want to go the extra step and have the slides shot by studio cameras, incorporating movement into the production by panning, zooming, tilting, and dissolving from camera to camera while taping the slides projected onto screens.

4. Multi-media presentations utilizing slides, movie projectors, and videotape. This type of presentation is extremely complex and usually left for the production studio; however, scripting is frequently done in house.

The audio-visual script should be easy to follow. Visuals appear exactly opposite their audio counterparts, often with numbers corresponding to the slide placed within the script narration to indicate the exact point at which the slide will be changed.

The major difference between audio-visual scripts and television spots is length. Slide presentations are usually longer with fewer visual changes. To keep them lively, count on changing slides every five to ten seconds. Much depends on the type of presentation. For instance, if you are presenting the annual budget report, you might be severely limited as to the type and number of slides shown. If the slide contains written information, gauge the amount of time it will take to read it by reading it aloud. If you are dealing strictly with visual images, then the five to ten second time allotment should be just about right. Slides used for television presentation, especially, should change frequently, or some other sort of movement should be incorporated into the production to compensate.

Exhibit 8.10 is a slide/tape presentation that accompanies a fundraising appeal to corporate sponsors from a major university. See if you can discern where best to place the slides within the narration. What do you see as the theme or focus of this first page? Can you tell who the intended audience is from the tone and focus?

Broadcast Releases

Sometimes, you will be asked to provide a broadcast release with accompanying visuals. The format is very much like a television or slide script. **Exhibit 8.11** is based on a broadcast release from **Chapter 3 (Exhibit 3.5)** The visuals have been written in.

Exhibit 8.10—Slide/Tape Script

Slide Script
"Building the Future"   Page 1 of 5

1. Graphic—"BUILDING THE FUTURE ON THE PAST" over University coat-of-arms	1. BUILDING THE FUTURE ON THE PAST. THESE WORDS REFLECT BUTLER UNIVERSITY'S COMMITMENT TO INNOVATIVE RESEARCH AND EDUCATIONAL PROGRAMS.
2. Aerial shot of campus	2. A COMMITMENT TO DEVELOP THE PROMISE OF IDEAS INTO THE FOUNDATION OF HUMAN PROGRESS.
3. Same, with "RESEARCH" and "TEACHING" supered	3. THIS COMMITMENT TAKES MANY AND VARIOUS FORMS REFLECTING THE INTELLECTUAL DIVERSITY OF THE CAMPUS COMMUNITY.
4. Psychology researcher with experimental subject	4. IMPORTANTLY, THE BOLD AND UNCOMPROMISING INQUIRY SO TYPICAL OF RESEARCH AT THE UNIVERSITY MORE OFTEN THAN NOT PROVIDES THE BASIS FOR THE BEST IN TEACHING AND PUBLIC SERVICE.
5. IEC researcher testing solar cell	5. IT HAS BEEN SAID THAT THE FUTURE IS PURCHASED BY THE PRESENT.
	-more-

Exhibit 8.11—Broadcast Release Script

Society for Needy Children   Contact: Lucille Bevard
4240 Welxton Ave.   Day Phone: 555-8743
Newhope, MN 78940   Night Phone: 555-9745

SNC FUNDRAISER NETS $75 THOUSAND   For Immediate Release

:90 Seconds	A little girl stood for the first time today to
Tape Roll (SIL)	receive a new teddy bear and a check for $75,000 from the Society for Needy Children. Eight-year-old Mary Patterson accepted the check on behalf of the children at the St. Mary Martha's Children's Hospital. The money represents the culmination of a year-long fundraising drive by the Society.The money is earmarked for a new ward to be devoted exclusively to the treatment of crippling diseases in children. One of the first beneficiaries will undoubtedly be little Mary who has been disabled by congenital arthritis since birth. Along with her new teddy bear, Mary and the other children at the hospital will be using a new physical therapy center that was donated through a matching grant from the Friends of St. Mary Martha's. Hospital Administrator Lois Shelcroft says that the check and the new therapy center are just the first step...
(SOT: Shelcroft :20)	(CUT TO SHELCROFT INSERT OUTRO: "... continue next year.")
	The next fundraising drive, scheduled to begin in September, will provide money for a new lab.

# # # # #

Case Study: Associated Products Corporation

Use the background information provided in **Chapter 3** to complete these assignments.

Assignment 8.1: Television

You have been assigned to develop a complete promotional package that will be used by APC and NEA to stimulate interest in computer learning skills. As part of the package, write a 60-second television spot (in the form of a shooting script) employing the talents of a celebrity of your choosing. The spot should focus on the place of computers in today's society and the importance of computing skills to children of all ages.

The spot will be generic in nature and will not mention the new APC/NEA program. You have total control at this point as to the angle and message. Try to be as creative as you can. Try also to use the unique talents of whatever celebrity you have chosen to their fullest. It will be necessary to develop some sort of slogan or catch phrase that will be used in all of your broadcast media spots. The slugline for TV and subsequent radio spots will be:

For more information on computer learning skills and your child write:

The National Education Association
Box 1776
Washington, D.C. 20012

Before you begin the actual scripting, develop a treatment for your proposed script. It should be no more than one page and include preliminary ideas of narrative, talent, camera movement, shot composition, and sound effects.

Assignment 8.2: Television

Take the 60-second spot you have written and cut it to 30 seconds. In doing so, remember to include the most pertinent information and maintain the flavor of the original 60-second spot as much as possible. Focus on the main ideas and basic concept that make your 60-second spot work.

Assignment 8.3: Radio

You must develop, as part of a complete broadcast media package, radio spots on APC/NEA, using the theme you developed for your TV spots. You must first create a series of spot announcements to be read by radio station personnel. You will need 10-, 30-, and 60-second spots highlighting the information presented in your TV spot but without the celebrity.

Assignment 8.4: Radio

In addition, you will need to develop two "as-recorded" spots—one 30- and one 60-second—using your celebrity talent's voice in some way. Remember to maintain consistency of theme by keying on the main points and using a thematic slogan if possible.

Assignment 8.5: Radio

As part of your everyday work for APC, you have been assigned to produce publicity for a joint venture with the American Red Cross to sponsor a cardio-pulmonary resuscitation (CPR) education and awareness campaign. This campaign is to emphasize the importance of Red Cross CPR training to the community and to the individual. Other campaigns have been held around the country over the past eight months, resulting in approximately 50,000 individuals being trained.

The first event is to be a kick-off "CPR Awareness Day" to be held in Bellevue State Park on Sunday, November 4. Present will be members of paramedic units from the local area as well as Red Cross volunteers.

The "Day" begins at 1:00 p.m. with introductions and refreshments. An initial demonstration will be made to all attending, then individuals will break up into groups headed by the trainers. Each group will learn the basics of CPR. At the end of each hour-long training session, participants will receive certificates of completion in CPR training from the Red Cross.

At 5:00, the rock group "Plastic Umbrella" will perform.

Your assignment is to make up three promotional radio spots of 10, 30, and 60 seconds in length to be read live . Remember, these need to reflect a conversational style because they will be read aloud on the air. For the 60-second spot, you may want to create an interesting "hook."

CHAPTER 9

Print Advertising

...we by tracing magic lines are taught, how to embody and to color thought.

Anonymous

For writers, there can be no truer proving ground than the print ad. Aldous Huxley once remarked that trying, through words on paper, to sell something to someone who doesn't want to buy it is the hardest task a writer can set himself. The fact of the matter is, most print ads don't get read at all. Readers have a tendency to skip over ads that they find of no immediate interest. While television, and radio to an extent, play to "captive" audiences, not so a magazine or newspaper. Gone are the devices used by the electronic media to interest the reader. In print advertising, there is no catchy music score or flashy moving image; no slick camera angles or intriguing sound effects—only the printed word and the overall effect of layout and design. Don't feel, however, that print advertising is a waste of time. On the contrary, it offers the reader the luxury of perusing at leisure. Print can be most effective as a vehicle for information too complex or lengthy for television or radio.

Public relations practitioners do not usually spend a great deal of time writing for product or service advertising; however, corporate America spends billions of dollars a year in advertising aimed not at selling products but at creating or enhancing image. This means that more and more PR writers are responsible for producing ad copy. There is also a trend in public relations toward a more complete integration with other communication functions. Marketing, advertising, and public relations all share common goals when it comes to the organization in which they work. Flexibility is the key. Being able to produce copy for corporate advertising is just another aspect of being a complete public relations writer.

Writing Print Advertisements

Whether designed for broadcasting or for the printed page, corporate advertising falls into the same three forms mentioned in **Chapter 8**: public service, public image, and advocacy advertising. Although the focus of these forms is identical from broadcast to print, the format and execution is quite different. Print ads are composed of three primary elements: headline, visual, and copy.

Headlines

Like the press release, the print advertisement has to be sold on its appearance, but to a different audience—the public. To the writer, this means that the reader has to be hooked in some way into reading the ad. The best place to start is the beginning.

Aside from an eye-catching visual, nothing attracts a reader like a good headline. Recent research indicates that the headline is often the only thing read in a print ad. David Ogilvy, in his book *Ogilvy on Advertising,* says that "On the average, five times as many people read the headline as read the body copy."

Headlines come in all shapes and sizes and need be neither long nor short to be effective. What they do need to be is interesting. Consider the following headlines gathered from a number of consumer magazines.

YOUR DYING IS YOUR RESPONSIBILITY.

The Hemlock Society

THE WAY SOME OF US PERCEIVE AIDS,
YOU'D THINK YOU COULD GET IT
BY JUST TOUCHING THIS PICTURE.

Pediatric AIDS Foundation

FOR 50 YEARS,
TEXACO HAS BEEN HAVING A LOVE AFFAIR
WITH THE MOST PASSIONATE WOMEN.

FOR 50 YEARS,
TEXACO HAS BEEN ASSOCIATING
WITH THE MOST VILLAINOUS CHARACTERS.

FOR 50 YEARS,
TEXACO HAS BEEN SUPPORTING
THE MOST HEROIC MEN.

FOR 50 YEARS,
TEXACO HAS BEEN YOUR
TICKET TO THE MET.

(A series of small ads placed in the upper
right-hand corner of succeeding pages)
Texaco

Research conducted by Starch INRA Hooper, an advertising research firm, concludes that what the headline says is of more importance than its form or design. However, inclusion of certain elements was found to increase readership.

- A headline addressing the reader directly.
- A headline referring to a specific problem or desire.
- A headline offering a specific benefit.
- A headline offering something new.

Of course, not all readers will be interested by all headlines. Print ads, like other forms of communication, are intended for a target public. A print ad for the preservation of bald eagles by the Sierra Club may not get much readership among nonconservationists (or poachers). All good headlines, however, have certain attributes in common.

- They should be specific. Try to avoid vague phrases or references that mean little or nothing to your reader.
- They should be believable. If you make them appear unbelievable, you should do so only in an effort to entice the reader into reading further.
- They should be simple. A good headline sets forth one major idea. The time to elaborate is in the body of the ad, not the headline.

There are several ways to construct your headlines to help them attract readers.

- Introduce news value into your headline. News invites readership. Any time your ad can appear newsworthy, your readership will increase. The headline "Why reforming our liability system is essential if America is to succeed in overseas markets," appeared on a two-page ad by AIG. Headlines such as these appear as lead-ins to articles and appeal to readers who are interested in informative advertising.

- Target your message by using a selective headline that pinpoints the exact public you are trying to reach. An ad run by Metropolitan Life featured a small child on crutches and the headline, "If you forget to have your children vaccinated, you could be reminded of it the rest of your life." This headline obviously appeals to its target audience—parents. It might or might not appeal to people with no children.

- The testimonial approach features a firsthand quotation. "Rock the boat!" is the headline on one of a series of ads featuring first-hand employee testimonies about Texaco and its products. This ad features a chemist talking about innovation. A testimonial headline is particularly useful if spoken by a celebrity. Many nonprofit agencies now utilize the talents of celebrities to sell ideas. Paul Newman speaks out against nuclear weapons, Charlton Heston speaks on behalf of the nuclear deterrent, and numbers of celebrities urge us to become foster parents or pen pals to underprivileged children.

- The curiosity headline invites the reader to read further in order to answer a posed question. "Do we really want to return to those good, old-fashioned days before plastics?" comes from an ad on recycling from Amoco.

- The command headline orders the reader to do something. "Make a life or death decision" refers to the right to die and is from a series of single-column magazine ads from the Hemlock Society. In most cases, this type of headline isn't actually commanding you to do something, it is simply suggesting that you think about it.

Of course, there are other types of headlines less used than these, but most fall into one of these categories. Remember, the headline is the hook. Write a good headline, and half your job is already done.

Visuals

You don't absolutely have to have a visual in a print ad, although most of us are used to seeing one. Many good advertisements have been carried off with words only. For instance, the Chase Manhattan Bank once ran an ad with a very large headline comprised of a single word "WOLF!" The rest of the ad, run without a visual, spoke of the necessity of "crying wolf" occasionally in order to draw attention to the vanishing capital situation in the U.S. today.

If you do decide that you need a visual, make it a good one. The choice of visual is not always the prerogative of the writer. (The ad in **Exhibit 9.1**, for example, uses visuals effectually.) In most cases, that part is taken care of by the art department or agency; however, every writer of print advertising has something in mind when creating an ad. It is virtually impossible to come up with snappy copy and have had no visual in mind. It is your job to communicate your ideas for visuals to the people who will be charged with producing the final ad. You don't have to be an artist—all you need to do is provide a rough sketch (a *thumbnail*) and a narrative description of the visual with the ad copy. The headline, visual, and body copy should work together to make a single point.

Body Copy

Good body copy is hard to write. Don't let anybody tell you otherwise. You can bet the best examples of good ad copy are the ones that took the most time, effort, and revision. Good body copy is easy to spot. It uses a minimum of adjectives and relies heavily on nouns. It uses verbs to keep things moving along. Most of all, it follows a logical order of presentation.

Good body copy begins with a bridge from the headline (an expansion of the headline idea), continues with the presentation of major points, and ends with a recapitulation of the main point, a call for action (overt or implied), or both. Sometimes, a device known as a "kicker" is used to reiterate the message of the headline. A kicker is usually a slogan or a headline-type phrase coming at the end of the body copy. Consider this ad (written by a student) concerning nuclear waste disposal.

BURYING THE MYTH ABOUT NUCLEAR WASTE IS TOUGHER THAN BURYING NUCLEAR WASTE.

One of today's biggest misconceptions is that nuclear waste can't be disposed of safely. This just isn't true. With today's technology, we can safely bury nuclear wastes deep underground, imprisoning them in a series of safeguarding barriers designed so that even if one should fail, the waste would still be contained. Nuclear waste disposal can be as safe as taking out the trash. It simply requires good sense. So please, bury the myth, and we'll bury the waste.

Exhibit 9.1—Using Visuals

Here's a simple ad using simple graphics and but a few words. It was designed for a self-congratulatory image campaign in papers such as The Wall Street Journal.

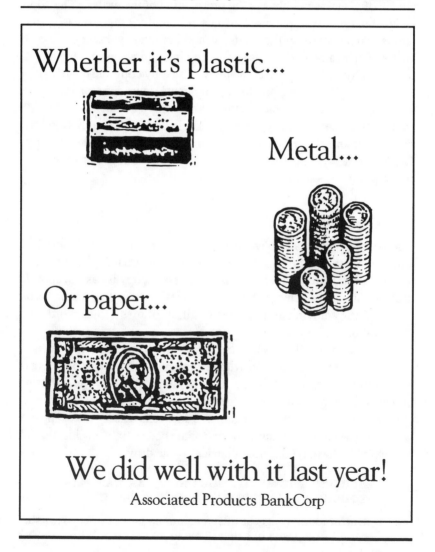

Notice, first of all, that the headline is interesting and plays on the term "burying" to designate both the disposal of nuclear waste and the disposal of a misconception. The lead sentence in the body copy elaborates on the headline by explaining exactly what "myth" is referred to. A presentation of the main points follows the lead sentence and explains how technology helps ensure safety. The ad wraps up with a direct reference back to the headline and a call for action. All of the components necessary for a successful ad are present.

Notice too that the copy is limited. "Brevity is the soul of wit" to the ad copywriter. Unfortunately, not all public relations advertising can fit so neatly into so few words. It is the nature of public relations to be informative. This often requires detail of the kind that can only be presented in the print media and at length.

Longer public interest ads—often running to one or more pages—can provide detailed explanations and will be read, but only by those intensely interested in the topic. Others, not interested enough to read through an entire ad of this type, might still skim it for highlights or, at the very least, appreciate the fact that the sponsoring agency felt that the issue was important enough to spend money advertising it.

Aside from logical order of presentation, there are some basic guidelines that will help you to write good body copy.

1. Stick to the present tense when possible. This will make your message seem timely and active.

2. Remember that you are speaking to one person. Unlike television and radio ads, which reach a mass audience simultaneously, print is read by one person at a time. Use a familiar voice. Use personal pronouns. Involve the reader. Say "we" or "our" instead of "the Company" or "the industry." Make the readers understand that you are one of them.

3. Use the active voice. Don't say "A proposal was made whereby nuclear waste can more effectively be disposed." Say instead, "We've proposed a new method for disposing of nuclear waste."

4. Use words that will be familiar to your readers. On the other hand, don't speak down to them. Assume that they know something about your subject but are looking to your ad to increase their knowledge. If you use a necessarily difficult word or phrase, explain it. Remember, readers like to think that the people explaining or giving advice are smarter than they are, but not a whole lot smarter.

5. Although the average sentence length for ease of readability is about 16 words, vary your sentence length for variety. Varying paragraph length, too, will lend your ad an appearance of readability. Many readers who do not have time to pore over long, unbroken passages will read shorter paragraphs. To this end, subheads are useful to point to especially informative passages.

6. Use contractions. People talk that way, so why not write that way—as if you were speaking to them. An exception would be the contracted form of *there is—there's*. The contraction reads awkwardly and is too often used ungrammatically instead of *there are*.

7. Always punctuate properly, even in headlines. Think about what punctuation does. It makes the reader pause and denotes a change or variance in emphasis. Stay away from the exclamation point and try not to use ellipses or "leaders."

8. Avoid clichés and try not to use vague words or phrases. People like to feel that they understand you.

9. Never say anything controversial that you don't back up with facts or evidence. Unsupported statements will hurt your credibility.

Formatting Print Ads

Ad Copy Format

Print ads, like other forms of public relations writing, require the proper format for presentation. Most print ads, however, will not be sent directly to the media as mere copy but rather as a complete ad, ready to be published (camera-ready). Nevertheless, it is necessary to format your ad copy so that the agency or department handling the assembly of the final product understands what it is you are trying to do. Fortunately, the format for ad copy is similar to other formats such as brochures, posters, and direct mail pieces. It is easily adapted to any form of copywriting that requires a mixture of headlines, visuals, and text. The key is to make sure you designate clearly all of the elements at the left-hand margin so that a reader can see what element of the ad he or she is reading at the time (see **Exhibits 9.2, 9.3, and 9.4**).

Exhibit 9.2—Print Ad Format
The ad copy and the laid-out ads on the next three pages clearly show the relationship between the format and the final layout.

Nuclear Waste
Quarter-page Newspaper Ad

HEADLINE: Burying the myth about nuclear waste is tougher than burying the waste.

VISUAL: Silhouette of grass with cutaway for copy – implying copy is placed in hole in ground simulating nuclear waste.

COPY: One of today's biggest misconceptions is that nuclear waste can't be disposed of safely. This just isn't true. With today's technology, we can safely bury nuclear wastes deep underground, imprisoning them in a series of safeguarding barriers designed so that even if one should fail, the waste would still be contained. Nuclear waste disposal can be as safe as taking out the trash. It simply requires good sense. So please, bury the myth, and we'll bury the waste.

SLUG: The Committee for Clean Energy

-30-

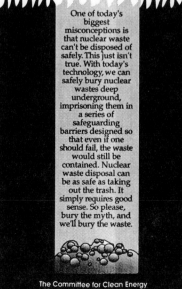

Burying the myth about nuclear waste is tougher than burying the waste.

One of today's biggest misconceptions is that nuclear waste can't be disposed of safely. This just isn't true. With today's technology, we can safely bury nuclear wastes deep underground, imprisoning them in a series of safeguarding barriers designed so that even if one should fail, the waste would still be contained. Nuclear waste disposal can be as safe as taking out the trash. It simply requires good sense. So please, bury the myth, and we'll bury the waste.

The Committee for Clean Energy

Exhibit 9.3—Print Ad Format

Associated Products Corporation &
the National Education Association
Textbook: Full-page Magazine Ad

HEADLINE: Does this look like a textbook to you?

VISUAL: Blackboard with headline next to simple drawing of
            computer

COPY: To thousands of school children all over the United
            States it does. They are learning traditional subjects in a
            whole new, and stimulating, way—through computers
            in the classroom. They are preparing for a future that is
            increasingly demanding knowledge of new technology
            along with the basics of math, English, history, and
            science.

            And computers are helping solve the problems of
            overcrowded classrooms by supplying the individual
            attention and instant feedback busy teachers can't
            always provide. Computers not only help teach
            children, they ask them questions
            and correct them when they are
            wrong. Not many textbooks can
            do that.

            If your school doesn't have
            computers in its classrooms,
            perhaps it should. In today's world,
            a classroom without computers is
            like a school without books.

            SLUG: Computers in education: A
            new look to an old subject.

            # # # # #

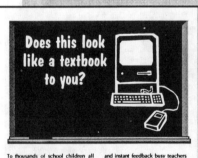

Does this look like a textbook to you?

To thousands of school children all over the United States it does. They are learning traditional subjects in a whole new, and stimulating, way—through computers in the classroom. They are preparing for a future that is increasingly demanding knowledge of new technology along with the basics of math, English, history, and science.

And computers are helping solve the problems of overcrowded classrooms by supplying the individual attention and instant feedback busy teachers can't always provide. Computers not only help teach children, they ask them questions and correct them when they are wrong. Not many textbooks can do that.

If your school doesn't have computers in its classrooms, perhaps it should. In today's world, a classroom without computers is like a school without books.

Computers in education: A new look to an old subject.

Exhibit 9.4—Print Ad Format

Northrim Associates
Quarter-page Newspaper Ad
"You Probably Know"

VISUAL: Cartoon line drawing of grizzly bear with fly fishing gear and waders standing in stream.

HEADLINE: You probably know that the Alaskan Grizzly eats hundreds of pounds of salmon a week.

COPY: But did you know that he is also a superb fisherman, catching dozens of salmon a day from mountain streams? If your sport is fishing and wildlife watching, come to Alaska this summer. Aside from some of the best fishing in the world, we've also got some of the most beautiful scenery, friendly people, and "wild" life.

If you've never been to the "Last Frontier," you'll find it the experience of a lifetime; and if you're coming for a return visit—welcome back! Consider Alaska this summer. Start by writing:

Department of Tourism,
State of Alaska,
Juneau, Alaska
99504

We can help with all your travel arrangements, and even find you a campground—free of bears.

KICKER: Alaska: The first choice. The last frontier.

# # # # #

Ad Layout Formats

Some public relations writers, especially those in limited-budget non-profit organizations, find themselves in sole charge of some forms of advertising and must design ads as well as write the copy for them. It is best to know how to proceed *before* you're assigned the task. Even if you don't lay out your own ads, it's a good idea to become familiar with the most common ad formats so that as you write, you can conceptualize exactly how your copy will fit into the finished product. The following represent the most common print ad formats in use.

Picture window is probably one of the most popular styles for print ads. The visual dominates this format and usually takes up the top or bottom two-thirds of the page. Normally, the headline is a single line followed by body copy in two or three columns.

Copy heavy places the emphasis on the copy rather than on the visual. For messages that are complex in nature and require detailed explanation, this is one of the best formats to use. In corporate advocacy advertising, copy-heavy ads are very common.

Silhouette or **copy fit** usually has the copy "wrap around" an open (as opposed to framed or bordered) piece of art. Copy fit takes an expert in typesetting. This isn't something a beginner will normally feel comfortable with, but a good copy fit ad can exude an air of unity that may not be found in other layouts.

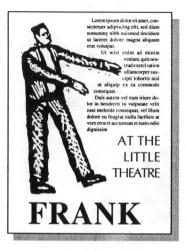

Mondrian is named after the Dutch artist who developed the style. This style is, again, not for the beginner. Mondrian divides the ad space into rectangles of various sizes into which headlines, copy, and visuals are placed. Balance is the key here.

Frame or **donut** refers either to framing copy with a visual or framing a visual with copy. If the perimeter is open at either the top or the bottom, the layout is sometimes called **horseshoe**.

Circus is definitely the domain of graphic designers. It takes an expert to balance this layout well. This format often utilizes both framed and silhouetted visuals along with copy-fit body copy and numerous subheads.

Multi-panel or **cartoon** is exactly what it says. In this format, the panels are usually of equal size. Sometimes the panels tell a sequential story. Multi-panel does not always have to frame each picture in the sequence. Some multi-panel layouts use a series of open or silhouetted visuals—often a repeated image that changes gradually as it progresses.

Type specimen relies on the effect of a special or enlarged typeface in place of or as the primary visual element. Again, it takes an expert designer or typographer to handle a type specimen design.

Case Study: Associated Products Corporation

Use the information provided in Chapter 3 for the following assignments.

Assignment 9.1: Print Ad

As part of an overall promotional package for APC/NEA, including television, radio, and now print, you are to write copy for a full-page magazine ad to be run four color. The theme should be the same as or linked to the theme you developed for the radio and television spots to add continuity to your promotion. You will need to come up with a headline, visual idea, and body copy. You may or may not choose to include a kicker or some other standard ending device. Include a thumbnail sketch in the upper right-hand corner of your copy indicating placement of headline, visual, and body copy.

Assignment 9.2: Print Ad

Restructure your full-page, four-color magazine ad for newspaper. The visual will be in black and white—the size of the finished ad is to be 5 x 9 inches. The typeface will be 12-point Goudy Oldstyle with 1-point leading. You first need to determine if your original copy will fit in this reduced space. It is up to you to come up with a copy block shape and size. If you need to trim your copy to fit the space, do so. If you need to rethink the visual and come up with another one, do that too; but remember to try to keep your components consistent. The format for the copy is the same as for the last assignment. Attach your formulas for working out the copyfitting to the copy. Include all measurements. Be sure to include a thumbnail sketch on the copy.

CHAPTER 10

Speeches & Presentations

There are two times in your life when you are totally alone:
When you die, and just before you give a speech.

Anonymous

S peech writing is putting words into someone else's mouth; and that's not an easy task. It requires that you know the person for whom you are writing intimately. You need to know his or her style of speaking, body language, tone of voice, speech patterns, and, most important, personality. When you write a speech, you become the person you are writing for, and, to an extent, that person will become you at the moment he or she begins to speak your words.

Thus, speech writing is a truly collaborative effort. It requires the absolute cooperation of all parties involved. Think of famous speeches you have heard or read: Patrick Henry's "Give me liberty or give me death," Winston Churchill's "Blood, sweat and tears," John F. Kennedy's "Ask not what your country can do for you," and Martin Luther King's "I have a dream." Often, famous speeches such as these were written by the speakers themselves, but just as often, they were collaborative efforts by the speakers, professional speech writers, and others with valuable input into the process. As in other forms of public relations writing—everybody has something to say about what you write.

Types of Speeches

The public relations speech is as varied as are the purposes to which the speech will be put. In fact, speeches are usually classified by purpose.

- A speech to inform seeks to clarify, instruct, or demonstrate.
- A speech to persuade is designed to convince or influence and often carries a call to action.
- A speech to entertain covers almost everything else including celebrations, eulogies, and dinner speeches.

The type of speech you use will be determined largely by the topic and the audience. The method of delivery and the degree to which the speech relies on audio-visual aids will also depend on these factors.

Modes of delivery

There are four basic modes of delivering a speech:

- extemporaneous delivery
- impromptu delivery
- scripted delivery
- memorized delivery

In the first two types, the public relations writer is responsible primarily for the research and compilation of information, usually in outline form. The speaker then studies the notes carefully and is theoretically prepared to speak knowledgeably and fluently on the topic. Speeches to be delivered from script or from memory can be written entirely by the public relations writer. For all modes of speaking, the primary responsibility of the public relations practitioner, after the speech is prepared, is to coach the speaker. This means, of course, that you must know how to give a good speech yourself. If you don't, and many public relations people don't, find someone who can and have that person coach the speaker. This often means hiring outside professionals to do the job, which may be costly, but in the long run, may be well worth the effort.

Preparation and Writing

Preparation is the most important element in any type of presentation. Although some of us are able to speak "off the cuff," it is a dangerous habit to get into. Think of the politicians who have lost elections because of candid "off the record" remarks or unwise ad libs. It is extremely important that you prepare in advance everything that you will say and do during a presentation. Don't leave anything to chance.

The "nuts and bolts" of an effective presentation include:

- Specific purpose;
- Clear understanding of your audience;
- Well organized ideas;
- Adequate support;
- Effective delivery.

Specifying Your Purpose

Keep two important principles in mind. First, the speech should be results oriented. Think of the effect you want it to have on the audience. Decide whether you want your audience to be persuaded, informed, or feel entertained by your presentation.

Second, the purpose of your presentation should be the basis for all the other decisions you make. This means that the way you organize your ideas, the kind of audio-visual support materials you use, even the way you deliver the presentation, will hinge on why you are giving it in the first place.

Analyzing Your Audience

Your presentation is given for your listeners. Even if you think it is the best presentation you have ever given, if it doesn't affect them, it will have failed.

Analyze the occasion: the reason why this group is together at this time and what they expect to hear from you.

Analyze the people: what experience and knowledge about the subject do they bring to your presentation? What is their attitude toward the subject? Toward you?

Organizing Your Speech

Good organization lets your audience know that you know what you're talking about. A seemingly confused speaker loses credibility, and wastes valuable time. Remember, no one will sit still for long— especially if you're not making sense. And the only way to make sense is to be organized.

It is worth repeating that the best way to organize a speech is to think of its *purpose*. Use that purpose as the basis for deciding what goes in your speech, how you structure it, what data you present, even for deciding your style or wording.

Here is a typical speech format.

Introduction
- Attention-getter—Tell people why they should listen.
- Establish rapport—Create a bond with your audience. Show them what you have in common.
- Preview—Tell people what they are going to hear.

Body/discussion
- Main points, arranged logically (usually in order of importance).
- Data supporting each main point.

Conclusion
- Review—Summarize the key points the audience has heard.
- Memorable statement—Create a desired "frame of mind" that will stay with the audience.
- Call for action (if applicable).

Building a speech is like building anything else. You've got to have a solid foundation. It helps if what you build has a look of continuity, coherence, and completion. No one likes a structure that looks haphazard or loosely constructed. For speechmakers, a solid structure implies a solid idea.

You can see from this outline that in speeches, it pays to be repetitious. Tell people what you are going to do, do it, then tell them what you have done.

Most writers find it easier to work on the body of the presentation first, before thinking up a snappy introduction and conclusion.

The body of a speech may be developed in a number of ways:

- Chronological—Organized by time. For example, cover first this year's events, then next year's.
- Spacial—Organized by direction. For instance, talk about your company's development as it moved from the East Coast, across the nation to the West Coast.
- Topical—Organized by topic. Cover ideas that are related to each other together, then move on to the next set of ideas.
- Cause and effect—Organized by need/fulfillment. Describe "what we need" and then "how to get it."
- Problem/solution—Organized by question/answer. Describe the problem and then the solution, or vice versa.

Pay attention to how you word the main points you want to make. Work for parallelism, balance, and good transitions between main points. (Notice how the five types of organization described above begin with parallel openings. Notice, too, that they are balanced in both length and sentence structure.)

With the body of the presentation in hand, attack the introduction. A good introduction is relevant to the audience and occasion, involves the audience personally, positively disposes them toward your presentation, and stimulates them.

A good introduction does not begin with "Today I want to talk to you about...," nor does it necessarily include a joke. Good introductions can be questions, unusual facts, good examples, stories, illustrations, metaphors, analogies, or any one of a number of other devices.

Now to the conclusion of your presentation. Remember the advice: Tell them what you are going to do, do it, then tell them what you have done. The conclusion is the time to tell them what you have done. You should summarize or reiterate the main points of your presentation. Finish with a memorable statement that makes the purpose of the speech clear and positions the audience firmly on your side.

Supporting Your Ideas

Look at every presentation as though it were a plant. The roots are the good ideas you have. The stalk or stem is the organization of those ideas so that they flow well and fit nicely. Now for the fine detail: the pattern of the leaves, the shape and texture of the flower.

The detail or support you use to fill out your presentation must be sufficient to ensure that your listeners know precisely what you mean but should not be so overwhelming that you lose your audience in detail.

Your support must be relevant to your listeners. If it makes no sense to them you will fail to get their attention, gain their good will, or persuade them to your view. Use any kind of support that is appropriate to your purpose and ideas. Facts and statistics are almost mandatory for many business presentations. Examples and illustrations, however, can often make those hard numbers "come alive." Quotations from a source your listeners respect can add proof that what you are saying is true. Analogies and metaphors can often be used to make concrete that which is abstract by bringing the abstraction down to human terms. Preachers use these two devices all the time. Remember, use enough support and detail to do the job but no more.

One of the best ways to organize is to develop a summary sheet. Include at least the following information:

- **The audience:** Ages, size, educational background, demographic characteristics?

- **The purpose:** Inform, persuade, reinforce attitudes, entertain "After listening to my speech, audience members will..."

- **Organization of the speech:** Chronological, spatial, topical, cause and effect, problem-solving?

- **Supporting materials:** Statistics, quotations, case histories, analogies, hypothetical illustrations, anecdotes?

- **Purpose of introduction and conclusion:** Gain interest, create need for listening, summarize, call for action?

- **List of visual aids:** Which media, what content, integration into speech?

Delivery

Finally, you are standing in front of your listeners. Now it is your job to make your ideas come alive. The secret of effective delivery is thorough preparation and lots of practice.

You cannot deliver a presentation effectively if you don't know what you want to say. That requires preparation. The only way you can become a fluent speaker is to practice. There is no shortcut!

Okay. You are thoroughly prepared and well practiced. Now you must stand and do two things. First, stick to what you have practiced. Don't get distracted. Don't "throw away" your prepared presentation for an impromptu effort. Second, keep your eyes on your audience. Look at them. Watch their reactions to what you say. Don't get engrossed in your script. In fact, try not to use a script. Use an outline or brief notes instead.

Don't get engrossed in your audio-visual material. Watch the audience, not the screen. Even if you are using 35 mm slides in a black room, look out at your audience. You won't be able to see them well, but it is important they get the feeling that you can.

Another piece of advice: look relaxed, even if you aren't. Smile, frown, move your arms, look around the room at everyone. Try to feel as though you are in the middle of a lively conversation with a group of friends. It will do wonders for your delivery.

Using Audio-visual Support

We live in an increasingly visual society today. Most of us watch TV or go to the movies. Our magazines and newspapers are increasingly visually oriented. It's hard for an audience to maintain attention, even with the most persuasive of speakers, without something to look at. Used as integrated components of a speech, audio-visual materials can help keep the audience's attention and add valuable information.

Use audio-visual support for impact—to develop audience interest and hold attention. Use it for effectiveness—to help your listeners remember more, longer. Don't use it simply because it is there. Use it only if it enhances your presentation.

Briefly, if you do use audio-visual support:

- Be sure it adds to your presentation.
- Do not let the support control the presentation. Your ideas must come first.
- Be sure to rehearse the presentation with the audio-visual materials. Learn how to use them.
- Do not talk to the visuals, talk to the audience.
- Talk louder—you are competing with the visuals for audience attention.
- Stand clear—remember, visuals must be seen to be useful.

The most common support materials used with speeches are:

- **Visual support**: Charts, graphs, diagrams, samples, handouts, photographs.
- **Audio support**: Recordings.
- **Audio-visual support**: Films, videotapes, slide/tape programs.

Slide Shows

A good slide presentation can add zip and clarity to information that may be otherwise dull. It requires that you be well organized, know your audience, and follow a few simple rules.

Rule 1: Define your objective. Be sure you know what you want to accomplish; what changes you want to take place in your listeners; what behavior you want to affect.

Rule 2: Analyze your audience. Are they ignorant or expert? Do you aim for the "lowest common denominator"? The middle? The top? The more you know about them, the easier it is to make that decision.

Rule 3: Work from an outline. Keep it simple and make it a concise summary of the major points and supporting materials needed to reach your objective with this audience.

Rule 4: Decide what mood or treatment you want. A light, humorous treatment may mean cartoons and a comic narration. Are you going to threaten? Cajole? Be low-key? Mood makes a difference in how you use color and pacing.

Rule 5: Write a script, if you plan to use one.

Rule 6: Plan your slides.

- Convert material originally designed for publication to slide format.

- Use a series of slides or charts, disclosed progressively, to build up complex ideas.

- Keep all copy and symbols simple and legible. Projected letters should be at least two inches high and one-half inch wide. The number of feet from presenter to rearmost viewer, multiplied by .04, is the minimum height of a letter projected on a screen. (30 x .04 = 1.20 feet)

- Make all copy slides short and to the point. Include no more than 15 or 20 words or 25 or 30 pieces of data per slide.

- Keep slides simple and bold, Limit each slide or chart to one main idea.

- Use charts and graphs rather than tables. Tables almost always look complicated and confusing.

- Use variety in layout, color, charting, and graphics for change of pace.

- Avoid mathematical formulas or equations on slides.

- Keep photographs uncluttered.

- Plan to keep moving. Leave slides up only long enough for the audience to read. Remember, they are there to supplement and support your words and ideas.

- Enlist the aid of a competent audio-visual specialist.

Rule 7: Edit your slide presentation. Ask yourself the following questions:

- Are all major points covered?
- Does the content of each slide fit the narration?
- Are all slides legible?
- Are colors and visuals bold and effective?
- Does each slide depict one idea only?
- Is there good continuity from slide to slide?
- Does the program add up to form a visually coherent and pleasing presentation?

Rule 8: Rehearse, rehearse, rehearse.

Rule 9: Be sure to visit the room where you will be making the presentation prior to your presentation time to make sure the projector is there and in working order. Run through your program to make sure all is as you want it.

Rule 10: Slide programs are almost always given in darkened rooms. The only other light may be the one on the lectern you use. That means you must make a special effort to force yourself to look out into a blackened room at people you may be unable to see. Don't lose eye contact with them, because they can see you just fine.

Handling the Q & A Session

Anticipation is the key to successful question and answer (Q & A) periods. If you're the type of speaker who has to have everything written out in advance, then Q & A is not for you. You need to know whether you can handle thinking, analyzing, and speaking off the cuff before you "throw yourself to the lions." The best hedge against blowing a Q & A session is practice. It's advisable to have someone who is familiar with the topic you cover in your presentation work with you on possible questions in advance. That way, you have at least some idea of what to expect when you face the real thing. The following advice will help you when you do.

1. Repeat the question or paraphrase it in your own words.

2. Make sure you understand the question before answering it. Seek clarification if necessary.

3. Don't lie, fabricate or distort information. If you don't know the answer, say so—but don't appear flustered. Offer to find the answer and get back to the questioner. Confidence breeds credibility.

4. Refer to any visual aids that will help you answer the question.

5. Be concise—don't give another speech.

6. Don't allow a questioner to take you on a tangent. Stick to the main points of your speech..

7. Don't allow an individual questioner to monopolize the Q & A session.

Case Study: Associated Products Corporation

Background for Speech Assignment

The corporate level group of Associated Products Corporation is considering a three-day retreat. The purpose of the retreat is to:

- "Energize" corporate staff;
- Delve into interpersonal issues affecting productivity (for example, trust, openness, sensitivity, political power plays);
- Create increased group cohesiveness;
- Provide an opportunity for staff members to learn more about one another; and
- Discuss long-range corporate strategy in a relaxed setting.

The Company and Staff

Use previous background on the company. In addition, look at the following specifics about the corporate staff.

The corporate staff is composed of 48 people: 30 men and 18 women. APC prides itself on being young and innovative. The median age of the corporate staff is 34. Thirty percent have college degrees.

Members of the corporate staff have strong feelings—pro and con—about having a three-day retreat. Many have expressed the view that the retreat could turn into a "warm and fuzzy" group encounter.

APC has never gone on a company retreat. James Sutton, the president, recently read in an airline magazine that corporate retreats might be a good idea for some companies. He has sent a copy of the article on to all members of the staff. The following are excerpts from the article.

- Of the companies who have gone on company retreats, 70 percent report unqualified success; they are already planning next year's retreat.
- Some company officials return from the retreat as casualties. They learn things about themselves that may be traumatic.
- The best retreats are those that have an agenda.
- None of the companies reported allowing spouses to attend. And some spouses expressed concern about their mates attending the three-day retreat.

- Many of the companies (30 percent) reported using an outside consultant to design and "lead" the retreat.

- The 70 percent who report unqualified success point to such indices as increased profits, increased staff commitment, healthier and more productive working climate, and lack of game playing and political maneuvering.

- Retreats are usually held outside the city where the home office is located within a two-hour driving radius.

- All corporate officers surveyed agreed that, if held, the retreat must be compulsory, not voluntary.

- Retreats cannot "cure" a sick company. Sick companies tend to return from retreats sicker than they were before. "Healthy" companies, or those on the road toward health, tend to return from retreats healthier.

- Successful retreats are predicated upon individuals opening up and disclosing those issues that trouble them.

- The average cost of a retreat in 1993 was $80.00 per staff member per day.

- Many companies view a retreat as a fringe benefit for employees.

- Progressive companies believe in the value of retreats more that conservative ones.

- Successful retreats require advance preparation within the corporate staff itself. Staff members approach the retreat with the "right" attitude.

- Over the last ten years, the number of companies that have held retreats has declined slightly.

Assignment 10.1: Speech

You head a task force that will review the pros and cons of holding a corporate retreat. Present the case that APC should go on the retreat, *or* present the case that APC should not go on the retreat.

You will present your speech to the corporate staff of which you are a member. The staff will vote after hearing all proposals.

Your presentation should be 10 minutes in length and you can use any visual aids that you deem necessary. It will be delivered in the small company auditorium, which has an amphitheater arrangement. Complete the Summary Worksheet that follows. This worksheet may also be used as a guide in preparing future presentations.

Summary Worksheet

Preliminary questions

I. What are the expectations of this audience?

Toward me?

Toward my topic?

Toward this specific situation (Are there any extenuating circumstances that should be considered)?

II. How do I expect my audience to be affected by my presentation?

The general purpose of my presentation will be to inform, persuade, reinforce certain ideas, entertain?

The specific thesis: After listening to my speech, the audience will...

The body of the speech

III. What is the best structure to follow given I and II above?

Should my presentation be arranged chronologically? spatially? topically? By cause and effect? By problem/solution?

The structure I have chosen is the best in this particular situation because...

IV. What are the three or four main points suggested by the specific structure?

A.

B.

C.

D.

V. How will I support the main points?

Will I use statistics, examples, analogies, case studies, direct quotations?

A will be supported by:

B will be supported by:

C will be supported by:

D will be supported by:

VI. How should I adapt my language and word choice to suit audience expectations?

To what extent should I use jargon and "buzz words"?

To what extent should I be conscious of defining certain words?

VII. Should I use any visual aids?

What should be visualized?

How should it be visualized?

Why should it be visualized?

VIII. How should I introduce the speech?

Why should my audience listen to this message?

How will my audience benefit by listening to me?

How can I make my audience want to listen?

You should listen to me because...

IX. How should I conclude the speech?

How do I relate the conclusion to the main points I have covered?

In conclusion...

Once you have completed the worksheet, write the speech. Begin with the body of the speech and leave the introduction and conclusion until last.

CHAPTER 11

Working
with
Printers

Knowledge is of two kinds. We know a subject ourselves,
or we know where we can find information upon it.

Samual Johnson

The relationship between the writer-designer, typesetter, and printer is supposed to be a symbiotic one. This might lead you to conclude that everyone in the trio gets along. Don't believe it for a minute. Typesetters and printers are professionals in their own rights, and, as such, are very likely to have their own, often very different ideas, of what you need.

The trick to working successfully with typesetters and printers is to know what you are talking about. There's no substitute for knowledge. The key is to try out several typesetters and printers and work with those who not only give you the best deal, but who also are willing to give you guidance. This is not an easy process, but it does pay off in a lower frustration factor in the long run. Knowing how to spec type and select the proper typeface will help you out with typesetters. They are generally willing to do exactly as you specify, no matter what it looks like when finished. Their job is to set in type what you have given them as copy according to your written and verbal explanations. Well-marked copy will go a long way toward alleviating any misunderstandings between you and your typesetter. You have to know a bit more about the printing process, however, in order to get along with your printer. Every writer can tell you horror stories about printers who, after seemingly understanding exactly what *you* want, proceed to print exactly what *they* want. This is not to say that it is hard to get along with printers. It simply means that you have to know what you want and be able to explain it in printer's terms.

Printers can be an invaluable aid in selecting papers, inks, printing methods, bindings, and so on. You can get what you want if you know how to ask for it.

Printing Processes

Many writers simply entrust the choice of printing method to the printer. Although there are a number of printing processes available to you, probably the two you will have most contact with will be **offset lithography** and **quick printing**. Most collateral pieces and many newsletters are simply offset printed, which is one of the fastest and cheapest methods to get good quality printing today. Other quick-print methods will usually result in a loss of quality. Other, more detailed printing jobs, such as embossing or special paper shapes, may require specialty printing. Be advised that specialty printing is costly. Make sure that you are willing to bear the extra cost before you decide on that gold-foil stamp on the cover of your new brochure.

Offset Lithography

The most common printing process used today is offset lithography. The process is based on the principle that oil and water don't mix. In offset lithography, the nonprinting area of the printing plate accepts water but not ink, while the image, or printing, area accepts ink but not water. During the printing process, both water and ink are applied to the plate as it revolves. It is named *offset* printing because the plate isn't a reverse image as in most printing processes. Instead, the plate transfers its right-reading image to an offset cylinder made of rubber (which reverses the image), and from there to the paper (see **Exhibit 11.1**). Because the plate never comes in contact with the paper, it can be saved and used again and again, saving cost on projects that have to be reprinted periodically—unless, of course, you make changes.

Most PR documents will be printed this way. It is relatively inexpensive, compared to other processes, and it results in a high-quality image. Although small press runs of 1,000 or less can be made using offset lithography, it is especially cost-effective for larger runs, because presses are capable of cranking out hundreds of copies a minute.

Exhibit 11.1—Offset Printing

Offset gets its name from the indirect, "offsetting" printing process, in which the printing plate's image is "offset" to a rubber blanket that puts the ink on the paper. Notice how the type and image go from right-reading to reversed to right-reading again.

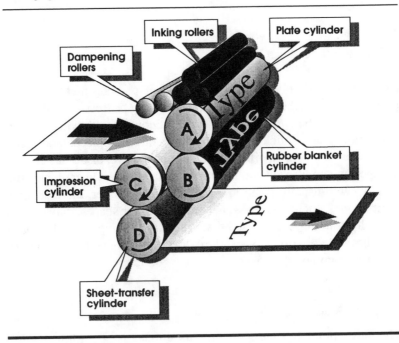

Quick Copy and Quick Print

The *quick copy* or *quick print* process involves two methods of reproduction.

Quick print involves a small cylinder press using paper printing plates. The plates are created using a photo-electrostatic process that results in a raised image created with toner (much like the toner used in photocopy machines). This raised image takes the ink and is imprinted directly onto the paper.

Quick copy is really xerography, and has made tremendous inroads into the quick print area. The larger model photocopiers used in this process can rapidly produce multiple copies, collate, and often staple them.

Neither of these processes is useful for two-color work, but both are cheap and fast. If you are going to use quick copy, reserve it for rush projects or those that won't suffer from single-color xerography. Be aware, also, that there can be major differences between photocopiers, and even between copies run on the same machine. A copier that ran your last job beautifully may not repeat the same quality the next time if the toner hasn't been changed recently. Don't be afraid to ask for a test print of your most difficult page to make sure the blacks are really black and there is no fade out on any part of the page.

Choosing Paper

Paper choice is one of the most important aspects of producing effective PR documents, particularly a collateral piece such as a brochure. Your choice of paper may determine whether your brochure is picked up and read, whether it lasts more than one or two days before it falls apart, or whether it even works well with your chosen type style, graphics, and ink color.

When choosing a paper, you will need to consider two major criteria. First, does the paper suit the use to which it will be put? In other words, does it have the right look, feel, color, durability, and so on? And, second, how much does it cost?

Suitability

In judging the suitability of your paper choice to your job, you must first determine the nature of your information. Do you want your printed piece to last and be passed from reader to reader? If you do, you'll want to choose a durable stock that will take constant opening, closing, and general handling without tearing. Some pieces are printed on relatively cheap and lightweight stock and are meant to be thrown away soon after reading (flyers, announcements, etc.). Others need to be more permanent. A brochure outlining company benefits to employees, for example, is one that probably will be kept and used over and over again. It will need to be on a heavier and more durable stock. A company magazine printed in four-color will need a durable paper because the publication will probably be passed on to other readers.

Aside from durability, three other factors need to be considered in judging the suitability of your paper: weight, texture, and color.

Weight. Papers come in various weights. Weight is determined by taking 500 sheets of the paper and weighing it. Although a heavier weight usually indicates a thicker stock, it doesn't have to. One 25-pound bond paper may be thicker than another. Likewise, one 60-pound book paper may be lighter and less durable than another. The best way to judge weight versus thickness is to handle the paper for each type of stock personally. Most printers have hundreds of samples of paper stock and can help you select the weight and thickness you want for your job.

Texture. Texture is also an important consideration when choosing a paper. Heavily textured paper may impart a feeling of quality or a feeling of roughness, depending on the paper stock and the method of manufacture. Basically, papers break down into two broad categories for texture: *matt finish* and *coated stock*. Matt finish ranges from a paper with a rather smooth but nonglossy surface to heavily textured paper. *Coated stock* refers to any paper that is "slick" or "glossy." Again, the range is considerable. Photographs often reproduce better on coated stock, which is what most magazines use. On the other hand, using a matt stock will soften the color and give a photograph an entirely different feeling. Some heavily textured stocks may not take ink well but may be perfect for foil stamping or embossing. The best way to tell if your idea will work on a certain texture stock is to ask the printer, look at some samples, and come to an informed decision.

Color. Paper color has to complement all the other graphic elements of your collateral piece: typeface, ink color, photographs, and artwork. It will also set the mood of your piece. Color preference is a very personal matter. Remember, however, that you are producing pieces to be read by certain target publics who may or may not like your color choice. Thus, to an extent, color choice is a matter of gauging your intended audience's reaction to a particular color. Research has shown, for instance, that business people will not respond to questionnaires printed on hot-pink paper (not much of a surprise). They will respond to beige and various shades of white, but respond very little to pale blue and green. All colors carry connotations for most people. You need to stay away from outrageous combinations and any color you judge might not get the response you want from your information piece.

Cost

The determining factor in your paper choice may well be cost. Don't despair, though, just because your budget may be limited. Paper comes in thousands of weights, colors, and textures; and one of them will fit your cost restrictions. Also remember that a few extra dollars on a good grade paper may well pay off in the long run by impressing your readership.

Selecting Paper for Computer Laser Printing

Paper is probably the least thought-about part of laser printing. Most of us simply opt for whatever is handy. The fact is, some papers are made specifically for laser printers, and some papers definitely should be avoided.

Ask yourself three questions when you pick laser printer paper.

- Will the laser copy be used as a finished piece or for reproduction?
- Does the paper say what you want it to say? In other words, what is its look and feel?
- Does the paper run well in your printer?

Keeping in mind the paper specifications presented earlier in this chapter, the following rules of thumb should help you select the proper paper for your needs and your printer.

- Brighter paper reproduces well on laser printers. (This doesn't mean *whiter* paper; there are varying degrees of brightness even among white papers.) Brighter papers are also good for reproduction masters. In fact, several manufacturers make papers specifically for laser printer output that will be used for reproduction. Also, because it's hard to predict the degree of darkness of your printer, the brighter the paper, the more contrast you're likely to have between the print and the paper. In general, avoid colored paper; however, some interesting effects can be obtained with lighter colors such as gray and beige.
- Stay away from heavily textured paper. The heavier the texture, the more broken your type will look, because it will be harder for the toner to adhere to the paper's surface. Texture also affects any large, dark areas such as screens and display type. Some texture, like that found in bond paper and linen stock, is fine. The trick here is to experiment.
- Avoid heavy papers like cover stock, generally 90 pounds or more, unless you like removing jammed paper from your printer. On the other hand, extremely light papers, such as onion skin, may stick to the rollers or jam as they feed into the printer. Don't experiment much here. Just settle for a text-weight paper (generally around 60 pounds) and consign the choice of cover paper to your commercial printer.
- Use a fairly opaque paper, especially if the laser-printed copy is to be your final version. If you use a paper with high opacity, be sure it isn't also heavily textured.

- Don't expect heavily textured papers to retain their texture. Unlike offset presses, laser printers flatten the paper as it moves through the printer. In most cases, any texture will be lost.
- By the same token, don't use embossed or engraved papers in your laser printer because they might jam the mechanism and will flatten out anyway.
- Make sure your paper is heat resistant. Because laser printers work in temperatures of around 400° F, certain letterhead inks may melt or stick and any metal or plastic will certainly ruin your printer. Above all, don't use acetate in your laser printer unless it has been specifically designed for your particular printer.

Choosing Ink

Choosing an ink can be a nightmare for the novice. Even the most experienced designers often have a short list of their favorite inks. Inks come in virtually limitless color combinations. And, each color will be affected by the paper it is printed on. Coated (slick) paper will result in brighter colors while matt finish paper will soften the color. The texture of the paper also affects ink color, as does using colored paper.

There are no easy ways to learn what inks to use. The best way for a beginner to choose an ink is to look at other work done using the same ink/paper combination. Also, obtain a copy of the Pantone Color Matching System. It's really just a color sample book, like the ones you see when you pick out a house paint, but it is the most commonly used system among printers and designers. You'll be amazed at the variety of colors available to you. Don't be embarrassed, however, to stick to the basic colors to begin with. They are usually the safest to work with. Your printer will usually have a Pantone book you can use while there. Pantone's address is on the sample book. Just write them and ask about obtaining your own copy.

If you don't want any surprises, ask to see samples of work your printer has done using different papers and inks. Most printers take great pride in their work and will be more than happy to share it with you.

Color Printing

Color brings an added dimension to any publication, whether it's as simple as a second color to help accent, unify, or dress out a publication, or as complete as full-color. To use color effectively, you should have a rudimentary understanding of how the different color processes operate.

Spot Color

Spot color is the placement of a second color (black—or whatever the primary inking color—being the *first*) in a publication. (Note that in printing, black is counted as a color.) Unless you're using a multicolor press, applying the second color means an additional press run. That translates to more ink, materials, handling, and press time and money.

In two-color printing, two sets of printing plates are made, one for each color run. Often, a designer will use the second color for the art and graphic highlights—such as dropped-initial letters—and use the black (or other first color) for the type. This also means that you have to create two originals, one for the black plate and one for the second color. This is not an easy process for most people and is usually left to a designer or printer. Check with your printer first and see what their requirements are for two-color printing.

Process Color

Process color or **four color** is used for reproducing full-color artwork or photography. This illusion of full color is accomplished by optically mixing the three primary colors—yellow, red (actually *magenta*) and blue (called *cyan*)—along with black. Four color plates are shot through a screen to reduce solid areas to printable, graduated dot patterns. Because each color is shot through a slightly different angle screen, the screened halftone of each blends through the overlaid dot patterns.

During printing, each color is applied separately, one plate at a time and one color atop the others. The quality of this four-color overprinting method largely depends upon the quality of the original work, the quality of the cameras, plates, and printing press used, and upon the skills and professionalism of those who operate the equipment. Process color is best left to your printer to handle for you. As always, ask in advance.

Binding

With binding, as with everything else, if you want to know what to expect, ask your printer, and seek out samples on your own. Basically, there are two types of binding: that used for relatively thin publications such as magazines and pamphlets, and that used for thicker publications such as books. We'll only discuss those most applicable to public relations output here.

Regardless of what you are binding, it will probably be organized into **signatures**. Signatures are groupings of pages printed on both sides, usually sixteen to a signature, but sometimes less, as long as they're in multiples of four (pages printed for binding are usually printed four to a two-sided sheet of paper).

After signatures have been collated, they may be bound. Among the most common bindings that public relations people are likely to use are **saddle stitching, perfect binding,** or **spiral binding** (see **Exhibit 11.2**). More traditional forms of binding, such as *case binding* (for hardcover books) are reserved for publications you want to last longer than you.

Most quick printers can do saddle stitching and spiral binding; however, only larger printers will be able to do perfect binding.

Exhibit 11.2—Common Binding Methods

Saddle stitching is a simple, inexpensive procedure that nests the signatures atop one another and drives two to three staples through the spine and cover of the publication. Magazines and annual reports are most often bound this way.

Stitching

Trimmed and glued signatures

Cover is glued to signatures

*Publications that are expected to receive a great deal of use and/or be around for a while are more likely to be perfect bound. In **perfect binding**, the backs of the collated signatures are trimmed or ground off and dense adhesive is applied. While it's still sticky, a bonding/lining is placed atop the adhesive and the cover is glued on. The adhesive maintains its flexible bonding strength for a long time. Most paperback books and some hardcover books are perfect bound. Hefty magazines and annual reports are sometimes bound this way as well.*

Spiral binding is not attractive, but it does have the benefit of opening flat. Any reference publication would benefit from spiral binding. Holes are drilled or punched through the gutter of the publication after the signatures have been collated and trimmed, and either wire or plastic is inserted or "spun" through the holes.

Trimmed signatures, hole-punched and spiral bound

Swipe Files

One of the best ways to tell your printer or typesetter what you want is to show them an example. A **swipe file** is a collection of your favorite pieces done by other people or companies. They will help you a great deal with design, layout ideas, and writing style, as well as with communicating your ideas to typesetters and printers. You may find a particular brochure, for instance, that is exactly the right size and design for the information piece you want to produce. You may decide to use similar paper, ink color, or even design. Most graphic artists, designers, and printers use ideas generated from a variety of sources. However, don't plagiarize your source. Don't steal the artwork right off the source brochure. Be careful to differentiate between emulation and plagiarism. If you do decide that you must "borrow" directly from another piece, obtain permission from its originator in advance of the publication of your piece.

Keep a swipe file of samples to show your typesetter and printer. If you find a piece that you would like to emulate, show it to the typesetter and printer to get an idea how much it will cost to produce. They can tell you what the type is, whether your copy will fit in that size, what the paper stock is, weight, color ink, and mechanical needs—all of which will affect the price. For the beginner, a sample is worth a ten-thousand word explanation.

Preparing Computer Layouts for Printing

The final stage of layout is the *mechanical*, the finished camera-ready layout that goes to the printer. The computer has revolutionized this process. If you are diligent, exact, and working with a limited range of graphics, you can present your printer with a mechanical in one piece—with no pasted-up parts. Computer imagesetters, such as the Linotronic, print out your layouts onto paper exactly as you have designed them, ready to be shot into printer's negatives. You can even go directly to negative film from an imagesetter, saving the cost of shooting negatives from a positive mechanical—but only if you are completely satisfied with your layout.

Assuming you are working in black and white, there are several ways to construct your mechanical.

1. You can have it run entirely off an imagesetter, either from your computer disks or through a network or telephone line hookup.

This requires that all of the elements on your mechanical be computer generated—word-processed text and display type; borders, boxes, and rules produced in your page-layout program; photos scanned, cropped, and sized in either a photo manipulation program—such as *Adobe PhotoShop*—or right in your layout program; illustrations created in a paint, draw, or illustration program and imported or placed in your layout program; and any color separations already performed by your software.

2. You can run the basic mechanical (text, display type, rules, and boxes) on an imagesetter and have photos and art shot separately and stripped into the negative before the printing plate is made. If you don't have a scanner or access to electronic clip art, this is probably the closest you'll get to having the whole thing done in one step. Even at this level, the savings in typesetting and pasteup alone are worth it.

3. You can run your mechanical on a laser printer at either of the above two levels (see **Exhibit 11.3**). This assumes you either don't have access to an imagesetter, or you don't feel that the extra quality is needed for your particular publication. Some very nice newsletters and brochures can be offset printed directly from laser-printed mechanicals. Most office-quality laser printers are capable of printing to plain paper at approximately 300 dots per inch (dpi) resolution. The difference to the trained eye (or anyone with a magnifying glass) is the type. It bleeds badly at larger point sizes and can even look fuzzy at smaller sizes. But if you're on a shoestring budget, this is a great compromise. Some of the newer laser printers print 600–800 dpi and make excellent mechanicals for phtocopying.

An imagesetter can print either to resin-coated paper positives or directly to right-reading film. Printing to film greatly enhances resolution, especially of scanned photographs, because it eliminates one step in the printing process—the shooting of negatives from camera-ready copy. When imagesetting directly to film, always ask for a proof prior to final printing.

Exhibit 11.3

A basic computer-printing configuration below shows a digital scanner for entering photographs and other artwork into a computer-readable format and the computer itself, linked to a laser printer and an imagesetter.

Scanner or other peripheral devices

Computer/CPU

Imagesetter

Laser printer

Laser copies on plain paper

Resin-coated (RC) paper positive

Film negative (right-reading)

CHAPTER 12

Public Relations Writing & the Computer

And now I see with eye serene
The very pulse of the machine.

Wordsworth

Every day in the United States, and around the world for that matter, hundreds of thousands of publications are created for and by organizations. These publications are aimed at a variety of audiences: employees, shareholders, members, volunteers, communities, and countless others, and come in dozens of shapes and sizes—newsletters, brochures, magazines, annual reports, pamphlets, booklets, posters, flyers, and direct mail pieces are just a few.

Anyone assuming the responsibilities of putting together a publication for an organization has quite a lot to learn. However, the availability of computer software and hardware designed specifically to augment that task has made the job, if not easy, at least manageable by a single person.

Probably the most revolutionary invention of the last century has been the computer. Scarcely fifty years ago, a computer able to do the simplest calculations took up an entire room. Today, even the most complex work can be done at your desk. When the microcomputer became commonplace only a very few years ago, life changed for millions of people. For the publishing industry, however, the most significant change followed invention of the hardware itself. The microcomputer changed the way we do nearly everything; page-layout software programs changed the way we think about and execute publications.

One of the earliest page-layout programs was *PageMaker*, invented by Paul Brainerd (now president of Aldus Corporation) and a handful of friends. Its original target audience was newspaper publishers. When that audience proved to be unreceptive, Brainerd turned to business. As it turned out, page-layout software revolutionized the way organizations thought about in-house publication. What once had to go through the traditional writing, editing, typesetting, pasteup, and printing processes could now be done in a few, simple steps.

What Is Desktop Publishing?

Although it took several long years for "desktop publishing" to catch on, it is now sweeping the country. The term **desktop publishing** is a bit of a misnomer because "publishing" involves much more than just the writing and laying out of a publication—which is all the software does. True publishing entails all the stages of printing and production, testing the product in its respective markets, creating a marketing and distribution plan, and the myriad other details that make publishing a complex and often risky business. What this software, and the increasingly sophisticated hardware, allow is the involvement of fewer intermediaries in the publication process.

As Paul Brainerd once quipped, "A desktop publishing program won't make you a designer." What the revolution in computer publishing has done is provide the writer, editor, and designer with another tool to better accomplish their respective jobs. Without the knowledge and experience gained through a study of the basics of writing, editing and design, however, even the best computer hardware and software won't help you.

The computer has made a tremendous difference. Word processing programs, once cumbersome and nearly impossible to work with, allow us to write, delete, move whole copy blocks, copy between files, index, outline, and do other tasks that once took hours and days to accomplish on a typewriter. The computer has allowed writers and editors to facilitate their work through the on-line interchange of information (or exchange of disks). Editors can now edit on screen, and the writer can watch—if he or she or he has the nerve. And the designer and artist can see their work come to life on the screen and have it delivered into their hands as fast as a laser printer can print. Working together, writers, editors, designers, and artists have made the most of this revolutionary tool.

Desktop Publishing and Public Relations

The greatest benefit of desktop publishing is that it allows you to control your own output, right down to the printing. Its greatest drawback is that it allows you to control your own output, right down to the printing. In other words, its greatest asset is its greatest deficit, and you are the deciding factor. Unless you become skilled at not only writing and editing but also layout and design, the complete benefits of desktop publishing may never be realized for you. But that's okay. What you really need to do is to realize exactly what you can do, what you are willing to learn to do, and how much you can afford to spend to get it all done. Remember, everybody has to begin somewhere, and, fortunately for us, there is a wealth of programming to fit every need.

We could spend a lot of time and space here learning about the latest software and hardware, but I've discovered very quickly that anything I write here will most certainly be outdated by the time you read it. My advice? Seek out a consultant. Almost every town and village has a computer "expert" around, either in the business of helping people understand computing, or simply willing to give free advice when asked.

Find yourself a reputable and knowledgeable consultant, and ask all the questions you can think of. Come prepared with a list of things you want to accomplish with a desktop publishing system, and be ready to learn about the many options available.

The Proof is in the Publication

Ultimately, your final, printed publication is going to determine how successful your desktop publishing system is—and a lot of that success depends not on your hardware and software, but on you.

You are the final ingredient in this system. Your energy, talent, interest, and organizational abilities will be the final determinant in the success or failure of your ads. Truthfully, you can get by on a lot less than you think you can if you possess the right attitude and the requisite abilities. Fancy hardware and expensive software only enhance and streamline a process you should already have down to a fine art.

The fact is that many excellent publications are still laid out the "old-fashioned" way. Nothing substitutes for being able to accomplish the task this way. Don't get the wrong idea—computers have made and are continuing to make a tremendous difference in publishing. Just remember—that multi-thousand dollar system you sit down in front of every day is only a tool. The system doesn't make you an artist, just as sitting in front of a typewriter doesn't make you a writer. Dedication, hard work, and talent do.

Take a hard look at your layouts and ask yourself a few questions:

- Are they already the best they can be without the addition of desktop publishing? If they are, you probably already know the basics and are ready for desktop publishing. If they're not, why not? Will the technology help the look or simply add to the clutter? Be honest. Don't expect desktop publishing to give you something you don't already possess.

- What, exactly, do you expect desktop publishing to add to your layouts or the process of developing them? Again, if you're looking for an answer to your design problems, check out your own abilities first. On the other hand, if you're expecting the technology to streamline the process and save you some money—it probably will.

- Will the savings you accrue be offset by the cost of the system? It takes a lot of savings in typesetting to counterbalance a $25,000 investment.

- Are you willing to take the time needed to make you an expert on your system? If you aren't willing to become an expert, you're wasting your money. Anyone can learn the basics (or just enough to cause trouble), but if you're serious about desktop publishing, you'd best dedicate yourself for the long haul. Be prepared to immerse yourself in the process, the programs, and the machinery. The more you know, the more streamlined the process becomes.

Above all, don't set yourself up for frustration. Realize the limitations of your system and of desktop publishing in general. Understand how it works and why it does what it does. You don't have to become a "computer nerd" to gain a fairly complete understanding of your hardware and software. The more you know, the less frustrated you'll be when something does go wrong. Most of the frustration of working with computers comes from not knowing what's happening in software or hardware problem situations. Keep those technical support hotline numbers close at hand and use them. Don't be afraid to ask questions, but read your manuals first so you'll know what to ask.

Finally, take it all with a grain of salt. Don't talk to your computer. You probably don't talk to your typewriter. They're both just tools of the trade. Misuse them, and your shortcomings will become apparent to everyone who looks at your work. Use them wisely, and they'll show off for you.

## CHAPTER 13

The Basics of Grammar

Let schoolmasters puzzle their brain,
with grammar, and nonsense, and learning;
good liquor, I stoutly maintain,
gives genius a better discerning.

Oliver Goldsmith

Writing is a technical skill as well as an art and, as such, it demands a thorough understanding of grammar. Unfortunately, most of us still have some rather uncomfortable memories of grammar lessons in either grade school or high school. Others believe that we can write intuitively, without any formal knowledge of grammar. This is a dangerous belief because it leads to a false sense of security and often a misunderstanding of the basic rules of grammar.

The simple fact is, those who know and understand grammar are better writers than those who don't. Obviously, no one wants to start at the beginning of a grammar text and wade all the way through it in order to gain a better understanding of how to use a comma. The following brief discussion of grammar is offered as a shortcut.

This is not a definitive text. It is merely a collection of helpful hints and a few rules of thumb that will serve to set you on the right track. The key, of course, is recognizing when you need help. As a public relations writer, you will never want for editors who point out your errors, even though some are no better at grammar than you are. It is in your best interest to learn the rules and use them. Writing without a knowledge of grammar is like falling into the water without a knowledge of swimming—in either case, your chances of surviving in the medium are slim.

Parts of Speech

The parts of speech are simply the categories in which words belong. Most words are classified in three ways:

- By their grammatical function (such as *subject*, *object*, etc.);
- By their grammatical form (such as the *s* form added to the end of plural nouns);
- By their meaning (such as the names of things as in the case of *nouns*, or statements of action as in the case of *verbs*).

No matter what category we place words in, some of them will end up as more than one *part of speech*. Take the word *place,* for instance.

> *As a noun*
> This advanced version of PSO-1 will certainly take the *place* of older compounds in plastics manufacturing.

> *As a verb*
> In a startling move, John Rivers, Mayor of Edmonton, has decided to *place* his hat in the ring for the governor's race.

> *As a modifier*
> *Place* settings of plastic spoons were totally inappropriate at the company picnic, considering that roast beef was being served.

Parts of speech are categorized according to what they do. The following groups represent the basic parts of speech in English.

Nouns

Nouns are words that name a person, place or thing. Subjects of sentences are usually nouns, as are objects of verbs and prepositions.

> Associated Products *Corporation* (APC) of *Syracuse, N.Y.* today announced a joint *venture* to educate American school *children* in the *uses* of *computers.*

Keep in mind that although most nouns form the plural by simply adding *s*, some, such as *sheep*, and *woman*, are irregular.

Pronouns

Pronouns substitute for nouns, but in order to understand exactly what noun a given pronoun is substituting for, we have to look for its antecedent, the preceding noun to which the pronoun refers.

> Tom said that *he* was going out for a while, but *he* left no
> forwarding address or indication when *he* would return.

In this sentence, it is clear that the pronoun *he* refers to the antecedent,
Tom.

Indefinite pronouns (*everybody, anybody, someone*) do not refer
to particular persons or things and therefore take no antecedent. These,
like *one* in the following sentence, refer to whoever takes the action.

> *One* would have to be a fool to come to work dressed for the
> weather outside when the air conditioner still insists it's
> winter.

Verbs

Verbs are action words, as we were told so many times in grade school; but
what they really do is make a statement about the subject of the sentence.
For public relations writers, choosing the right verb tense is important. For
instance, stating that the president of APC "has announced" an important
project has a different effect on readers than saying he "announced" an
important project. Both use a past tense form, but the first is more
immediate. The nuances are subtle, but they are definitely there.

The following tenses are the most common for regular verbs.

- **Present tenses** express actions that are happening now or that are
  habitual. The *simple present tense* might most commonly be used
  in print ad copy.

  > Associated Products Corporation *Announces* a Break-
  > through in Educational Software.

  The present progressive tense uses a *present participle* (the *-ing*
  form). This implies immediacy and is not generally used in press
  releases because it would imply the action is taking place right now.

  > James L. Sutton, a native of Deerborn and president of
  > Associated Products Corporation of Syracuse, New York,
  > *is announcing* the development of a new educational
  > software line as we speak.

- **Present perfect tense** indicates an action carried out before the
  present and completed in the present. It can also be used for an
  action that was begun in the past and continues in the present.

  > James L. Sutton, a native of Deerborn and president of
  > Associated Products Corporation of Syracuse, New York,
  > *has announced* the development of a new educational
  > software line.

This tense is the perfect choice for some press releases because it implies immediacy, yet ties the action to the past. It has the benefit of being nonspecific and doesn't call for the inclusion of a date.

- **Past tenses** express actions that took place in the past.

    > James L. Sutton, a native of Deerborn and president of Associated Products Corporation of Syracuse, New York, *announced* the development of a new educational software line at a two o'clock press conference today (May 25).

Again, note that the use of the past tense in this lead is followed by a specific time.

The **past perfect tense** expresses actions completed *before* other past actions occured. Compare the use of the past perfect and the simple past tense in this press release lead.

    > James L. Sutton, a native of Deerborn and president of Associated Products Corporation of Syracuse, New York, *had announced* the development of a new educational software line just before he *announced* his resignation from the company.

- **Future tenses** express an action that will occur in the future.

    > James L. Sutton, a native of Deerborn and president of Associated Products Corporation of Syracuse, New York, *will announce* the development of a new educational software line at a two o'clock press conference today (May 25).

A specific time is called for here, too.

The **future perfect tense** indicates actions that will be completed before a specified future time.

    > James L. Sutton, a native of Deerborn and president of Associated Products Corporation of Syracuse, New York, *will have announced* the development of a new educational software line before he resigns.

Obviously, some of these tenses are more common than others in public relations writing. The point, however, is that they each impart a special nuance to your writing and should be chosen with care.

Adjectives and Adverbs

Adjectives and **adverbs** are the modifiers. Adjectives modify nouns or words acting as nouns, and adverbs modify other adverbs, adjectives, verbs, and most other words. We will look in detail at these parts of speech later on.

Prepositions and Conjunctions

Prepositions and **conjunctions** are used to connect parts of a sentence. A *preposition* usually relates a noun, pronoun, or phrase to some other part of the sentence.

> The ancient cities *of* Sodom and Gomorrah have long since vanished *from* its shores. (*Cities* is related to *Sodom and Gomorrah*; *vanished* is related to *shores*.)

> Sitting *behind* a cluttered desk, boxes scattered *around* the office—some still unopened—is the new head of the Law Department. (*Sitting* is related to *desk*; *boxes* is related to *office*).

A **conjunction** is used to join words, phrases, or clauses together. In using conjunctions, never forget that these simple words carry meanings of their own as well as show relations between the sentence parts that they connect.

> The project is a joint effort of the National Education Association *and* Associated Products Corporation of Syracuse, New York. (*And* joins the *NEA* with *APC*.)

> The Lincoln High School graduate has been chief systems engineer since 1974, but he says the new project has given him a rare opportunity to work with designers outside the computer field. (*Since* links the first clause with a specific date; *but* joins two main clauses.)

Sentences and Clauses

Words are the basic unit of written English. Good writers string these units together to form coherent clauses, which in turn form complete sentences. The type (and therefore the complexity) of sentence we write depends on the type and combination of clauses we choose to make up the sentence.

Independent Clauses

Independent clauses, sometimes called **main clauses**, always have a subject and a verb and make a statement independent of the rest of the sentence. A sentence always has one independent clause, and sometimes it has more than one.

There are several frequently used words that serve to separate independent clauses. These are called **coordinating conjunctions**. The most common coordinating conjunctions are *and, but, so, for, yet, or, nor*. A comma is usually used before a coordinating conjunction separating independent clauses.

> A recent study shows that students between the ages of 7 and 14 have the ability to acquire computer skills readily, *yet* many school do not have computer teaching facilities.

> The program is designed to benefit a small segment of the public, *but* the public relations "fallout" will be apparent for years.

Conjunctive adverbs, like coordinating conjunctions, join complete clauses that are linked by a common idea. And, like coordinating conjunctions, they possess meanings of their own. Make sure that you are using the correct conjunctive adverb for your transition—one that indicates the relationship between the clauses. The most common conjunctive adverbs are:

accordingly	however
also	likewise
besides	moreover
consequently	nevertheless
else	otherwise
furthermore	then
hence	therefore

> The announcement came as a complete shock to those present; consequently, few questions were asked. (*Consequently* implies that the second clause is a result of the first.)

> There are many possible excuses for not getting to work on time; however, John chose to say he had been kidnapped by terrorists and was only released an hour ago. (*However* indicates that what happened in the second clause happened in spite of what happened in the first.)

Subordinate Clauses

Subordinate clauses, sometimes called dependent clauses, contain ideas that are less important than those in the independent clause. A subordinate clause relies on an independent clause for meaning, and is frequently introduced by a **subordinate conjunction** such as:

although	unless
as	until
because	when
how	where
though	whether

Subordinate clauses also act as parts of speech (adjectives, adverbs, nouns). The sentence must contain an independent clause or it will not be a complete sentence.

> When he arrived... (Subordinate clause, but not a sentence.)

> When he arrived, the meeting was already underway. (Subordinate clause followed by an independent clause, thus a sentence.)

> The meeting was already underway when he arrived. (Same here except that the subordinate clause is positioned last.)

Sentences are classified by the number of subordinate or main clauses they contain. The basic classifications are: **simple, compound, complex,** and **compound complex.**

A **simple sentence** has a single main clause.

> You can do something to help save the whales.

A **compound sentence** has two or more main clauses.

> You can do something to help save the whales, and you can earn money doing it.

A **complex sentence** has a main clause and one or more subordinate clauses.

> By doing something to help save the whales, you can also earn money.

A **compound-complex sentence** contains two or more main clauses and one or more subordinate clauses.

> If you do something to help save the whales, you can earn money and they can continue to live in peace.

Case

Case is used to indicate the function of nouns and pronouns in a sentence. For instance, in the sentence "He gave me a week's vacation," the *nominative* case form *he* indicates that the pronoun is being used as subject; the *objective* case form *me* shows that the pronoun is an object; the *possessive* form *week's* indicates that the noun is a possessive.

Personal pronouns (*I, you, he, she, it*) have different forms for the nominative, possessive, and objective cases. The following table will help clear up the differences.

Singular

	Nominative	Possessive	Objective
First Person	I	my, mine	me
Second Person	you	your, yours	you
Third Person	he, she, it	his, her, hers, its	him, her, it

Plural

First Person	we	our, ours	us
Second Person	you	your, yours	you
Third Person	they	their, theirs	them

Probably the most troublesome use of case involves the **relative pronoun** *who*. In both the singular and plural forms, *who* is the nominative case, *whose* is the possessive case, and *whom* is the objective case.

Nominative

Use the nominative case to indicate the subject of a verb. In formal English (which usually means anything you write short of a personal memo or note), try to adhere to the following rules.

1. Use the nominative case of the pronoun after the conjunctions *as* and *than* if the pronoun is the subject of an understood verb.

   > Hoffman obviously felt that they were better off than he (was). (*He* is the subject of the verb *was*, which is understood.

2. Use the nominative case for the subject of a clause even when the whole clause is the object of a verb or preposition. (Compare this rule to the use of the objective case discussed later.)

   > Sutton has stated that he will give a bonus to whoever accomplishes the task first. (*Whoever* is the subject of the verb *accomplishes* in the clause of which it is a part.)

3. Use the nominative case of the personal pronoun after forms of the verb *be* (*is*, *are*, *were*, *have been*). This is a tough rule to follow, however, because even good speakers these days tend to use less formal forms. In this instance, it is usually permissible to be more informal, especially when a contraction is involved. Let the expectations of your audience be your guide.

> *Formal:*
> It was I. I thought it was he. It was not we.
>
> *Informal:*
> It's me. I thought it was him. It wasn't us.

4. Use the nominative case following the infinitive *to be* when the infinitive has no expressed subject. Again, the informal form is commonly used instead.

> *Formal:*
> I would not want to be he.
>
> *Informal:*
> I would not want to be him.

Possessive

Most nouns have a common form that is changed to show possessive by simply adding *'s*, as in *worker/worker's*. In the possessive case, *'s* should be used with nouns that are animate objects. For inanimate objects, use the *of* construction.

> Sutton's leadership has inspired a number of workers in their creative endeavors.
>
> The value of the dollar has increased dramatically over the past month.

Objective

The objective case is particularly troublesome for some writers. Following a few basic rules should iron out the difficulties.

1. Use the objective case for the object of a verb, verbal (gerunds and participles), or preposition.

> *Whom* did you see about the irregularity in your typewriter? (*Whom* is the object of the verb *see.*)
>
> I saw *him.* (*Him* is the object of the verb *saw.*)
>
> Visiting *them* was the highlight of the convention. (*Them* is the object of the gerund *visiting.*)

Two of *us* were reprimanded for being late this morning. (*Us* is the object of the preposition *of*.)

Whom does he want to nominate for president? (*Whom* is the object of the infinitive *to nominate*.)

As a contrast, consider this sentence:

Who do you suppose convinced him to run? (*Who* is the subject of the verb *convinced*, which has the object, *him*.)

2. In formal English, *whom* is always used in the objective case; however, informal English permits the use of *who*. We have become so used to using who, it is now difficult to switch to *whom* in formal writing. Again, think of the expectations of your audience.

Formal:
Whom are you seeing this morning?

Informal:
Who are you seeing this morning?

3. One of the more confusing constructions is the use of the objective case after the conjunction *and*.

They found Sheila and me locked in an embarrassing grip behind the filing cabinet. (Not *Sheila and I. Me* is the object of the verb *found*.)

You must choose between him and me. (Not *he and I. Him* and *me* are objects of the preposition *between*.)

4. After the conjunctions *than* and *as*, use the objective case only if it is the object of an understood verb.

This company needs him more than me.

By using the objective case, the sentence is understood to mean "This company needs him more than it needs me." If we were to use the nominative case, the meaning of the sentence would be altered:

"This company needs him more than I (need him)."

Adjectives and Adverbs

Adjectives and **adverbs** are words that qualify meanings. Without them, descriptive writing would be impossible. Consider the following sentence:

> Sutton is a *neat* and *energetic* man who speaks *glowingly* of his *latest* project.

Remove the adjectives and adverbs and you are left with:

> Sutton is a man who speaks of his project.

The key to the proper use of adjectives and adverbs in PR writing is to avoid overusing them. The more adjectives and adverbs you use, the less credible your writing becomes.

> Sutton is an excruciatingly neat man who speaks in absolutely glowing terms of his latest project.

Adjectives are words that modify nouns or noun substitutes. Never use an adjective to modify a verb, another adjective, or an adverb.

> *Wrong:*
> She was terrible upset when he spilled coffee on her new dress. (*Terrible* is an adjective and thus cannot modify *was upset.*)

> *Right:*
> She was terribly upset when he spilled coffee on her new dress. (*Terribly* is an adverb.)

> She jumped very quickly to her feet when he spilled the coffee. (*Very* is an adverb modifying the adverb *quickly.*)

There are two basic types of adjectives: **descriptive** and **limiting**. **Descriptive adjectives** name some quality of an object, such as a *white* house; a *small* car; or a *worn* carpet.

Limiting adjectives restrict the meaning of a noun to a particular object or indicate quantity. There are five kinds of limiting adjectives:

> *Possessive: My* suit; *their* office

> *Demonstrative: This* suit; *that* office

> *Interrogative: Whose* suit? *Which* office?

> *Articles: A* suit; *an* office; *the* office

> *Numerical: One* suit; *second* office

Nouns as Adjectives

Sometimes a noun can be used as an adjective, but it is advisable to avoid this use, other than in such commonplace uses as *horse* race, *theater* tickets, *show* business.

And, make sure that you are using the proper form of a noun when you intend it as an adjective:

Wrong:
The Taiwan plant opened on schedule in October.

Right:
The Taiwanese plant opened on schedule in October.

Linking Verbs

One of the most confusing areas of adjective/adverb usage comes when we have to deal with linking verbs. *Linking verbs* connect the subject of the sentence with the subject complement (the word that modifies the subject).

The most common linking verbs are *be, become, appear,* and *seem.* Others pertain to the senses, such as *look, smell, taste, sound,* and *feel.* Modifiers that follow linking verbs refer back to the subject and should be in the form of an adjective and not an adverb.

> Joan looks pretty today. (*Pretty* modifies *Joan.*) Joan looks great, but she smells bad. (*Great* and *bad* both refer to *Joan.*)

One of the most common errors is "I feel badly" in place of the correct form, "I feel bad."

> *Wrong:*
> I felt badly about the loss of your mother.

> *Right:*
> I felt bad about the loss of your mother.

The selection of an adjective or adverb as a modifier will alter the meaning of your sentence. Use an adverb after the verb if the modifier describes the manner of the action of the verb.

> The man looked suspiciously at her. (The adverb *suspiciously* modifies the verb *looked.*)

> The man looked suspicious. (The adjective *suspicious* modifies the subject *man.*)

In the first example, the verb *looked* expresses action and must be modified by an adverb. But in constructions like "He looks tired" or "He feels well," the verbs serve, not as words of action, but as links between the subject and the adjective.

The choice of an adjective or an adverb thus depends on whether or not the verb is being used as a linking verb. Ask yourself whether you want to modify the subject or the verb. And, be careful not to alter the meaning of your sentence.

Degree or Quantity

Adjectives and adverbs also show degree or quantity by means of their **positive**, **comparative**, and **superlative** forms.

- The **positive** form expresses no comparison at all: *slow, quickly.*

- The **comparative** form permits a comparison between two (and only two) nouns by adding *-er* or the adverb *more* to the positive form of the word: *pretty, prettier; rapid, more rapid.*

- The **superlative** form involves a comparison between three or more nouns by adding *-est* or the adverb *most* to the positive form: *pretty, prettiest; rapid, most rapid.*

As a rule of thumb, most adjectives and a few one-syllable adverbs form the comparative and superlative forms with *-er* and *-est.* Two-syllable adjectives often offer a choice, as in *lovelier, loveliest* and *more lovely, most lovely.* Adjectives and adverbs of three or more syllables usually use *more* and *most* (*more assiduous*, not *assiduouser*).

Some adjectives and adverbs are absolute in their meaning and can have no comparison. These are words like *final, unique, empty, dead,* and *perfect.* However, you may imply that something is *not quite empty* or *not quite perfect* by using the adverb *nearly.* (This letter is *more nearly* perfect than the other.)

Agreement

Subject/Verb

What's wrong with the following lead?

> The National Education Association (NEA), in cooperation with the Associated Products Corporation (APC), are co-sponsoring a program that is designed to educate school children with computers.

The verb *are cosponsoring* doesn't agree with the subject, the *National Education Association.* The problem is that the writers have mistakenly assumed a *compound subject,* which normally requires a plural verb form. In this sentence, *Associated Products Corporation* is the object of the prepositional phrase *in cooperation with.* A singular subject requires a singular verb and a plural subject requires a plural verb.

The following types of constructions often cause trouble in subject-verb agreement.

1. When words or phrases come between the subject and the verb, the verb agrees with the subject of the sentence, not with the noun in the intervening expression.

   Wrong:
   The first two hours of the day was boring.

   Right:
   The first two hours of the day were boring.

2. When a sentence has a singular pronoun, the singular pronoun takes a singular verb.

   Wrong:
   Everyone involved in the transfer think that APC made the right move.

   Right:
   Everyone involved in the transfer thinks that APC made the right move.

3. A sentence that has two or more subjects joined by *and* always uses a plural verb.

   Wrong:
   Both the IRS and Associated Products considers the agreement fair.

   Right:
   Both the IRS and Associated Products consider the agreement fair.

   However, when the parts of the subject refer to the same thing, the verb form is singular.

   Right:
   His editor and friend recommends that he pursue a career other than writing. (Assumes that the editor and friend are the same person.)

   Right:
   His editor and friend recommend that he pursue a career other than writing. (Assumes that the editor and friend are two different people.)

   Right:
   My husband and lover was there to help me.

   Wrong:
   My husband and lover were there to help me. (Unless, of course, they are two different people.)

4. In a sentence that has two or more subjects joined by *or* or *nor,* a verb agrees with the subject nearest it.

Wrong:
Neither the board members nor the CEO were there.

Right:
Neither the board members nor the CEO was there.

5. In a sentence with a *collective* noun (*assembly, committee, jury, mob, herd*) a singular verb should be used to indicate that individual members of the group are acting collectively.

The *committee* has reached a consensus.

If you wish to indicate the individual actions of a collective group, use an additional noun.

The committee *members* have returned to their offices.

6. In a sentence with a *predicate noun* (one that usually follows the verb but says something about the subject) the verb agrees with its subject, not the predicate noun.

Wrong:
Status and pay is reason enough for most corporate climbers.

Right:
Status and pay are reason enough for most corporate climbers. (*reason* is the predicate noun.)

Antecedents

An **antecedent** is a word or group of words referred to by a following pronoun. The following general rules apply to the selection of proper pronouns for agreement.

1. Use a singular pronoun to refer to antecedents such as:

any	man
anybody	neither
anyone	one
each	person
either	somebody
every	someone
everybody	woman
everyone	

Everybody held *his* breath as the ball dropped signifying the new year had begun.

Each of the participants brought *his* own expertise to bear on the problem.

The problem with sentences such as this is that the use of *he* as a pronoun will probably be construed as sexist. The use of *he* or *his* to denote a group of unspecified gender composition is a delicate one. There are basically three ways to avoid this most common use of sexist language. One is to use a *he or she, him or her* construction.

> A PR person can get ahead if he or she works hard.

Another is to recast the sentence in the plural, making sure the pronoun is also plural.

> PR people can get ahead if they work hard.

The most common mistake made in this construction is to leave the singular noun antecedent while changing the pronoun to a plural.

> A PR person can get ahead if they work hard.

Finally, the pronoun can be deleted altogether.

> A PR person can get ahead by hard work.

2. With a collective noun as an antecedent, use a singular pronoun if you are considering the group as a unit. If you are considering the individual members of the group separately, add another noun to indicate individual actions.

> The *committee* has finished its work for the day.
>
> The committee *members* have decided to finish their work for the day.

3. If two or more antecedents are joined by *and*, use a plural pronoun to refer to them. If two or more singular antecedents are joined by *or* or *nor*, use a singular pronoun to refer to them. If one of two antecedents joined by *or* or *nor* is singular and one plural, make the pronoun agree with the nearer.

> Jack and Jim have finished their work.
>
> Neither Jack nor Jim has finished his work.
>
> Neither the department head nor the secretaries have finished their work.

Faulty Pronoun References

Faulty references of pronouns frequently present problems. The answer is to avoid sentences in which there are two possible antecedents for a single pronoun.

Unclear:
Jack told Carl that he was ungrateful. (Is *he* Jack or Carl?)

Clear:
Jack said to Carl, "You are ungrateful."

Clear:
Jack confessed to Carl that he was ungrateful.

Also avoid the indefinite use of *they*, *you*, and *it*.

Informal:
In smaller offices, they do not have great problems of communication.

Formal:
In smaller offices, the problems of communication are not great.

Informal:
In some states you are not permitted to walk against traffic.

Formal:
Some states do not permit pedestrians to walk against traffic.

Informal:
It says in the newspaper that Monday will be warmer.

Formal:
The newspaper says that Monday will be warmer.

Dangling Constructions

A **dangling construction** is one in which the second clause in a sentence does not logically modify anything in the first, although it seems to at first glance. Most people will, however, understand the sentence despite the dangling construction.

Two of the most common types of modifiers are **participles** and **gerunds**. These parts of speech are called **verbals** and are words that are derived from verbs but are normally used as nouns or adjectives. Verbals often cause trouble because they look like verbs; however, they can act only as modifiers or as nouns. They can never, by themselves, transmit action.

A **participle** is the form of a verb that ends in *-ing* in the present form and in *-ed* or *-en* in the past form. A participle can act as an adjective.

> Perspiring heavily, the man ran wild-eyed into the oncoming truck. (*Perspiring* is an adjective modifying *man*.)

When using participles as adjectives, make sure that they relate to a noun or a noun substitute; otherwise, there is nothing to modify and a dangling construction results.

> *Dangling participle:*
> While hunting in the woods, several deer were shot. (This means, literally, that several deer were hunting in the woods.)
>
> *Corrected version:*
> While hunting in the woods, we shot several deer.
>
> *Dangling participle:*
> The afternoon passed quietly, watching the words on the screen of the word processor scroll slowly by. (This means, literally, that the afternoon watched the word processor.)
>
> *Corrected version:*
> She passed the afternoon quietly, watching the words on the screen of her word processor scroll slowly by.

A **gerund** is the form of a verb that ends in *-ing*. The gerund is always used as a noun.

> Taking your medicine is better than avoiding the consequences of your acts. (*Taking* is a noun and the subject of the sentence.)

One of the most common problems with verbals is that we often think we are using a gerund (as a noun and therefore as the subject of a sentence) when we are really using a participle (which requires a subject).

> *Gerund as subject:*
> Reading a good novel is a thoroughly engrossing experience.
>
> *Dangling participle:*
> Reading a good novel, time passed quickly. (This means that time was reading the novel.)
>
> *Corrected version using a participle:*
> While reading a good novel, Tom didn't realize that time was passing so quickly. (*Reading* modifies *Tom.*)

Corrected version using a gerund:
Reading a good novel causes time to pass quickly. (The subject of the sentence is *reading a good novel.*)

Parallel Structure

Another common problem for writers is handling **parallel structure** correctly. In a sentence that has parallel structure, each of the phrases and clauses is structured in the same way. This helps keep the meaning of sentences clear.

Notice the correct use of parallel structure when the elements in a sentence are joined by a coordinating conjunction.

Wrong:
Bob likes working late and to take charge of everything.

Right:
Bob likes working late and taking charge of everything.

Or:
Bob likes to work late and to take charge of everything.

Wrong:
Ginny is bright, with a quick wit, and has a college degree.

Right:
Ginny is bright, shows a quick wit and has a college degree.

Or:
Ginny is bright, with a quick wit and a college degree.

In sentences that make comparisons, parallel structure is sometimes difficult to achieve. Make sure that you complete *all* comparisons. This often can be done simply by repeating a word or two.

Wrong:
He is as pernicious, if not more pernicious, than I am.

Right:
He is as pernicious as, if not more pernicious than, I am.

If you read the first sentence without the parenthetical comparison, you'll see that it doesn't make much sense.

He is as pernicious than I am.

Now read the corrected version the same way.

He is as pernicious as I am.

Another common mistake is to leave out one of the terms of the comparison. This can alter the meaning of a sentence.

Wrong:
I admire her more than Jane.

Right:
I admire her more than Jane does.

Or:
I admire her more than I admire Jane.

In some sentences, the meaning may be drastically altered by omitting a necessary word.

> Mr. Grant helps around the office by filing and making coffee. (Does Mr. Grant file coffee?)

> Mr. Grant helps around the office by filing and *by* making coffee.

Difficulties also arise in sentences that use *and/who* or *and/which* clauses.

Wrong:
They bumped into Marge at the top of the stairs, an unlit passageway at best and which is dangerous at worst.

Right:
They bumped into Marge at the top of the stairs, which is an unlit passageway at best and which is dangerous at worst.

The second *which* can be left out as long as the first is present. Another option might be:

> They bumped into Marge at the top of the stairs—an unlit passageway at best, and dangerous at worst.

The **correlatives** *either/or, neither/nor, not only/but also, both/and*, and *whether/or* require parallel constructions.

Wrong:
You are either late or I am early. (This makes the adjective *late* parallel with the clause *I am early.*)

Right:
Either you are late or I am early. (Now we have two parallel clauses.)

Wrong:
Philbert not only has been understanding to his secretary, but also to his wife. (A verb parallel with a preposition.)

Right:
Philbert has been understanding not only to his secretary, but also to his wife. (Two parallel phrases.)

Larger elements also need to be parallel. This is especially important in writing where lists or "bulleted" items are used. It is necessary
that all items in a series be kept parallel. Note the following problems
with parallel structure.

> In using the following program, we have set certain long-
> range objectives. These include:
> * Informing children of the voting process.
> * Increasing voter participation in the future.
> * Increasing voter understanding in the future in the home
>   as well as in the classroom.
> * Promote patriotism by having people become involved in
>   the U.S. government.
> * Promote teaching of the governmental processes in
>   schools and in the home.

The problem is that the first three items begin with gerunds and the last
two begin with verbs. Change the last two to gerund forms (*promoting*)
and the structure is parallel.

> General Goals:
> * Gear programs to specified target audiences.
> * Program elements to be evaluated.
> * Design a program that is easy to use and understand and
>   is interesting.
> * Testing of all elements by target audiences.

The problem here is that two of the items begin with verbs, one begins
with a gerund, and one begins with a noun. To correct this structure, the
second item should read, "*Evaluate* program elements," and the fourth
item should read, "*Test* all elements by target audience."

> Some notable economic/financial highlights of 1983 were:
> * Increased GNP of approximately 6.2% (fourth quarter to
>   fourth quarter)
> * A drop in unemployment from 10% to 8.2% by year-end
>   —Inflation (C.P.I.) of approximately 4.0% (December to
>   December)
> * Corporate profits up approximately 15% on average and
>   still rising
> * A strong U.S. dollar.

By converting each of the items to a phrase beginning with a noun, we
would achieve parallel structure. Thus:

> * An increased GNP...
> * A drop in unemployment...
> * A rise in corporate profits...
> * A strong U.S. dollar

Related to parallel structure is the problem of *mixed construction.* The most common error results from shifting from one verb tense to another or from one "person" or "voice" to another in pronoun references.

Mixed:
My secretary told me she *would* have the letter for me as soon as she *can* get to the word processor.

Fixed:
My secretary told me she *would* have the letter for me as soon as she *could* get to the word processor. (or *will/can.*)

Mixed:
People are always making mistakes. *You* could avoid most of them by thinking before *you* act.

Fixed:
We are always making mistakes. *We* could avoid most of them by thinking before *we* act.

Mixed:
A *man* (or male of the species) *is* a complex being, and *he is* quite territorial. *They are* constantly on the alert for competitors.

Fixed:
A *man* (or male of the species) *is* a complex being, and *he is* quite territorial. *He is* constantly on the alert for competitors.

Punctuation

Internal punctuation is possibly the most complex area of grammar because it is so open to interpretation.

Internal punctuation marks indicate the relationship of elements within a sentence. In English, five punctuation marks are used for this purpose: **commas, semicolons, colons, dashes,** and **parentheses.** Using these marks correctly requires adherence to certain rules. The only options are those that allow the writer nuances in meaning. For example, consider this unpunctuated sentence:

Woman without her man is an animal.

Now, place two commas setting off *without her man* as a parenthetical element and you have:

Woman, without her man, is an animal.

Place a period setting off *woman* as a statement, make *without her* an introductory phrase, and you have:

Woman. Without her, man is an animal.

As you can see, punctuation is important to meaning. How well we punctuate may mean the difference between being understood and being misunderstood.

Commas

The simplest reason for using a comma is to indicate a pause. Commas are most commonly used to separate independent clauses joined by a coordinating conjunction.

I was tied up all morning with work, and I had a meeting just before lunch.

Marvin could not make it to the ten o'clock meeting, but he sent his secretary to take notes.

The only exception to this rule is when one or both of the clauses are very short.

Just ask me and I'll go.

If in doubt—use a comma. It is better to use punctuation than leave it out and possibly cause confusion.

Don't mistake a compound *subject* for a compound *sentence*, however. A compound subject does not require a comma.

Both the obnoxious tasting potato salad and the equally horrible hot dogs were provided by the company food service crew.

Commas are used to separate introductory clauses and phrases from a main clause.

When he saw the approaching storm, he quickly ran to the cellar and locked himself in.

In an office of so many functions, she remains functionless.

The comma may be omitted, however, after very short introductory clauses or phrases unless this omission may lead to misunderstanding, as in the following examples.

Unclear:
After dark streets in the poorer section of town begin to empty.

Clear:
After dark, streets in the poorer section of town begin to empty.

Unclear:
When you return gifts will be waiting for you under the tree.

Clear:
When you return, gifts will be waiting for you under the tree.

Commas are used to set off transitional expressions such as *for example*, *on the other hand*, *in fact*, or *second*. Normally, these occur at the beginning of the sentence and are followed by a comma.

In fact, Jones was so intoxicated that he couldn't even sign his name.

For example, the number of schools receiving aid under the new computer loan program has doubled in the past six months.

Commas also separate items in a series (usually called a **coordinate series**).

Eudora spoke haltingly, quietly, and quickly.

The woods are quiet, dark, and deep.

It is a dark, dank, foreboding place to work.

There is an option in this case. Many people always include the final comma after the *and* in a coordinate series (called the **serial comma**). Others always leave it out. It's up to you, of course, but remember to leave it in if there is any chance of confusion.

Perry used his windfall to purchase a number of new items including an automobile, a new television, some antique books and furniture. (Was the furniture antique too?— insert a comma.)

Remember to group items joined by *and* and separate these groupings by commas.

Perry used his windfall to purchase a number of new items including an automobile and tires, a new television and VCR combination, and a remodeled sailboat.

Use a comma to separate **coordinate adjectives** (adjectives that all modify the same noun). A good rule of thumb is, if you can insert *and* between the adjectives without altering the meaning, use commas.

He sat behind a large, black, metal desk and smiled his best Cheshire Cat smile. (All adjectives modify desk. Removing the comma after *black* would make *black* modify *metal*. The difference may be subtle, but it is there.)

All coordinate adjectives refer to the noun they precede. If one or more of the adjectives refers to another adjective in the series, don't separate it from the adjective to which it refers with a comma.

> It was a dark red house. (The house wasn't dark. It was a dark shade of red.)

Set off **nonrestrictive elements** with commas. Do not set off **restrictive elements** with commas. A nonrestrictive element is a word or group of words that is a supplement to, rather than an integral part of, the basic word or group of words it modifies. If the word or phrase can be omitted without changing the meaning of the sentence, it is nonrestrictive and must be set off by punctuation. If the word or phrase cannot be omitted without impairing the sense of the sentence, it is restrictive and must not be set off.

> Bank employees, who are highly paid, can afford vacations to the Virgin Islands. (Here, *who are highly paid* applies to all bank employees and is therefore nonrestrictive.)

> Bank employees who are highly paid can afford vacations to the Virgin Islands. (Here, *who are highly paid* applies only to some bank employees and is therefore restrictive.)

It's appropriate here to mention two words—*that* and *which*— that often cause some confusion. The key to understanding exactly when each should be used is knowing whether they represent a restrictive or nonrestrictive element within the sentence. *That* is the restrictive or defining pronoun, and *which* is the nonrestrictive or nondefining pronoun.

> The copier *that* is broken is on the third floor. (Indicates which copier we are talking about.)

> The copier, *which* is broken, is on the third floor. (Indicates some additional information about the copier in question.)

A good rule of thumb is, if the phrase can be set of with a comma without changing meaning, use *which*.

When speaking of people, always use *who*.

> That crowd from the Marketing Department, *who* are on the third floor, just barricaded themselves in the lounge. (*Who* refers to the people from marketing who are forming this particular crowd, not the entire department.)

> That crowd from the Marketing Department, *which* is on the third floor, just barricaded themselves in the lounge. (*Which* refers to the whole department.)

> That crowd from the Marketing Department *that* is on the third floor just barricaded themselves in the lounge. (Refers to a specific Marketing Department among several.)

Semicolons

Semicolons are normally used as substitutes for commas when a relationship exists between two clauses yet the ideas are strong enough to appear almost as separate sentences. Semicolons can be used in place of commas when separating main clauses joined by a coordinating conjunction, especially when the clauses already contain commas.

> Joan, the best secretary in the office, won the secretary of the month award; but Anne, Becky, and Ruth were all given honorable mentions.

Semicolons should also be used to separate main clauses not joined by a coordinating conjunction, especially if the two clauses show a strong relationship of ideas.

> Fred is a total nerd; every day he proves it more.

Never join sentence elements of unequal grammatical rank with a semicolon. Always make sure both clauses are main clauses.

> *Wrong:*
> Fred is a total nerd; although he is sincere.
>
> *Right:*
> Although he is sincere, Fred is a total nerd.

Use a semicolon to separate main clauses joined by a conjunctive adverb.

> John was late for work this morning; however, he brought doughnuts.
>
> Dr. Howard has published several works over the past ten years; therefore, he is considered an authority.

Colons

Colons are overused in most writing. The colon is most appropriately used to separate two main clauses, the second of which amplifies the first.

> On the door of the men's room was posted a sign: Off limits due to bi-functional overload.

Note that the first word of a complete sentence following a colon may be capitalized or not—one of the few options in the correct use of grammar. The most common use of the colon is as a means of introducing a list.

> Sales of the "Gaftex" plastic elbow have increased as follows:
> * 20% in January
> * 30% in May
> * 10% in July.

A colon should not be used, however, to introduce a list that is an object of an element in the introductory statement.

> A number of new applications have been discovered, including automotive, industrial, aerospace, refined foods, and retail sales.

Dashes and Parentheses

Dashes and parentheses are used in place of commas to either add or subtract emphasis. They are used to set off parenthetical expressions that abruptly interrupt the structure of the sentence. The choice of which marks to use is entirely up to you. Most writers, however, use dashes to set off statements that they wish to emphasize, and parentheses to set off less emphatic statements.

> *Emphatic:*
> The bottom line—as the boss often said—is the bottom line.

> *Less Emphatic:*
> The bottom line (as the boss often said) is the bottom line.

> *No Emphasis:*
> The bottom line, as the boss often said, is the bottom line.

Dashes can also be used to prevent confusion when commas might lead to a misreading.

> *Confusing:*
> Two women, Jane and Myrna, run the entire department from the confines of a small office on the third floor. (This could be misread [and there is always someone who will misread it] to mean four women— two unnamed and Jane and Myrna.)

> *Clear:*
> Two women—Jane and Myrna—run the entire department from the confines of a small office on the third floor.

When using parentheses, make sure to include any punctuation that normally would be used in the sentence without parentheses.

> Because she went to lunch early (nine o'clock), she was docked one hour's pay.

If the matter within parentheses is a complete sentence, place a period within the parentheses.

> Whatever the reason, Fred chose not to attend. (He frequently pulls this maneuver.)

Don't confuse brackets with parentheses. Brackets are used to set off editorial corrections or explanations within quoted matter. They are sometimes necessary (but only rarely) to set off another item from an item already set off by parentheses.

> The letter opened, "Dear Fiends [sic] and Romans."

> He [the manager of public relations] spoke at great length and with something less than aplomb.

> The bottom line (as the boss [Mervin Smirks] often said) is the bottom line.

Quotation Marks

Quotation marks are almost always properly used. What are misused are the punctuation marks placed either inside or outside the quotation marks. In the United States, internal punctuation, such as commas, is placed inside the quotation marks.

> "There is no use in working today," he said.

Periods are also placed inside quotation marks.

> According to Tom, "Work is the only true medicine for depression."

Colons and semicolons should be placed outside the quotation marks.

> According to Tom, "Work is the only true medicine for depression"; however, Tom is frequently wrong.

Place a dash, question mark, or exclamation point inside the marks when it applies only to the quotation. Place it outside the quotation marks when it applies to the whole statement.

> He said, "Will I see you tomorrow?"

> Did he say, "I'll see you tomorrow"?

Do not to place a punctuation mark after the quotation marks if another punctuation mark has been used inside the quotation marks.

> The program, entitled "Johnny can learn to read!" will be available to most of the country this fall.

Normally, you would be required to put a second comma setting off the parenthetical element; but, in this case, that would leave you with three punctuation marks. The comma can be eliminated without disturbing the message.

Apostrophe

The apostrophe is used to denote several different things. For example, use an apostrophe to indicate the omission of letters or numbers.

> can't
> the summer of '42

Use an apostrophe to form the plurals of letters, numbers, and words used as words.

> Cross your *t*'s and dot your *i*'s.
> Count to 10,000 by 2's.
> Don't use so many *and*'s when you write.

Don't use an apostrophe before the *s* indicating decades.

> 1960s
> 1980s
> the '90s

Use an apostrophe to indicate the possessive form of a word. Place it before the *s* in the singular form and after the *s* in the plural form.

> The boss's desk was absolutely spotless. (Only one boss.)
> The bosses' desks were absolutely spotless. (Many bosses.)

Hyphen

The hyphen is a useful punctuator, but is often confused with the dash when typed on a typewriter. (Most computers have both a dash and a hyphen.) On a typewriter, two hyphens (--) equal one dash (—).

Use a hyphen for compound words that are not yet accepted as single words. Many of the words we accept today as being single, unhyphenated words started as two separate words, and then became compound words joined by a hyphen.

> base ball > base-ball > baseball

The only accurate way to determine whether a word is hyphenated or not is to check a recent edition of a dictionary.

Use a hyphen to join two or more words that act as a single adjective before a noun. Don't hyphenate two adjectives if they follow the verb.

> Arthur is a well-known philanthropist, which is amazing considering that he only makes $10,000 a year.

> That Arthur is a philanthropist is well known.

Omit the hyphen when the first word is an adverb ending in -*ly*.

> He managed to glue the entire typewriter back together using quick-drying cement.

> He managed to glue the entire typewriter back together using quickly drying cement.

Use a hyphen to form compound numbers from 21 through 99 and to separate fractions.

> twenty-nine
> two-thirds

Use a hyphen with the prefixes *self, all, ex,* and the suffix *elect.*

> self-important
> all-conference
> ex-mayor
> president-elect

And use a hyphen to avoid ambiguous or awkward combinations of letters.

> *belllike* should be *bell-like*
> *recreate* means to enjoy leisure time; *re-create* means to create anew.

Mechanics

There are several areas we haven't touched on yet that serve to complete this discussion of grammar. They are the use of italics, capitalization, and numbers.

Italics

Italics are a tricky business for the public relations writer. When writing news releases, for instance, the PR writer has to act as, and follow the guidelines of, a journalist. According to the *Associated Press Style*

Book and Libel Manual, for instance, there are several rules for using italics (or underlining, which is the typist's substitute for italics).

For example, AP style does not allow for italics for the titles of books, records, and newspapers. It would have you place these in quotation marks. *The New York Times* thus becomes "The New York Times." And, for magazines, *Newsweek* would become, simply, "Newsweek."

Now, AP style is anything but consistent and is intended largely for journalists and, as public relations writers, there are times when we have to write in acceptable journalistic style. However, most PR writers probably spend as much, or more, time writing copy for items that will be printed (house magazines, newsletters, brochures, etc.) as they do writing releases for the print media. As any typesetter will tell you, anything that is to be set in italics is so designated by the copywriter by underlining. In the long run, it will probably be to your benefit to become familiar with both AP style and accepted standard usage for italics. It will undoubtedly save you and your typesetter some problems later on.

The following rules, therefore, reflect standard English grammar usage—not AP style—for italics and use of quotation marks for publications.

- Use italic (underlining) to indicate the titles of entire publications.

  The New York Times
  Time magazine (The entire name of the magazine is *Time*, not *Time Magazine*.)

  The Sun Also Rises (Note that the movie version of this book would also be set in italics.)

- Use quotation marks to indicate a chapter from a book, an article in a newspaper or magazine, or a cut from a record album (the title would be in italics as it is a complete publication).

  The article "I Was a Teenage Corporate Executive" appeared in the June issue of *Forbes*.

  Billy Joel has had several number one hits, including "Keeping the Faith" from his album *Innocent Man*.

- Italicize letters, words, and numbers used as words.

  Your *r*'s look very much like your *n*'s.

  When you use the word *dedicated*, exactly what do you mean?

- Use italic to add stress or emphasis to certain words, but don't overuse it.

    I was speaking of *your* bad habits, not mine.

Capitalization

Capitalization is tricky unless you adhere to some basic rules of thumb. First of all, capitalize proper nouns and common nouns used as proper nouns.

1. Specific persons, races, and nationalities:

    William, Mary, American, Asiatic

2. Specific places:

    Dallas, Iran, Peoria

3. Specific organizations, historical events, and documents:

    Democratic National Committee
    Taft-Hartley Act
    Civil War
    NAACP

4. Titles when they precede a proper noun:

    Professor Wilson
    Dr. James Arlington
    President George Bush

    When titles follow the name, capitalize them only if they represent a title and not a job description.

    John Smith, President, Bank of the North

    John Smith, the president of the Bank of the North, was conspicuously absent from the meeting.

5. Common nouns when used as an essential part of a proper noun.

    University of Delaware (Not in "The university was overrun with bigots.")

    General Motors Corporation (Not in "The corporation stands to lose millions this year.")

6. An exception is usually made for state and federal governments.

    The state encompasses some three-million square miles. (Speaking of the state as a land mass.)

The State refused to reinstate voting rights to over 400 criminals. (Speaking of the government.)

The Federal Government ran roughshod over the territory for over 40 years.

7. Capitalize geographic locations when they refer to the locations themselves and not to a compass direction.

The Northeast is seriously overcrowded yet maintains a vast amount of virgin forest.

If you travel northeast from here, you are bound to come to a fast food restaurant.

Numbers

Numbers are a sticky subject. Different style and grammar books approach numbers in a variety of ways. Probably the best method to use is laid out in *The Associated Press Style Guide*. What follows is a distillation.

1. Spell out all numbers from one through nine. The numbers 10 and above should be written as numerals. There are, of course, exceptions.

- Spell out numbers at the beginning of sentences, regardless of the size of the number. (This doesn't apply to dates.)

  Forty people attended the meeting, which was held in a closet-sized room.

  1986 is going to be a good year.

- Spell out numbers that represent rounded figures or approximations.

  About two or three hundred were in attendance.

  He was obviously in his nineties.

- Spell out fractions.

  one-fourth, two-thirds, seven-eighths

- Spell out numbers preceding a unit-of-measure modifier containing a figure.

  five 9-inch toothpicks

  seven 1/2-inch pieces of plastic

2. Use figures to represent numbers in the following cases:

- When numbers below 10 appear in the same sentence but refer to the same general subject as larger numbers.

    Melissa sent out for 3 sandwiches, 20 cups of coffee, and 4 small bags of pretzels, but she wanted them within five minutes. (The number five does not refer to the same general subject and so does not have to be written as a numeral.)

- When numbers refer to parts of a book, they should be figures.

    Chapter 2, page 75, paragraph 4

- When numbers precede units of time or measurement, they should be written as numerals.

    3 x 5 card
    9 o'clock or 9:00
    15-yard penalty

Spelling

Spelling is a problem for many of us. We simply cannot spell. Part of the problem is our language. English, historically, is made up of many languages: Latin, French, Dutch, German, and many others. Often there seems to be no logic to the way words are spelled in English.

For instance, the letter *a* can have many different phonetic sounds, as in *ran, air, day, papa,* or *lathe.* On the other hand, different combinations of letters are often sounded alike: *rec(ei)ve, repr(ie)ve, rep(ea)l.* There seems to be no logical reason for the difference in the sound of *c* in *citizen* and *cat* or the *g* in *regal* and *regency.* Some letters don't seem to belong in the word at all as in *i(s)land, recei(p)t,* and *de(b)t.* And then there are the words for which pronunciation would seem to be impossible if we didn't grow up knowing the difference: *through, bough, trough, though.*

Of course, knowing all this doesn't help the chronic poor speller. Knowing that *sight* comes from Anglo-Saxon, *site* from French, and *cite* from Latin doesn't help us unless we spell by context and recognize the differences in meanings of these words.

For the problem speller, there is, however, some hope. That hope lies in correct pronunciation, recognition of differences in meanings and spellings, and the memorization of some of the rules of spelling.

Correct Pronunciation

Correct pronunciation can act as an invaluable aid to spelling. Many words are commonly mispronounced, leading to misspelling. The following list is by no means exhaustive, but it does contain some of the most often mispronounced words.

arctic	interest
athletics	irrelevant
boundary	mathematics
candidate	mischievous
cavalry	nuclear
comparable	prejudice
desperate	quantity
disastrous	temperature
grievous	veteran
incidentally	

Note that some of these words do have more than one pronunciation. If you have trouble spelling them, you should cultivate the pronunciation that helps you with spelling.

Many words in English sound alike but are spelled differently. These are called homonyms, and the spelling must be derived from the meaning within the sentence.

ascent = a climb	assent = to agree
all ready = everyone is ready	already = by this time
all together = as a group	altogether = entirely
altar = a place of worship	alter = to change
capital = governing city, or wealth	capitol = a building
council = an assembly	counsel = to advise
bare = stripped or naked	bear = to carry or a stuffed Teddy
course = a path or way	coarse = rough textured
complement = that which completes	compliment = praise
principal = chief or most important	principle = a belief or rule
stationery = writing paper	stationary = not moving
weather = the elements	whether = if

Spelling Rules

Unfortunately, the only way for many of us to improve our spelling is to memorize the rules. This may sound impossible, but knowing some of the rules that pertain to your particular area of weakness can aid you immeasurably.

1. Write *i* before *e* except after *c*, or when sounded like *a* as in *eighty* or *sleigh*.

      belief   neighbor
      ceiling   receive
      deceive   thief
      feign   vein
      field

Naturally, there are some exceptions: *financier, species, fiery, weird.*

2. When using prefixes, add the prefix to the root of the word without doubling or dropping letters.

      *dis*appear
      *dis*satisfaction
      *un*necessary

3. Drop the final *e* before a suffix beginning with a vowel but not before a suffix beginning with a consonant.

      care + ful = careful
      come + ing = coming
      entire + ly = entirely
      fame + ous = famous
      ride + ing = riding
      sure + ly = surely

In some words, keep the final *e* to keep a *c* or *g* soft before an *a* or *o*.

      change + able = changeable
      courage + ous = courageous
      notice + able = noticeable

Again, there are some exceptions: Some words that take suffix *-ful* or *-ly* drop the final *e*.

      awe + ful = awful
      due + ly = duly
      true + ly = truly

And some words taking the suffix *-ment* drop the final *e*.

      acknowledge + ment = acknowledgment
      judge + ment = judgment

4. The final *y* is usually changed to *i* except before a suffix beginning with *i* (usually *ing*).

      cry + ing = crying   funny + er = funnier
      happy + ness = happiness   hurry + ied = hurried
      hurry + ing = hurrying   study + ing = studying

5. Double the final consonant before a suffix that begins with a vowel when a single vowel precedes the consonant, and the consonant ends an accented syllable or a one-syllable word.

> format + ed = formatted (a is a single vowel preceding the consonant but the word is accented on the first syllable.)
>
> sad + er = sadder (a is a single vowel preceding the consonant and the word is one syllable).
>
> stoop + ing = stooping (The word is one syllable but the consonant is preceded by two vowels.)

6. Sometimes, adding a suffix like -ity, -ation, or -ic can help you spell the base word by showing you the pronunciation.

> similar   similarity
> moral   morality
> symbol   symbolic
> grammar   grammatical

The bottom line is that good spelling can become a habit. Once you have learned to spell a word correctly, you shouldn't have any more trouble with it. Here are some steps that might help you to spell troublesome words, however, and prevent you from using ingrained misspellings.

1. Look closely at a word that is giving you trouble and say it to yourself, taking care to pronounce it carefully and correctly.

2. Divide the word into syllables, taking care to pronounce each one.

3. Try to visualize the correct spelling before you write the word.

4. Write the word without looking at the correct spelling.

5. Then look the word up to see if you spelled it correctly. If you did, cover the word and write it again. Write it one more time just to be sure you have it down. If you've written it correctly all three times, chances are you won't have any more trouble with it in the future. If you had some problems with any one of the three writings, go over the word again starting with step one.

6. Finally, make a list of words that give you trouble. Go over the list frequently using the above method until you have eliminated them one by one. If you are a chronic misspeller, this can seem an almost never-ending job, but it is well worth the effort.

## CHAPTER 14

The Basics of Style

Proper words in proper places,
make the true definition of style.

Jonathan Swift

Why study style? The problem is, not many of us learned to write the way we do in school—instead, we learned on the job, picking up bad habits as well as good ones and having those habits further ingrained by people who couldn't put it down much better than we could. That's why it's important to pause for a few moments and check our writing style to see if we have acquired any bad habits that we should correct.

That's the purpose of this section—to help you understand some of the accepted methods of "good" style and to apply those methods to your personal writing style. We don't want you to change an already good writing style. What we would like to accomplish is an increased awareness of how to change those things that you would like to change while leaving the good parts intact. I've tried to make this section as painless as possible by providing you with the most appropriate areas of style in the most abbreviated way.

Working with Words

Formal vs. Informal

All of us think we know how to use a dictionary. It's part of every writer's library. The problem is that a lot of people don't *use* their dictionaries to check the meanings and spellings of the words they use. This leads, of course, to misinterpretation of written materials by readers.

One of the biggest problems in using dictionaries is deciding whether or not a word is appropriate in context. For instance, a word that might be entirely appropriate in informal English might not be appropriate in formal English. Dictionaries can be of some help. Most provide guidance in selecting the right word. For instance, a dictionary might label the word *swipe* as a colloquial or informal alternative to *steal* or *plagiarize*. You wouldn't want to use it in a formal, business letter. This brings us to our first rule: Avoid using informal words in formal writing.

> *Informal:*
> It seems that Mr. Jordan swiped the information on the new plastic widget from a brochure he found in his files.
>
> *Formal:*
> It seems that Mr. Jordan plagiarized the information on the new plastic widget from a brochure he found in his files.

It's usually safe to assume that if a word is unlabeled in your dictionary, it is considered to be in general usage and therefore formal.

For the public relations writer, contractions (which are usually considered informal usage) can be useful. Frequently, you can take on a familiar tone with your target audience by using contractions. For strictly formal documents, however, it is still a good rule to write out the complete word or phrase instead of its accepted contraction. Words like *can't, won't, isn't* should be written out as *cannot, will not,* and *is not.*

Jargon

All industries have their jargon, or specialized vocabulary. Banks call Certificates of Deposit "CDs," journalists call paragraphs "graphs," police call a record of arrests a "rap sheet," and highly technical industries develop an entire dictionary of shorthand notations. Jargon should not be used for external information pieces unless they are to be read only by experts in the field. For internal pieces, jargon is usually acceptable. For the lay reader, use jargon only if you are able to explain it in lay terms. It is wise to follow this procedure unless you are sure that your jargon has become accepted general usage.

When jargon becomes cumbersome, it overrides meaning. What we commonly refer to as "legalese" and "bureaucratese" are really overuse of jargon. The result is ambiguity.

> *Jargon:*
> Do not discharge your mechanical device releasing its base-metal projectile until such time as the opposing force has

decreased the distance between your two positions to a point allowing visual recognition of the delineation between the occular components of the aforesaid opponent and recognition of the opaque, globular housing thereof.

General:
Don't fire until you see the whites of their eyes.

Words like *impact* and *input* have now become jargon to many industries. They sound "trendy" to many people and give them a false sense of belonging to a select group of "experts."

Jargon:
I have asked Ms. Pomeroy to input the latest cost figures so that we may have the results by 4:00 this afternoon. (A noun misused as a verb.)

General:
I have asked Ms. Pomeroy to enter the latest cost figures so that we may have the results by 4:00 this afternoon. (A verb used correctly.)

Jargon:
The severe downturn in the economy has negatively impacted our industry. (A noun misused as a verb.)

General:
The severe downturn in the economy has negatively affected our industry. (A verb used correctly.)

Did you recognize any other use of jargon in the above examples? What are they, and how would you change them to a more general style?

In your efforts to write clearly and concisely, remember that the object of written communication is to communicate. In other words—don't "fuzzify."

Exactness

Exactness is an art. Most of us tend to "write up" when we assume a formal style. But when we "write up," we lose precision. What we should strive for is clarity, and clarity can be achieved most easily by using exact words. Most of our writing is read by people who know something about us and what we do, but we cannot always assume that to be the case.

Denotative and connotative meanings. One way to avoid confusion is always to use words whose denotative meanings most closely match those understood by our audience. The *denotative* meaning of a word is its "dictionary" meaning and, of course, the best way to determine that is to look the word up. The first example following uses the wrong word.

> *Wrong:*
> The employees were visibly effected by the president's speech. (*Effect* means result.)
>
> *Right:*
> The employees were visibly affected by the president's speech. (*Affect,* in this case, means emotionally moved.)
>
> *Wrong:*
> As a manager, Marvin was fine; but as a human being, he had some severe problems dealing with sex differences among his department members. (*Sex* usually refers to biological differences or the act itself.)
>
> *Right:*
> As a manager, Marvin was fine; but as a human being, he had some severe problems dealing with gender differences among his department members. (*Gender* has become the accepted term for the differences in roles related to the total experience of being either male or female.)

Connotative meanings are those your audience may associate with words in addition to or instead of their dictionary meaning. Connotation is the result of automatic associations your audience makes when interpreting some words. For example, you may intend the word *dog* to mean a four-footed, warm-blooded animal of the canine species. To audience members whose past associations with dogs have been positive, a picture of a particularly friendly dog may pop into mind. For some who may have had negative experiences—such as being bitten by a dog—the association may be entirely the opposite of what you intend. Although there is no way to guard against all such associations, there are certain words or phrases that you should avoid as being *too* vague in connotation to be useful to you as a communicator.

Think of the different connotative meanings for words such as *liberal, conservative, freedom, democracy, communism,* and *patriotism.* Words with multiple connotations may not be the best words to select if you are striving for exactness.

Some words or phrases may have little or no connotation, such as *place of birth.* The denotative meaning of this phrase is clear, but there is little connotative meaning. However, if we replace the phrase with the word *hometown,* not only does the denotative meaning become clear, but the word also gains a definite connotative meaning—usually a positive one.

Specific words vs. general and abstract. Exactness requires that you be specific. When we read something that has been written in general, nonspecific terms, we can't help but feel that something is being left out—perhaps on purpose.

General words are indefinite and cover too many possible meanings, both denotatively and connotatively. Specific words are precise and limited in definition.

General	Specific
car	Honda Accord LX
people	Delawareans
animal	cat
precipitation	rain

Abstract words deal with concepts or ideas that are intangible, such as *freedom* or *love*. Use these words, but make sure that they are not open to misinterpretation.

> "Enjoy the freedom of 7-Eleven!" (Does *freedom* mean that you pay lower prices, can shop 24 hours a day, have ample parking, preserve the American way each time you shop there, or what exactly?)

One of the parts of speech affected the most by inexactness is the adjective. A number of adjectives are extremely general and impart little or no additional meaning to a noun, thus negating their function.

> *General:*
> Marisa, please take this report to word processing and tell them it's a rush job. (Show me something that isn't a rush job!)

> *Specific:*
> Marisa, please take this report to word processing, and tell them we need it by 3:00 this afternoon. (Now, word processing has a specific deadline.)

Keep it fresh. At one time, all expressions were original; however, today we're frequently stuck with many trite or overworked expressions or clichés. The problem with these is that they may be entirely overlooked by your reader, who has probably seen them a thousand times.

> *Trite:*
> Nine out of ten times Harcourt is wrong in his instant analysis of a problem.

> *Better:*
> Most of the time Harcourt is wrong in his instant analysis of a problem.

Trite:
Harcourt is claiming his latest plan is a viable option in controlling employee absences.

Better:
Harcourt is claiming his latest plan is a solution to the problem of employee absences.

Public relations, like many other forms of writing, including journalism, has developed certain stock expressions that some might consider to be clichéd. Many of these, however, are acceptable shortcuts that aid understanding.

John Smith, *a native of* Chicago...

or

Chicago *native* John Smith...

Generally, these semantic shortcuts impart the correct meaning without being vague or appearing trite. Other phrases have become clichéd through overuse, and have consequently lost their meaning.

The head of programming says this new product will keep APC *on the cutting edge.*

James Sutton, president of Associated Products Corporation, *announced today* (May 25) the release of a new line of plastic widgets.

The key is to recognize trite, overused expressions and clichés and understand when they can be useful and when they can hurt your message. Remember, good writers avoid worn-out words and opt instead for fresh usage.

Wordiness

Being too "wordy" is a habit that most of us fall into at one time or another. Perhaps, as was mentioned above, we once thought it meant we were writing in a formal style. Actually, the opposite is true. Formal English should be no more wordy than informal English. In fact, it should be even more precise because it is formal. As a writer, you will find that the best way to eliminate wordiness is through editing. You probably already have more editors than you need, but your best editor is still you. You can eliminate a lot of shuffling of papers up and down the channels of communication for approvals if you perform some surgery early on. When you edit, strike out the phrases and words that add no additional information to your work, and clarify with precise words.

> *First draft:*
> I would appreciate it if you would set up a meeting for sometime in the late afternoon, mid-week, for our next, important get-together.

> *Revised draft:*
> I would appreciate it if you would set up a time sometime late Wednesday afternoon for our next meeting.

> *Final draft:*
> Please set up a 3:00 meeting for next Wednesday.

> *First draft:*
> We would like to attempt to schedule our very next company picnic to be held in or around the city of Wilmington in order to facilitate transportation by employees to the site.

> *Revised draft:*
> We want to schedule our company picnic in Wilmington to make it easier for employees to get to.

Of course, you don't want to be brief to the point of abruptness, but you can see what exactness can do in the editing process. The key is to make sure that all important information is covered in enough detail to be useful to the reader.

Unfortunately, we often over-clarify in an attempt to make our messages understood; however, much of what we write is simply redundant or not needed for clarification.

> The in-basket is completely full. (How can it be incompletely full?)

> Johnson has come up with a most unique design for dismantling the employee pension fund. (It's either unique or it's not—*most* adds no meaning.)

> The meeting date has been set for March 31, the last day of the month. (The final phrase is redundant.)

Emphasis

Organization of words within a sentence, sentences within paragraphs, and paragraphs within a larger work is key to clear writing style. We typically organize based on the importance or weight assigned to these words, paragraphs, or larger elements. By placing them in a prescribed order, we give the thoughts they represent emphasis.

Following are some of the standard methods for gaining emphasis.

- Place the most important words at the beginning or end of the sentence.

  Unemphatic:
  There was a terrific explosion in the Xerox room that shook the whole building. (*There* is an unemphatic word in an emphatic position.)

  Emphatic:
  A terrific explosion in the Xerox room shook the whole building.

- The end of a sentence is also a strong position for emphasis.

  Unemphatic:
  I know Tom was the one who stole the stapler.

  Emphatic:
  I know who stole the stapler—Tom.

- Increase emphasis by arranging ideas in the order of climax. Rank items in a series by order of importance, building from the least important to the most important.

  Jill was abrasive, lazy, undedicated, and generally ill-equipped to deal with her co-workers. (In this case, *ill-equipped* is used to sum up Jill's other attributes.)

  Watch out for an illogical ranking of ideas. If done unintentionally, this could cause some unwelcome hilarity, as in the following example.

  Because of his brief exploration of the casinos, Jerry became morose, despondent, melancholic, and lost twelve dollars.

- Gain emphasis by using the active rather than the passive voice. The active voice indicates that the "doer" of the action is the most important element in the sentence; the passive indicates the "receiver" is the most important.

  Unemphatic:
  Not much is being done by the employer to defray health benefit costs.

  Emphatic:
  The employer is not doing much to defray health benefit costs.

  Unemphatic:
  The study, accomplished by the Financial Department, showed a sharp decline in quarterly earnings.

Emphatic:
The Financial Department's study showed a sharp
decline in quarterly earnings.

- Add emphasis by repeating key words or phrases. Such repetition not only adds emphasis, but often serves as a memory stimulant.

    I am afraid that these negotiations gave rise to false
    hopes, false indications of changes that may not occur,
    and false expectations on the part of management as to
    its ability to fulfill false promises.

Don't mistake repetition for emphasis with redundancy. The difference is in the added strength of the statement.

- Add emphasis by balancing sentence construction. Balanced structure occurs when grammatically equal elements are used to point to differences or similarities. The usual construction is one in which two clauses contain parallel elements.

    Knowing the health hazards and still smoking is free-
    dom of choice; not knowing and smoking is victimiza-
    tion.

    Working here is boring; not working here is unemploy-
    ment.

Working with Sentences

Sentence Length

Constant sentence length creates monotony, and monotony creates disinterested readers.

The key to good style is to vary sentence length. Don't string together short, choppy sentences if they can be joined to form more interesting compound sentences.

Monotonous:
Harvey walked into the office. He sat down. He began to
type on his 1923 Underwood. It was the typewriter with the
black, metal carriage. Harvey hated typing this early in the
morning. He was never fully awake until at least 10 o'clock.

Varied:
Harvey walked into the office, sat down and began to type
on his 1923 Underwood with the black, metal carriage. He
hated typing this early in the morning, since he was never
fully awake until at least 10 o'clock.

Notice that related ideas are linked as compound sentences. Linking unrelated ideas is an easy mistake, and sounds silly.

> Harvey walked into the office, sat down and began to type on his 1923 Underwood. It was the typewriter with the black, metal carriage, and he hated typing this early in the morning.
> (What does his typewriter having a black, metal carriage have to do with Harvey's dislike for early-morning typing?)

Be careful, however, not to make your sentences too long. Short sentences are easier to read. A good rule of thumb for determining proper sentence length is to keep sentences down to about 16 words long. Naturally, you're not going to count each word you write, but you get the idea. Shorter sentences in the context of longer ones can aslo increase emphasis, as in the following examples.

> I have discovered that the content employee is dedicated, remains on the job longer, suffers fewer illnesses, creates fewer problems, and rarely complains. In short, he is productive.

> I understand. You have a number of assignments due simultaneously, your secretary is out sick, your copier is broken, and you cannot get an outside line. I still need it now.

Another easy method of preventing monotony is to alter the beginnings of your sentences. In other words, don't always write in the subject-verb-object order. One of the best ways to vary this order is to use a subordinate clause first.

> Because of his dislike for early-morning typing, Harvey never showed up at work prior to 10 o'clock.

> Starting out early, Harvey walked two blocks at a brisk pace, then collapsed.

> Before you start on that report, come into my office for a little chat.

And don't forget—beginning a sentence with a conjunction is perfectly acceptable. Remember, though, that even conjunctions have meanings and usually infer that a thought is being carried over from a previous sentence.

> Not only was Harvey later than usual, he was downright tardy. And I wasn't the only one to notice. (Implies that the information is being added to the previous thought.)

> Not only was Harvey later than usual, he was downright

tardy. But I was probably the only one who noticed. (Implies a contrast with the previous thought.)

With a little reworking, however, even a series of strung-together clauses can be fixed up. Conjunctions can be useful but not if they are overused.

> *Clauses strung together:*
> Francine is always on time, and she frequently comes in before regular office hours, and she never leaves before quitting time.

> *Reworked into a complex sentence:*
> Francine is always on time, frequently coming in before regular office hours and never leaving before quitting time.

> *Clauses strung together:*
> He ran down the street, and then he stopped at the main entrance, and he took a deep breath, and then he went inside.

> *Reworked into a compound predicate:*
> He ran down the street, stopped at the main entrance, took a deep breath, and went inside.

Working with Paragraphs

As the sentence represents a single thought, so the paragraph represents a series of related thoughts. There is no set number of sentences you should include in a paragraph; however, paragraph length is shorter today than in the past. Short paragraphs invite readership while long paragraphs "put off" the reader. The key, of course, is coherence, which means that ideas must be unified. You can give unity to your paragraphs in several ways: by making each sentence contribute to the central thought, by arranging sentences in a logical order, and by making logical transitions between sentences.

Making each sentence contribute. The first sentence should generally express the theme of the paragraph. Although the thematic statement may actually appear anywhere in the paragraph, the strongest positions are at the beginning or the end; and the end is usually reserved for a transitional lead into the following paragraph.

> Our annual operating budget is somewhat higher than expected due to the increase in state allocations to higher

> education this fiscal year. The result will probably be an increase in departmental allowances, with the bulk of the increase showing up in the applied sciences. Although Arts and Sciences have been "holding up" well, we don't expect that they will be able to maintain this independence for long. As a result, their departmental budgets will also reflect this positive financial shift. Next year's outlook is a different story.

The lead sentence sets the theme for the entire paragraph, which is this year's budget. The final sentence indicates that the next paragraph will probably deal with next year's budget. What you want to avoid are unrelated sentences. If they are truly unrelated, then they deserve a paragraph of their own. If they are slightly related, then the relationship needs to be pointed out.

Logical sentence order. Arrange sentences in a logical order, and provide smooth transitions between them indicating their relationship. There are several ways to group sentences to show ranking: time order, space order, and order of climax.

Time order and chronological order are sometimes synonymous, although chronological order often implies a direct mention of time or dates.

> The growth of communication in the northernmost regions of America was rapid and coincided roughly with the development of the land itself. In 1867, shortly following the Civil War, the first telegraph line was strung between Dawson Creek and Whitehorse. By the turn of the century, the lines had been extended through to Seattle, on the southeastern coast, and Anchorage, along Prince William Sound. The first World War saw a flurry of development as military involvement increased in the region. With this involvement came a windfall of communication development that lasted until 1959.

Time order is appropriate when explaining the steps involved in an action.

> Changing a typewriter ribbon is a relatively easy task, even for an office executive on a Saturday afternoon. First, pull the ribbon-release lever, and remove the old ribbon. Throw it away. Remove the new ribbon from its box, insert it onto the spindles provided for it, and snap it down. Next comes the hard part. Pull out enough ribbon to place around the ribbon guides against the platen and thread it through the "slots" in the guides. Return the ribbon-release lever to its original position. You are now ready to type.

Space order implies movement from one location to another: right to left, up to down, east to west, high to low, and so on.

> It rained all day yesterday. The weatherman had shown in glaring detail how the jet stream would carry the warm, moist low front from the snow-filled Cascades of the Northwest, over the Rockies, onto the plains, and finally into my backyard on the Atlantic coast. Apparently, it hadn't lost anything in the transition.

Order of climax means that arrangement follows from the least important element to the most important element in the paragraph, in ascending order of importance. Most of the time, the climax is the concluding sentence.

> If the clerical staff members are uncomfortable with the workload, their immediate supervisors are the first to know. Middle managers are often reluctant to act on "workload" problems, but if pressured, will pass on complaints to executive officers. If the problem isn't handled to the satisfaction of all the parties involved by the time it reaches the executive level, a vice president may have to intervene; but pity the poor vice president who can't handle the problem. The president's office is a bastion of corporate sanctuary. Woe to him who would invade it.

When arranging sentences in order of climax, consider moving from the general to the specific or vice versa. Sometimes, moving from the familiar to the unfamiliar will soften the blow of dealing with a new idea.

> When we view each member of our office staff as an individual, we sometimes develop tunnel vision. We have to understand the larger picture in order to alleviate this problem. Staff members are all a part of a much larger organism. Together they form departments; departments form divisions. The larger company is composed of these divisions, and the company is part of a much larger conglomerate. To take the analogy further, the conglomerate is only one of the hundreds of such groupings that help make our system of economics one of the most successful in the world.

Logical transitions. Make logical transitions between sentences. Related ideas are given further unity by the use of logical transitions between sentences. A good transition usually refers to the sentences preceding it. Remember that a transitional word or phrase also has a meaning. Make sure the meaning adds to the understanding of the sentences or phrases preceding the transition.

The floor plan was completely haphazard; furthermore, it appeared to crowd an already crowded office area. (*Furthermore* indicates an addition to the thought begun in the first clause.)

Don Johnson was the first to try the new water fountain. On the other hand, he was the last to try the potato salad at the last company picnic. (The phrase indicates contrast.)

Fourteen employees were found to be in violation of company policies forbidding alcohol on the premises. Consequently, inspection of employee lockers will probably become commonplace. (Indicates that the second sentence is a result of actions in the first.)

The rate of consumption has tripled over the past 18 months. In short, we have a severe problem. (Indicates a summary or explanation.)

Jeremy covered the news desk. Meanwhile, Judy was busy copying the report before Wally returned and discovered it was missing. (An indication of time placement.)

One of the major problems with the use of transitional words and phrases is over reliance on a very few common groupings. Many people tend to use words such as *however* to bridge every transitional creek. After a while, its use becomes monotonous. The answer? Vary transitional phrases. There's always another word you can use. Think about it.

The same applies to transitions between paragraphs. Use words and meanings that tie the thoughts together and form a smooth bridge between subjects. After all, even dissimilar ideas need to be linked. If they were so dissimilar that you couldn't link them logically, they wouldn't belong in the same document.

Paragraph Development

There are a number of ways to develop your paragraphs to show unity and coherence. Notice that all of the examples below supply relevant details in support of a main idea.

You will often find that developing a definition will add unity to a paragraph.

There are a number of ways of viewing the office water cooler; however, to a social scientist, it is a communal gathering place at which ideas and information are freely disseminated. It is an informal location, usually outside the territorial boundaries of any one employee and therefore accessible to all on an equal footing. It is the traditional "oasis," shared by any who are in need of water and at which all are free to share. To imply that this communal ground is the "property" of any one individual or department is to negate its real value. At it, we quench not only our thirsts for liquid, but also for information outside the formal boundaries of protocol.

Frequently, classification will serve to relate like ideas in a paragraph.

There are three categories of clerical aid within the company. At the lowest rung of the pay scale is the clerk. A clerk's job includes light typing, no shorthand, much filing, and a tremendous amount of running around. Next up on the scale is the secretary. More typing is involved (at a much faster speed and with more accuracy), much filing, some shorthand, and a great deal of running around. At the top is the executive secretary. Typing is a must (at great speeds and accuracy), good shorthand, much filing, and more running around than the Stanford University track team.

The main idea can be made more coherent by comparing or contrasting it with a like idea.

Comparison:
A committee meeting is like a football game. The chair is the quarterback, and so is the directing force; however, the members are the players without whom no goal can be obtained. The key to the game plan, then, is to coordinate the players into a single unit with a single goal. The players must be made aware that a unified, or team, effort is integral to the accomplishment of that goal and that the quarterback is the director—he is not the coach. The director recommends; he does not command.

Contrast:
The typical office environment is orderly. Without order, little can be accomplished. Remember the recess periods of your school days? You were able to act freely, without consideration to the restrictive environment of the classroom. You were free to explore your voice, your agility, and your mastery of fast-paced games not suited to the indoors. Once inside, however, you were required to conform to the needs of the classroom—quiet and order. Within these confines, work can be accomplished with a minimum of disturbance; and the accomplishment of that work is as important in an office environment as in a classroom.

One of the best ways to develop a paragraph and its central idea is to show cause and effect. Most things in life are a result of something else. For most of us, though, it takes some thought to trace that development.

> The so-called "open office" environment popular in newer buildings today has its roots in several trends. Since the mid-1970s, energy conservation has been a major concern in the United States. The open office requires less heat in the winter and less cooling in the summer, due mainly to the lack of walls. In the place of these walls, we now have "dividers" which, although they serve to mask sound, allow for the free circulation of air throughout an entire floor. In addition to conservation, open offices serve to homogenize workers by removing the traditional boundaries of high walls and closed doors. Employees now have access to each other through a network of openings, yet maintain the margin of privacy needed for individual productivity.

Obviously, a paragraph need not be restricted to any single method of development but can benefit from a combination approach. The key, of course, is to be clear, and any method that promotes clarity is a good one.

Planning and Writing

A sentence usually contains a single idea. A paragraph contains a number of sentences related by a single theme. So too, a complete piece of writing, whether it's a press release, a backgrounder, or an article for the company newsletter, contains a series of paragraphs unified by a single theme and related by logical transitions.

For many of us, the writing is the easy part—planning is the snag. And the toughest part of planning is deciding exactly what to say and what to leave out. Most of us tend to overwrite. In the words of one observer: "Writing is like summer clothing—it should be long enough to cover the subject, but brief enough to be interesting."

The first task in writing, then, is to choose your subject and limit yourself to the information needed to cover it. There are several ways to accomplish this. One of the easiest ways is to work from a very general topic to a specific topic.

> banking → withdrawing and making deposits → avoiding waiting in lines → using automatic tellers → using automatic tellers in the lobby

This may seem simple, but it does help clear your thoughts and crystallize your ideas through the act of putting them on paper. Naturally, the theme of any piece is intimately tied to its purpose. If, for instance, your purpose is to encourage patrons to use the automatic tellers in the bank lobby, it may be necessary to come directly to the point in your pitch. However, in doing so, you will probably use one of the traditional writing approaches.

Most of us remember our high school English classes in which we were taught to write various papers for different purposes. Among the most common approaches were:

Exposition—used to inform or explain
Argumentation—used to convince or persuade
Narration—used mostly for entertainment value
Description—used to explain through verbal "pictures"

In public relations writing, narration is the least frequently used except in feature-type stories. The other methods are often used and combined to present information to readers. A lot depends on whether you are trying to be persuasive or are simply presenting information— the two most common goals of public relations writing.

The Central Idea

Once you have decided on the purpose of a particular piece, you should write down a central idea in a single sentence or *thesis statement*. Suppose, for instance, that your goal is to convince employees to come to work on time each day. This will be a persuasive piece. The method you have chosen to use might be argumentation, which will convince your employees. What is your thesis statement? It might be something like this:

Coming to work on time puts you in step with the other employees who work with you, gives you time to adjust to your daily environment, allows you the leisure of some pre-work interaction with others, and impresses your employer.

So, in a single sentence, you have set down several controlling ideas that can now be elaborated upon. The next step is to develop a working plan or rough outline.

The Outline

Before you begin an outline, it helps to put down some ideas. These can be in the form of a simple list. For instance, to continue the previous example, perhaps you have decided to stress promptness by comparing the benefits of being on time with the disadvantages of coming in late.

Advantages of coming to work on time

— Allows time to adjust to daily routine
— Allows time for interaction with fellow workers
— Impresses employer
— Allows time to have coffee
— Allows time to read through the paper

Disadvantages of coming in late

— You are rushed into daily routine without adjustment period
— You have no time to interact informally with fellow workers
— You do not impress employer
— You have no time for coffee
— You have no time to read the paper

Now you have a starting point. It might be that you want to address the points one by one, covering the advantages first, then the disadvantages. Or perhaps you want to compare the advantages with the disadvantages one at a time.

Outline Organization

Outlines are extremely useful as a checklist of key points. You may use the outline simply to check your final written piece against to make sure you have covered all points regardless of final order, or you may have each point represent a complete paragraph or section of your finished document in the order presented in the outline.

In either case, make sure that your ideas are related within each paragraph and that each paragraph follows logically from the previous one. The same methods you used to arrange your sentences within the paragraph can be used to arrange your paragraphs within a larger composition: time order, space order, or order of climax.

Unity and Logical Thinking

Clarity

We've already learned something of unity by studying the placement of ideas in a logical order within sentences, paragraphs, and whole compositions. Now, let's turn to logic itself. In writing, we should try to present our ideas as logically as possible to enhance understanding.

A major problem hindering understanding is semantics. Semantics involves the meanings of words individually and as they appear in a context. We should be extremely careful to select words that hold the same meaning for the reader as for us. One way to do this is to define terms that are likely to be either misunderstood or not understood at all.

> The major cause of antenna malfunction is the lack of foundation stability. The antenna cannot be properly anchored due to permafrost, a permanently frozen layer of ice and soil some three feet below the surface.

> All copy to be printed by the in-house print facility should be camera ready (properly sized, clean, and pasted in place).

Often a word can be defined by inserting a synonym.

> The altercation, or fight, lasted only three minutes.

> Sled dogs are not only used to running over muskeg—boggy terrain—but often relish the softness of the ground.

Some words or concepts, however, require more careful treatment. Abstracts such as freedom, liberty, and democracy have meanings far beyond those found in the dictionary. We must be careful when we write to give some thought to a word's connotative meaning as well as its denotative, or dictionary, meaning.

> Productivity is the major responsibility of the individual employee. Although management is usually associated with and responsible for rises or drops in productivity, individual employees remain the sole determiners of these fluctuations. Do they arrive at work on time and refreshed, ready to work? Do they spend too much time on breaks or at lunch? Do they perform only the required duties, or do they work beyond those requirements? So, then, productivity is more than producing a greater number of "widgets." Productivity is a state of mind carried over into the workplace. Productivity means caring; and caring means taking responsibility.

The determining factor in deciding to go with a simple or expanded definition is knowledge of your target audience, and that is a concern of planning, not style.

Generalizations

A generalization is an assumption based on incomplete evidence. It is a belief that what is true of a few members of a group (regardless of how you categorize that group or what it composes) is true of the entire group.

Teenagers are irresponsible.

The British are very formal.

Football players are all dumb.

Tall people are good basketball players.

Generalizations can be harmless or they can be dangerous. In writing, generalizations such as these should be avoided. If you do make a generalization, you must support it. This means that you must present adequate evidence that what you are saying is true for most of a particular group.

> Nearly half of all women in the U.S. believe they are over-weight. A recent survey conducted by the National Center for Vital Statistics shows that 39 percent of all males and 49 percent of all females surveyed said they considered themselves overweight. The survey, part of the data col-lected in the most recent Health and Weight Loss Survey, was conducted on a random sample of men and women between the ages of 18 and 55. According to this survey, at any given time, at least 20 percent of the population are on some kind of weight-loss diet.

In this paragraph, the writer has made a generalization and given information enough to be considered adequate support.

Cause and Effect Relationships

Illogical statements often result when the writer fails to set up adequately a cause-and-effect relationship. We can construct such a relationship based on either inductive or deductive reasoning. *Inductive* reasoning proceeds from the particular to the general. A generalization is based on specific evidence that is deemed suffi-cient to support it. The results of scientific experimentation, for instance, are based on induction.

> A recent study by the Association for Scholastic Testing shows that school children between the ages of 7 and 14 learn quicker and absorb more knowledge when the lesson is interactive. Additional studies by National Employment Associates indicate that high-school students with com-puter skills attain higher-paying jobs upon graduation. It is clear that computer training is fast becoming a necessary component in the education process.

The *deductive* process involves working from the general to the specific. Specifics are usually determined from generalizations. If you know, for instance, that a high fever usually accompanies influenza, and you have a high fever during the flu season, then you might seek a doctor's care. You have deduced a specific need from a generalization. You may not, in fact, have influenza, but you have made a valid decision based on deduction. The basic assumption, however, must be sound for the deduction to be valid.

> It is clear that computer training is fast becoming a necessary component in the education process. Through this training, students will become better equipped to deal with a burgeoning technology. Teachers will be eased of the responsibility to be all things to all students, because of the interactive nature of computer learning. And students will ultimately benefit through higher-paying jobs.

As you can see, the deductive process in the preceding example was based on a previous inductive process. Most deductions are, in fact, based on previously collected information from which generalizations have been made.

The inductive and deductive processes are prone to problems in construction. The following guidelines will help you avoid the most common problems:

1. Because one item follows another chronologically, don't assume that the latter is a result of the former.

   > Helen came in late this morning, and everything has been going downhill since then.

   > Fred wouldn't be seeing Marge "on the side" if everything was all right at home.

2. Because one thing is true doesn't mean that you can infer another truth from it. This is commonly called a *non sequitur*.

   > The recent, sharp upturn in the economy will certainly result in lower unemployment.

   > Liz is something of an "air head." She'll never make it in the business world.

3. Don't beg the question. In other words, don't draw out an expected response by the way you ask a question. This happens when you assume the truth of a statement you are trying to verify. Sports interviewers frequently do this.

   > Champ? Was that the greatest match you ever fought or what? (Implies that the match *was* the greatest, thus biasing the response.)

> Janice snuck in at half past eight this morning. What do you suppose she's up to? (Maybe she slept late and isn't up to anything.)

4. Don't set up an either/or situation unless it really is one.

> Either you're going with me to the meeting or you're not. (Obviously a reasonable statement.)

> Either you're on my side or you're not. (Why can't I see the value in two different arguments without being on anyone's side?)

This is often called the all-or-nothing fallacy because it sets up a false dilemma, ignoring the fact that other variables or possibilities exist.

> Employees either come to work on time or they're simply not dedicated.

> School systems are either innovators because they acquire and use computers, or they're traditionalists who choose to ignore the future.

Finally, never argue a point that you can't back up with facts simply because you *believe* it to be true. Although much of what we believe is based on personal predispositions formed throughout our lifetimes, it is never too late to learn something new or to add facts to our existing knowledge.

If you are to be a good, persuasive writer, you must learn to be objective. For most writers, subjectivity indicates that you have a stake in what is being argued or, at least, a personal opinion. Opinions are best left for newspaper columnists or editors, who are paid to express their opinions. Objective writing is the hallmark of the logical writer. If you present the facts objectively, and they support your argument or point of view (whether that point of view is one that you personally hold or not) your argument will be logically sound.

Some Final Thoughts on Writing

Now that you have come to the end of this book, you should have mastered the basics of writing and produced most of the documents common to public relations. This will not, however, make you a good writer—it will simply make you a good technician. Good writing takes skill and imagination. Skill can be gained by practice. Imagination can only be gained by your willingness to experiment. Don't settle for the dry phrase or the lackluster sentence—bring creativity to every aspect of your writing.

Naturally, not every piece of public relations writing lends itself to greatness; however, as writers, we should always strive to present our ideas in the best possible light. In this way, even the most mundane may shine. It is not an easy task. As Alexander Pope said, "True ease of writing comes from art, not chance." Never look at writing as simply a job—it is an art and should be practiced with the care of an artist.

And read. Collect the writing of other professionals whose styles strike you. Read everything that you can in your field. Understand what you are writing about and never be afraid to experiment with your style. Of course you will be edited, and sometimes by those with less skill than you. Don't give up. In the end, good writing pays off—not only monetarily, but in the knowledge that you have the tools to write anything with the clarity and style of a professional, and an artist.

All the rest is mere fine writing.

Paul Verlaine

Glossary

Accompanying script. The version of a television script sent with the taped spot to the stations that will run it. The accompanying script is stripped of all but its most essential directions. It is intended to provide the reader a general idea of what the taped spot is about and is to be used only as a reference for broadcasters who accept the spot for use.

Actualities. Audio or video tapes that feature newspeople describing an event, interviews with those involved in the event, or ambience or background of the event itself for a voiceover.

Advertising. The controlled use of print or broadcast media ensuring that your message reaches your public in exactly the form you intended and at the time you want.

Annual reports. One of the most-produced organizational publications. Annual reports not only provide information on the organization's financial situation, they also act as a vehicle for enhancing corporate image among its various internal publics.

Articles and editorials. Usually for newsletters, house publications, trade publications, or consumer publications. In the case of non-house publications, PR articles are submitted in the same way as any other journalistic material. Editorials can be either paid for or submitted uncontrolled to vie for placement with other comments from other parties.

As-recorded spot. A radio spot produced by the originating agency and ready to be played by the stations receiving it. They are usually sent in the format used by the particular station or on reel-to-reel tape, which will probably be transferred to the proper station format. As with television spots, an accompanying script is sent along with the standard cover letter and response card.

Audio. Refers to the sound portion of a TV commercial or other video production.

Backgrounders. Basic information pieces providing background as an aid to reporters, editors, executives, employees, and spokespersons. This is the information used by other writers and reporters to "flesh out" their stories.

Body copy. Text material set in blocks in relatively small type. Distinguished from display copy (headlines and subheads).

Body type. Type set 12 points and smaller, used for body copy. Distinguished from display type, which is 14 points and larger.

Brochures. Technically called folders, brochures are usually formed of a single sheet of paper folded one or more times. The typical folded brochure is pocket sized. Brochures may be either stand-alone information pieces or part of a larger package.

Captions or **cutlines**. The informational descriptions that appear below or next to photographs or other illustrations.

Cliché. A word or phrase that has been used too often to be effective.

Collateral publications. These include brochures, pamphlets, flyers, and other direct marketing pieces. They are usually autonomous publications that should be able to stand on their own merits but which can be used as supporting information for other components in a package. They might, for instance, be part of a press packet.

Color separation. Process of breaking down full-color art into its primary color components.

Commercial. An announcement or spot. A radio or television sales message.

Compatibility. The degree to which different types of hardware or software interact successfully with each other.

Comprehensive (comp). A layout prepared to resemble the finished printed piece as closely as possible.

Consequence. One of the characteristics of newsworthiness of information. Relates to whether the information has any importance to the prospective reading, listening, or viewing public. Is it something that the audience would pay to know?

Controlled information. Information over which you have total control as to editorial content, style, placement, and timing. Examples of controlled information are institutional and advocacy advertising, house publications, brochures, and paid broadcast material. Preproduced public service announcements (PSAs) are controlled as far as message content is concerned, but uncontrolled as to placement and timing.

Corporate advertising. Advertising paid for by corporations, but not relating directly to products or services. Corporate or institutional advertising takes three basic forms depending on the purpose of the message.

- **Public interest advertising** provides information in the public interest such as health care, safety, and environmental interests. In order to have these ads placed free, they must meet stringent guidelines.

- **Public image advertising** tries to sell the organization as caring about its employees, the environment, the community, and its customers. Unlike the public interest ad, the public image ad will always focus on the company and how it relates to the subject.

- **Advocacy advertising** presents a point of view. This may range from political to social, and, by inference, positions, the company as an involved citizen of the community or the nation.

Daisy wheel printer. A printer utilizing a circular type element that rotates into place as each letter is chosen by the computer program.

Dateline. A brief notation at the beginning of a press release used to indicate the point of origin.

Demographics. The statistical description of prospects in objective terms, such as age, sex, occupation, marital status, education, household income, and so forth. See **Psychographics**.

Desktop publishing. The creation of publications utilizing computer hardware and software.

Display type. Type larger than 12 point, used for headlines and other emphasized elements.

Dot-matrix printers. Printers utilizing a fast-moving head to strike an inked ribbon, compiling letters and forms from individual bits.

Downward communication. Communication within an organization that imparts management's message to employees. Ideally, even downward communication channels such as newsletters permit upward communication through letters to the editor, articles written by employees, surveys, and so forth.

Drop shadow. A shadow created, usually behind a box, in a page-layout program.

Dummy. A mockup of the finished product, showing where the elements will be placed.

Exclusive. A press release or other information intended for only one media outlet. The same information may not be released to other outlets in any form.

Extemporaneous delivery. One of the four basic modes of delivering a speech. In this type, a speaker studies notes carefully and is theoretically prepared to speak knowledgeably and fluently on the topic.

Face. The style or design of type.

Feature style. A less objective style of writing that provides less hard information than straight news style. Features generally take a point of view or discuss issues, people, or places. The style is more relaxed, more descriptive, and often more creative than straight news style.

Flyer. A single sheet of paper, usually letter-size, printed on one or two sides and distributed either by hand or through the mail.

Font. A complete set of type characters of a particular typeface and size.

Formatting. Setting up guidelines for the placement of text within word-processing or page-layout programs. Indents, line length, and spacing are examples of formatting.

Four-color process. A printing process that reproduces a full range of colors using red, yellow, blue, and black. Full color.

Halftone. The traditional method of rendering a continuous tone photograph into a series of dots of varying sizes that can then be printed.

Hardware. The machinery of computing comprised of the computer itself and all physical peripherals attached to it.

Headline. Also *head*. Larger type lines, usually placed above other copy or art, used to get attention in an ad or other document. See **Subhead**.

Horizontal publication. Any publication distributed horizontally, across a narrowly defined group with a common interest: for example, newsletters on management techniques within a certain industry, or technical publications within an industry.

House publication. Any publication produced within and directed toward an in-house audience—typically employee publications such as newsletters and corporate magazines.

Illustration. Usually a drawing or a painting.

Importing/exporting. Transferring data from one software program into another.

Impromptu delivery. One of the four basic modes of delivering a speech. In this type, a speaker is expected to speak knowledgeably and fluently on a topic proposed on the spot.

Interest. One of the characteristics of newsworthiness of information. Relates to whether the information is unusual or entertaining. Does it have any human interest?

Laser printers. Printers utilizing a laser-read photo transfer method for reproducing text and graphics.

Lay out. To put the elements of an ad in a pleasing and readable arrangement in a given amount of space. *Layout* is the noun form, the resulting physical "blueprint."

Lead. The opening sentences of a straight news story or feature article. In a straight news story, the lead should include the who, what, when, where, why, and how of the story. Feature leads generally begin by setting the scene of the story to follow.

Live copy. The copy read by an announcer, in contrast to taped commercials.

Live tag. A message added by the announer to a prerecorded commercial giving local address, local price, and so on. Often used when a national manufacturer's radio commercials are aired by local stations.

Medium. A means of communicating: newspapers, magazines, television, radio, direct mail, outdoor advertising, and so on. Plural: *media*.

Megabyte (MGB). 1,048,576 bytes, equal to 1,024 kilobytes.

Memorized delivery. One of the four basic modes of delivering a speech. The speech is delivered from memory, but with cards or script as a backup.

Newsletters. A brief (usually four pages) printed publication distributed either vertically or horizontally. A newsletter usually contains information of interest to a narrowly defined target audience. The various types of newsletters include the following.

- **Association newsletters** help a scattered membership with a common interest keep in touch.

- **Community group newsletters** are often used by civic organizations to keep in touch with members, announce meetings, and stimulate attendance at events.

- **Institutional newsletters**, perhaps the most common type of newsletter, are usually distributed among employees.

- **Publicity newsletters** often create their own readers. They can be developed for fan clubs, resorts, and politicians.

- **Special interest newsletters** developed by special-interest groups tend to grow with their following.

- **Self-interest** or **"digest" newsletters** are designed to make a profit. The individuals or groups who develop them typically offer advice or present solutions to problems held in common by their target readers. These often come in the form of a sort of "digest" of topics of interest to a certain profession.

News releases. The most widely used of all public relations formats. News releases are used most often to disseminate information for publicity purposes and generally are of three types.

- **Publicity releases** cover any information occurring within an organization that might have some news value to local, regional, or even national media.

- **Product releases** deal with specific products or product lines and are usually targeted to trade publications within individual industries.

- **Financial releases** are used primarily in shareholder relations, but are also of interest to financial media.

Objective setting. A primary step in the planning process spelling out the purpose of your message or action. Objectives should be realistic and measurable. For public relations writing, there are three types of objectives: informational, attitudinal, and behavioral.

Offset lithography. A printing process in which the nonprinting area of the printing plate accepts water but not ink, while the image, or printing, area accepts ink but not water. During the printing process, both water and ink are applied to the plate as it revolves. The plate transfers its positive image to an offset cylinder made of rubber that then transfers the reversed image to the paper.

Output device. The device by which a computer document is printed. It can be a printer, imagesetter, graphic plotters, or other such instrument.

Pasteup. A layout in which all types and illustrative material are combined for reproduction as a single unit.

PC (personal computer). A generic term for a single-user microcomputer, typically an IBM or IBM clone.

Perfect binding. A binding for publications in which the backs of the collated signatures are trimmed or ground off and dense adhesive is applied, then a bonding/lining is placed atop the adhesive and the cover is glued on. The adhesive maintains its flexible bonding strength for a long time.

Pica. A unit of horizontal type measurement. Six picas equal one inch.

Placement agencies. Organizations that will take information, such as a press release, and send it out to media outlets using their regularly updated media lists and computerized mailing services.

PMT. Photo-mechanical transfer. A photostat produced without a negative (like a Polaroid process). Faster than screened print.

Point. A unit of vertical measurement of type. There are 12 points to a pica and 72 points to an inch.

Positioning. A marketing strategy that takes into consideration how consumers perceive a product or idea relative to competitive offerings.

Press kit. One of the most common methods of distributing brochures and other collateral information pieces. Press kits are produced and used for a wide variety of public relations purposes, including product promotion presentations, press conferences, and as promotional packages by regional or local distributors or agencies.

Process color or **four color**. Used for reproducing full-color artwork or photography. The illusion of full color is accomplished by optically mixing the three primary colors—yellow, red (actually magenta) and blue (called cyan)—along with black. Four color plates are shot using a screen to reduce solid areas to printable, graduated dot patterns. Because each color is shot through a slightly different angle screen, the colors in the overlaid dot patterns blend to form the full-color image.

Profile. A feature story written specifically about a person, product or service, or an organization or some part of it. It profiles the subject by listing facts, highlighting points of interest, and tying the subject to the organization being promoted.

Prominence. One of the characteristics of newsworthiness of information. Relates to whether the information concerns or involves events and people of prominence.

Proximity. One of the characteristics of newsworthiness of information. Relates to whether the information is local.

Psychographics. Refers to the description of prospects according to their personality and lifestyle traits. See **Demographics**.

Public service announcement (PSA). A radio or television spot providing an important message to its target audience. The PSA is reserved strictly for organizations that qualify as nonprofit under federal tax laws.

Pull quotes. A magazine or newsletter device of "pulling" out quotations from the text, enlarging the point size, and setting them off from the text to draw a reader's attention to a point within an article.

Quick copy. A xerographic printing process. The photocopiers used in this process can produce multiple copies, collate, and often staple them.

Quick print. A printing process involving a small cylinder press using paper printing plates. The plates are created using a photo-electrostatic process that results in a raised toner image that takes the ink and is imprinted directly onto the paper.

Rough. A preliminary sketch showing where type and art are to go on a printed piece.

Saddle stitching. A simple, inexpensive procedure for binding that nests the signatures atop one another and drives two to three staples through the spine and cover of the publication. Magazines and annual reports are most often bound this way.

Sans serif. In typography, a type that has no cross strokes or serifs at the tops and bottoms of characters.

Scaling. Enlarging or reducing an element in some increment of its original size.

Scene. In radio and television spots, a locale in which the spot takes place. A spot may be composed of several scenes.

Scripted delivery. One of the four basic modes of delivering a speech. The speech is delivered entirely from a script.

Serifs. The short cross strokes at top and bottom of characters in certain typefaces, especially those in Roman face.

Shooting script. A script constructed from a working script. A director will use it to produce a spot for television. It must include all of the proposed camera shots, transitions, narrative, audio of all types, and acting directions.

Shot. In radio and television spots, a camera or lens designation indicating location of action within a scene.

Signature. Groupings of pages printed on both sides, usually sixteen to a signature, but sometimes less, always in multiples of four (pages printed for binding are usually printed four to a two-sided sheet of paper, called "four up").

Slice-of-life spot. A television spot that sets up a dramatic situation complete with a beginning, middle, and end. In the slice-of-life spot, the focus is on the story, not the characters. The message is imparted through an interesting sequence of events incorporating, but not relying on, interesting characters. Slice-of-life spots usually use a wide variety of camera movements and post-production techniques, such as dissolves and special effects.

Slogan. Sometimes called a tagline. A cleverly written statement that quickly communicates everything a particular product or service represents.

Software. Computer programs.

Special. A press release or other information written in a style intended for a specific publication, but being released elsewhere as well.

Speeches and presentations. The interpersonal method of imparting a position or an image. Good speeches can inform or persuade and good presentations can win support where written methods may fail.

Spiral binding. A method of binding that allows the publication to open flat. Holes are drilled or punched through the gutter of the publication after the signatures have been collated and trimmed, and either wire or plastic is inserted or "spun" through the holes.

Spot color. The placement of a second color (black—or whatever the primary inking color—being the first) in a publication.

Spots. Broadcast messages, either paid-for advertising or PSAs.

Storyboard. An artist's rendition of a commercial, usually drawn on paper in separate frames.

Strategy. An approach to public relations problem solving aimed at defining target audience, competition, product/service benefits, and message.

Subhead. May be (1) a display line enlarging on the main headline, usually in smaller size, or (2) a short heading inside the copy used to break up a long blocks of text.

Swipe file. A collection of publications and designs done by other people or companies used to help with design, layout ideas and writing style as well as with communicating ideas to typesetters and printers.

Talking heads spot. A television spot in which the primary image appearing on the television screen is the human head—talking.

Target audience. Those prospects to whom the product you are communicating is most relevant.

Thumbnail. A rough layout in miniature, at the doodling stage.

Timeliness. One of the characteristics of newsworthiness of information. Relates to whether the material is current. If it isn't, is it a whole new angle on on old story? Remember, the word *news* means "new."

Tone. The attitude or expression of a message.

Trade journals. A publication produced for a specific industry that provides news and stories dealing with the concerns and products of that industry. Trade journals, or "trades," typically accept product press releases and articles that deal with any aspect of the industry they represent.

Treatment. In television, a written narrative version of a television spot. A treatment is not written in a script format but may include ideas for shots and transitions.

Typography. The field involving designing, setting, and using type.

Uncontrolled information. Information that, once it leaves your hands, is at the mercy of the media. The outlet in which you want it placed has total editorial control over the content, style, placement, and timing. Such items as press releases are totally uncontrolled. Others, such as magazine articles, may receive limited editing but are still controlled as to placement and timing.

Upward communication. Communication within an organization that provides employees a means of communicating their opinions to management.

Vertical publications. Any publication distributed vertically—that is, intended to be read by everyone up and down an organizational hierarchy.

Video news releases (VNRs). Originally prepackaged publicity features meant to be aired on local, regional, or national television, now VNRs are news releases designed as feature stories, usually for local television news programs.

Voice-over. The off-camera voice of an announcer who is heard but not seen.

White space. The space in an ad or publication page not filled with type or illustrations. An important design element in itself.

Word processing. Creating text with a computer. This text may be used as is or imported into a page-layout program.

Working script. In television, the working script includes all of the information necessary for a complete understanding of an idea. A first draft in which camera shots, transitions, audio—including music and sound effects—and approximate times are fleshed out.

Glossary of Grammatical Terms

Adjective. Adjectives modify nouns or words acting as nouns. There are two basic types of adjectives: **descriptive** and **limiting**.

- **Descriptive adjectives** name some quality of an object.

    white house; small car; worn carpet

- **Limiting adjectives** restrict the meaning of a noun to a particular object or indicate quantity. There are five kinds of limiting adjectives:

    Possessive: *my suit; their office*
    Demonstrative: *this suit; that office*
    Interrogative: *whose suit? which office?*
    Articles: *a suit; an office; the office*
    Numerical: *one suit; second office*

Adverb. Adverbs modify other adverbs, adjectives, verbs, and most other words. The most common way to recognize an adverb is by its *-ly* ending. Although not all adverbs end in *-ly*, most do.

Antecedent. An antecedent is a word or group of words referred to by a following pronoun.

Case. Case indicates the function of nouns and pronouns in a sentence. Personal pronouns (*I, you, he, she, it*) have different forms for the nominative, possessive, and objective cases. See **Chapter 13** for the proper uses of case, especially the troublesome use of *whom* versus *who*.

Clause. A group of words expressing complete thoughts which may or may not be a complete sentence. The two type of clauses are independent and subordinate.

- **Independent clauses**, sometimes called **main clauses**, always have a subject and a verb and make a statement independent of the rest of the sentence. A sentence always has at least one independent clause; however, it may have more than one.

- **Subordinate clauses**, sometimes called **dependent clauses**, contain an idea less important than that of the independent clause. A subordinate clause relies on an independent clause for meaning, and is frequently introduced by a **subordinate conjunction**.

Complex sentence. A sentence that has a main clause and one or more subordinate clauses.

Compound sentence. A sentence that has two or more main clauses.

Compound-complex sentence. A sentence that contains two or more main clauses and one or more subordinate clauses.

Conjunction. A word used to join words, phrases, or clauses together.

- **Coordinating conjunctions** serve to separate independent clauses. The most common coordinating conjunctions are *and*, *but*, *or*, *nor*, *for*, *yet*, and *thus*.

- **Subordinate conjunctions** such as *because, if, since,* and *when* join subordinate clauses with independent clauses.

Conjunctive adverb. Conjunctive adverbs, like coordinating conjunctions, join complete clauses that are linked by a common idea.

Degree. Adjectives and adverbs show degree or quantity by means of their **positive**, **comparative**, and **superlative** forms.

- The **positive** form expresses no comparison at all: *slow, quickly.*
- The **comparative** form permits a comparison between two (and only two) things by adding *er* or the adverb *more* to the positive form of the word: *pretty, prettier; rapid, more rapid.*
- The **superlative** form, which involves a comparison between three or more things, is achieved by adding *est* or the adverb *most* to the positive form: *pretty, prettiest; rapid, most rapid.*

Gerund. The form of a verb that ends in -*ing*. The gerund is always used as a noun.

Indefinite prounoun. A pronoun that does not refer to a particular person or thing and has no antecedent (*everybody, anybody, someone*).

Linking verb. A verb that connects the subject of a sentence with the subject complement (the word that modifies the subject).

Noun. Words that name a person, place, or thing. Subjects of sentences are usually nouns, as are objects of verbs and prepositions.

Parallel structure. Involves putting similar ideas into the same kinds of grammatical constructions.

Participle. A participle is the form of a verb that ends in -*ing* in the present form and in -*ed* or -*en* in the past form. A participle acts as an adjective.

Preposition. A word used to connect parts of a sentence. A preposition usually relates a noun, pronoun, or phrase to some other part of the sentence.

Prounoun. A word that substitutes for a noun. Common pronouns are *he, she, you, they,* and *it.* Pronouns usually take an **antecedent**—a noun usually preceding the pronoun to which the pronoun refers.

Simple sentence. A sentence that has a single independent clause.

Verb. An action word that makes a statement about the subject of the sentence.

Index